THE LIBRARY
OF HUMANITY

THE MOST INFLUENTIAL BOOKS
OF ALL TIME

Chiaretto Calò

The Library of Humanity

To Nubia, Valentina and Victor,
for their example of love.

CONTENTS

ACKNOWLEDGEMENTS

I warmly thank my first readers: my wife Nubia Arruda, Chiara Felici, J. Flowers-Olnowich, and Jill Paradis. Their thoughtful comments, valuable critiques, and constant encouragement were essential to completing the work. Special thanks go to Paul Bernasconi, whose expert editorial advice significantly improved the consistency of this work. The publication would not have been possible without the support and work of Susie Cioè, who helped me with the editing and revision. Her commitment and help were instrumental in bringing this work to the printing stage.

The Library of Humanity

PREFACE

Years ago, I made a significant transition in my life, moving my primary residence from a spacious house in the countryside, where a study filled with thousands of books brightened my days, to an apartment in a bustling city center. Unable to relocate the entire collection, I faced the dilemma of which books should accompany me to the new apartment.

The Bible, undeniably, emerged as the obvious choice – a timeless tome that has transcended generations, brimming with wisdom and knowledge that should grace every library. But what more? Philosophy, an essential pillar of human history and culture, beckoned me to include the works of other great thinkers like Plato and Aristotle. My quest for universality in literature led me to embrace narratives from diverse corners of the globe. These stories possess the power to unite readers, irrespective of their backgrounds or beliefs. I found myself drawn to Leo Tolstoy's poignant tales of war and William Shakespeare's enduring plays that have spanned centuries. I was captivated by Ernest Hemingway, a master of portraying life's struggles through extraordinary prose, and Gabriel García Márquez, who introduced us to magical realism and opened our eyes to new dimensions of reality. Yet, I also felt the pull of science, the gateway to progress. Hence, I incorporated groundbreaking works such as Charles Darwin's On the Origin of Species, which challenged conventional beliefs and illuminated the intricate laws of evolution.Furthermore, I welcomed the revolutionary contributions of Albert Einstein, whose *Theory of Relativity* redefined the very fabric of physics, transforming our understanding of the universe.

Each chosen book served a purpose: to enlighten us, the human race, about our collective past and, more importantly, to shape our future. These selections remind us of our common roots, regardless of our origins or the languages we speak.

This book is a guiding compass for those embarking on a journey to comprehend humanity's most influential literary works – written by authors who have indelibly shaped our perceptions of life throughout history. It explores themes of morality, humanity's relationship with nature, and the mysteries of the divine.

Appreciating and acquiring knowledge of the classics enables us to grasp the intricacies of history and, in turn, gain insights about ourselves, for we are all products of our shared heritage. This book offers concise and clear entry points into these great works, sparing readers from the daunting task of traversing entire volumes or centuries of material. Instead, it grants access to key concepts and ideas that bridge generations with brevity and clarity.

As you commence this literary expedition, the allure of these enthralling works may beckon you to dig further into their essence, immersing yourself in their entirety. The richness and profundity of these books can ignite an insatiable thirst for knowledge, compelling you to absorb each page and explore the profound ideas and revelations they hold. My greatest aspiration and wish are for this generative effect to take hold. The growth in the number of readers and the appreciation of the classics featured within these pages will yield an extraordinary outcome, justifying the effort invested in this book. It is my hope that the spread of knowledge and the cultivation of new ideas across all fields will contribute to a better humanity – more enlightened, less reliant on the sea of information devoid of genuine utility that inundates our modern existence.

That, dear reader, is the ultimate goal of this book – to serve as your guiding companion, selecting and preserving works from the past that are worthy of being handed down to future generations.

*"There is nothing for it but for all of us
to invent our own ideal libraries of classics.
I would say that such a library ought to be composed
half of books we have read
and that have really counted for us,
and half of books we propose to read
and presume will come to count
– leaving a section of empty shelves
for surprises and occasional discoveries."*

Italo Calvino, Why Read the Classics?

Notes for the Reader:

    a.   Works are presented in chronological order.

    b.   The title is the name of the work followed by, in parentheses, the author's name and the year of composition or first publication (generally adopted after the invention of the printed book)

    c.   In the description, titles of works are not italicized or quoted to improve overall readability in a short text.

    d.   BCE: *Before the Current Era*. CE: *Current Era*.

THE CLASSICS

The Library of Humanity

THE CLASSICS

Imagination has woven its threads into the fabric of our culture since the earliest days of human existence. It has fulfilled vital roles as a vehicle for communication, a form of self-expression, and a source of entertainment. Across civilizations and continents, people have gathered – around flickering campfires, in cozy corners, or awe-inspiring theaters – fascinated by the power of a well-told tale. Our ancestors used the art of narrative to pass down wisdom, preserve history, and ignite the sparks of imagination within each successive generation.

From ancient myths and legends that transcended time to the ageless classics that still grace our bookshelves today, stories have carried the weight of human experiences: offering insights into the human condition, exploring the depths of our emotions, and transporting us to realms that are at times familiar and at times fantastical. Stories have always had the remarkable ability to evoke joy, tears, and empathy; to challenge our perspectives; and to inspire introspection.

In the art of storytelling, the storytellers themselves have emerged as custodians of collective memories and truth. They have held the power to captivate audiences with their words, to paint animated pictures in the theater of the mind, and to leave indelible marks on the hearts of listeners. From bards and griots to playwrights and novelists, these masters of the craft have sculpted lines that resonate with our shared human experience.

Classical literature, which draws on the elements of rhythm, narration structure, rhyme, and metrics from earlier vocal forms, has endured for thousands of years. Its origins can be traced back some 4,000 years to Mesopotamia, where the *Epic of Gilgamesh* was first written on clay tablets in cuneiform characters during the reign of Sargon I (2334-2279 BCE) and his grandson Naram-Sin (2254-2218 BCE). Although this story likely existed as a myth or legend transmitted verbally among the Sumerians at least 500 years earlier, its transcription on clay tablets marked a significant turning point for storytelling, enabling tales to be preserved beyond memory and passed down through the generations.

Early epics served as a way for rulers and religious leaders to immortalize their deeds and teach moral lessons through histories that were easily retained due to the memorable characters and events. Supernatural elements, such as gods and goddesses interacting with humans, added intrigue and explained natural phenomena not otherwise understood.

The written language allowed authors greater freedom in creating their works than was possible with speech, but writers still drew inspiration from earlier recounted forms. For example, poems such as *The Odyssey* and *The Iliad*, heavily influenced by traditional Greek folktales, incorporated the rhythm and meter of their predecessors.

The Library of Humanity

The Epic of Gilgamesh

1. The Epic of Gilgamesh (Unknown, ca. 2100 BCE)

> *"The life that you seek you never will find:*
> *when the gods created mankind,*
> *death they dispensed to mankind, life they kept for themselves."*

— *Unknown, The Epic of Gilgamesh*

One of the first written texts to have come down to us is an epic poem about the legendary king Gilgamesh and his quest for immortality. The epic begins with Gilgamesh, the king of Uruk, who is two-thirds god and one-third human. He is a powerful ruler, feared by his people. To control Gilgamesh, the gods create an equal to him, a man named Enkidu, who is formed from clay and water. After a fierce battle between the two, Gilgamesh and Enkidu become friends and travel together on a series of adventures. The two heroes set out to defeat the monstrous Humbaba and gain access to the sacred Cedar Forest. Once there, Ishtar expresses a desire to marry Gilgamesh, but he refuses, fearing the same fate as her previous lovers. Ishtar seeks revenge by asking her father Anu to release the celestial Bull, but Gilgamesh and his companion slay it. Enkidu falls ill and dies (a consequence of the gods' anger due to the killing of the Bull of Heaven and Humbaba). Gilgamesh, mourning the death of his friend, begins a quest for immortality. He meets Utnapishtim, a man who was granted immortality by the gods, who tells him the story of the *Great Flood*. Utnapishtim challenges Gilgamesh to stay awake for six days, but Gilgamesh fails. However, Utnapishtim's wife convinces him to grant Gilgamesh a plant that restores youth. On his way back, Gilgamesh loses the plant to a serpent. Realizing the futility of his pursuit of immortality, he returns to Uruk, determined to leave a lasting legacy through his deeds and accomplishments.

The Epic offers a unique perspective on ancient Mesopotamian culture and mythology. This epic serves as a reminder that mortality is inevitable, but the legacy of a great ruler will live on.

2. Story of Sinuhe (Unknown, ca. 1875 BCE)

"Whatever god fated the flight be gracious, and bring me home!
Surely you will let me see the place where my heart still stays!
What matters more than my being buried in the land where I was born?"

—— *Unknown, Story of Sinuhe*

This work became a classic as early as ancient Egypt, and the story likely weaves historical elements with fictional embellishment. The ancient Egyptian text tells the story of Sinuhe, a nobleman of Pharaoh Amenemhat I, who decides (or is forced) to flee Egypt and resign from his powerful position to save his life when he learns of Pharaoh's assassination. The exact reasons for his flight are unclear, and the historical reconstruction is complex (there are even hypotheses of desertion or involvement in the assassination of Pharaoh). Crossing the eastern border, close to exhaustion, Sinuhe finds himself in the land of Retenu (present-day Syria), where he is taken in by a Bedouin tribe. The tribe's leader Amunenshi gives Sinuhe his daughter in marriage and grants him land in a place called Yaa. Sinuhe decides to stay and soon becomes an important figure because of his skills and knowledge. He prospers and has children and takes part in other military expeditions. As he grows older, however, gripped by the memory of his homeland, he pines to return to Egypt for his burial. Sinuhe sends letters to the Pharaoh, and the benevolent Senwosret I welcomes him back. Upon his return to Egypt, he still finds a place in the court. The final verses adopt a more ritualistic tone, in keeping with Egyptian funerary traditions. They describe the last joyful days in Egypt before his death and burial, fulfilling the ultimate wish of keeping his legacy alive in his beloved homeland.

Sinuhe's account reveals to us the value placed on their homeland by the Egyptians of the time: for Sinuhe's greatest desire, even after a fulfilling life in a distant land, is to be buried in Egypt.

3. Code of Hammurabi (Unknown, ca. 1800 BCE)

> *"Anu and Bel called by name me, Hammurabi,*
> *the exalted prince, who feared God,*
> *to bring about the rule of righteousness in the land."*

> — *Unknown, Code of Hammurabi*

The Code is an ancient legal document created by King Hammurabi of Babylon. It is one of the earliest known legal codes (the *Code of Ur-Nammu* could be considered earlier) and has been an essential source of inspiration for many subsequent legal systems throughout history. Hammurabi's Code is organized into 282 laws, divided into different sections. The laws cover various topics, ranging from property rights to criminal justice. The Code is known for using the *lex talionis* (*law of retaliation*) where punishments are often identical to the wrong committed. Punishments are prescribed according to the social status of the offender and the victim. The first section deals with property regulation, including inheritance, boundary, and debt laws. This section also outlines the responsibilities of citizens, which includes the payment of taxes and debts. In subsequent sections, the Code outlines criminal laws and punishments for theft, murder, and adultery. The code also covers family law, including marriage, divorce, and adoption. It also addresses what is akin to today's commercial law; it delineates the duties of merchants regarding taxation and payment of fines, and rules for trade and contracts regarding the rights of sellers and buyers. The Code concludes with exhortations for future rulers to preserve and not change legal norms, followed by a collection of curse formulas directed against anyone who ignores the admonitions. These maledictions also follow a structured pattern with the name of the deity, the relationship to Hammurabi, and the curse designated for the specific case.

The Code of Hammurabi is one of the earliest surviving codes of law, providing exact definitions of justice and establishing consistent rules.

4. Enūma Eliš (Unknown, ca. 1650 BCE)

> *"When on high the sky had not been named,*
> *the dry land below had not yet been named,*
> *there was nothing but the primordial Apsu,*
> *their generator, and Mummu-Tiamat,*
> *she who gave birth to them all."*

— *Unknown, Enūma Eliš*

Enūma Eliš is an ancient Mesopotamian epic poem written in the Akkadian language. The poem is a creation myth describing the universe's origin. It begins with the god Apsu (the *primordial indeterminacy* – personifying *fresh* water) and his consort, Tiamat (the *mother of all Cosmos* – personifying *salt* water), who create the other gods together. The successive generations of young gods become too rowdy and cause a disturbance in the universe, which enrages Apsu and Tiamat, who plan to kill them. The young gods learn of Apsu's intentions in the greatest bewilderment. Ea, the bravest among them and son of Anšar, uses magic to put Apsu into a deep sleep and then kills him. Having accomplished Apsu's murder, Ea settles in the *Waters of the Abyss* and builds his dwelling over Apsu's remains. After uniting with Damkina, they beget Marduk. The young god Marduk challenges Tiamat, offering to fight her and her monsters if the other gods make him their leader. The other gods agree, and Marduk defeats the original ancestress Tiamat in a great battle. Marduk then splits Tiamat's body, creating the heavens and the earth. He also creates the stars, planets, sun, and moon from her body, and invites the Anunnaki gods to build Babylon as his home. Marduk then appoints other gods to care for the different parts of the universe. The poem ends with Marduk being proclaimed the supreme god and the other gods praising him for his great deeds.

The poem offers a glimpse into the mythology of ancient Mesopotamia: the people's beliefs regarding creation, the gods' influence in crafting the cosmos, and Marduk's importance as a deity closely linked to the city of Babylon.

Enūma Eliš

5. The Vedas (Unknown, 1500-500 BCE)

"We have drunk Soma and become immortal;
we have attained the light, the Gods discovered.
Now what may foeman's malice do to harm us?
What, O Immortal, mortal man's deception?"

— *Unknown, The Vedas (Rigveda, Mandala 8, Hymn 48)*

The Sanskrit term *veda* means *knowledge* or *wisdom* and is derived from the Indo-European root 'weid-' for *see*, similar to *video* in Latin. The Vedas contain hymns, prayers, rituals, and philosophical texts. The four main collections of the Vedas include the *Rigveda*, the *Yajurveda*, the *Samaveda*, and the *Atharvaveda*. Central elements of the religious beliefs included *Rta* (the *Cosmic Law*), *Soma* (a sacred ritual drink), and the fire ritual. These elements often blended with features incorporated from local *Dravidian* cultures. The Rigveda, which is the oldest of the Vedas, is a collection of more than 1,028 hymns (referred to as *suktas*) that are dedicated to various gods, praising their power and strength. It was composed by multiple authors over several centuries before being compiled into a single text around 1500-1200 BCE. The Yajurveda contains sacrificial ritual instructions and *mantras* (incantations) used during ceremonies such as marriage or coronation rites. The Samaveda consists mainly of musical chants used in religious traditions, while the *Atharvaveda* focuses on magical and medical spells meant to heal and protect against evil forces or bring good fortune to individuals who recite them correctly. In addition to these books, there are also numerous other works associated with the Vedic tradition. They include the *Brahmanas* (commentaries), the *Aranyakas* (esoteric texts reserved for the hermits), and the *Upanishads* (philosophical dialogues).

The Vedas are a collection of sacred texts originating from ancient peoples who migrated to northern India around the 2nd millennium BCE. These early spiritual texts offer deep insight into ancient Indo-Aryan religion and profoundly influenced Hinduism, Buddhism, and Sikhism.

6. Hurrian Hymns (Unknown, ca. 1400 BCE)

> *"(Once I have) endeared (the deity),*
> *she will love me in her heart,*
> *the offer I bring*
> *may wholly cover my sin."*

> — *Unknown, Hurrian Hymns*

The Hurrian Hymns are a collection of religious songs from the ancient Near East, written in cuneiform writing and composed in the Hurrian language (the Hurrians, who settled in northern Mesopotamia, probably came from today's Armenia around 2300 BCE and disappeared around 1000 BCE). The hymns were discovered in 1950 at Ugarit, an ancient city-state on the northern coast of Syria. They provide insight into an early form of religion that precedes Judaism and Christianity. The texts consist of three main parts: praise for a deity or deities, prayers for protection or blessings, and supplication to various gods. Each hymn begins with an invocation addressed to one or more gods and then proceeds with verses praising their attributes and accomplishments. Many of these verses contain imagery drawn from nature, such as rivers, mountains, trees, animals, etc., which indicates that Nature worship was part of this early religion. In addition to the hymns, fragments contain instructions on how they should be performed, including musical accompaniment using lyres and drums and dance steps associated with each song. They suggest that music was essential in religious ceremonies during this period.

The Hurrian Hymns provide insight into religious practices and how worshippers conducted these rituals during this period. The lyrical content displays an intimate knowledge of mythology and musical composition, suggesting they may have been used for formal ceremonies. This type of structure is found throughout much of the work, implying there was some standardized way for priests or singers to present their offerings to each respective deity.

7. The Old Testament (Anthology, 1100 BCE-100 BCE)

"In the beginning,
God created the heavens and the Earth"

— The Old Testament (Genesis 1,1)

The Old Testament is a collection of sacred texts that form the *first part* of the Christian Bible and the *entirety* of the Hebrew Bible. It was primarily written in Hebrew, with portions of Daniel and Ezra written in Aramaic. In Jewish tradition, the texts are divided into three sections: the *Torah* (Law), *Nevi'im* (Prophets), and *Ketuvim* (Writings). The *Torah*, comprising the first five books (*Genesis, Exodus, Leviticus, Numbers,* and *Deuteronomy*), narrates the creation of the world; the early history of humanity; the story of the patriarchs; and the Exodus of the Israelites from Egypt under Moses' leadership; as well as the Mosaic law. The *Nevi'im* is subdivided into the *Former Prophets* (Joshua, Judges, Samuel, and Kings) and the *Latter Prophets* (Isaiah, Jeremiah, Ezekiel, and the *Twelve Minor Prophets*). These books relate the history of the Israelites entering the Promised Land; the establishment and development of the Kingdom of Israel; and the messages of prophets who communicated God's will to the people. *Ketuvim*, the Writings, includes diverse texts such as *Psalms, Proverbs, Job, Song of Songs, Ruth, Lamentations, Ecclesiastes, Esther, Daniel, Ezra-Nehemiah,* and *Chronicles*. These books encompass a wide range of literary genres including poetry, wisdom literature, and historical narratives. In the Christian tradition, the Old Testament is structured somewhat differently and sometimes includes additional texts known as the *Deuterocanonical books* or the *Apocrypha*.

Rooted in the Judeo-Christian spiritual heritage, the Old Testament is fundamental to Western civilization, containing rich historical narratives, moral teachings, and religious laws. Its timeless wisdom, compelling stories, and foundational values have shaped the spiritual, ethical, and cultural aspects of society, leaving an indelible imprint on our collective conscience.

The Old Testament

8. The Iliad (Homer, ca. 750 BCE)

> *"Sing, O goddess, the anger of Achilles, son of Peleus*
> *– that fatal wrath that brought countless ills upon the Achaeans."*

— *Homer, The Iliad*

The Iliad, attributed to the ancient Greek poet Homer, recounts a part of the *Trojan War* – a legendary conflict between the city of Troy and the *Achaean* (Greek) forces. The epic poem does not cover the entire war but focuses on a brief period prior to its conclusion. Central to the narrative is the *wrath of Achilles*, the greatest Greek warrior. The immediate cause of the war is the *abduction of Helen*, the wife of the King of Sparta Menelaus, by the Trojan prince Paris. However, the poem begins *in medias res* (in the middle of things) during the ninth year of the war. At this point, Agamemnon, the leader of the Achaean forces and brother of Menelaus, takes Briseis, a war prize, from Achilles. In his anger, Achilles withdraws from battle, which leads to a series of defeats for the Achaeans. The gods, who have their own allegiances and rivalries, play a significant role in the poem and often intervene in the battles. Athena supports the Achaeans, while Aphrodite and Apollo favor the Trojans. A turning point comes when Patroclus, Achilles' close friend, is killed by Hector, the Trojan prince and Troy's greatest warrior. Consumed by grief and rage, Achilles rejoins the battle. He fights Hector and kills him with the help of Athena. Achilles desecrates Hector's body by dragging it behind his chariot but later, moved by the pleas of Hector's father King Priam, returns the body for a dignified funeral.

Themes such as fate and destiny, heroism, the consequences of anger, and the transient nature of human life are woven through the epic. The Iliad is renowned for its compelling story, complex characters, and the psychological depth with which their motivations and emotions are portrayed. It is considered one of the greatest works of ancient Greek literature and has profoundly influenced Western culture.

The Iliad

9. Odyssey (Homer, ca. 750 BCE)

> *"I'd rather die at sea, with one deep gulp of death,*
> *than die by inches on this desolate island here!"*
>
> — *Homer, Odyssey*

The Odyssey is an epic poem that follows the adventures of Odysseus as he tries to return home to Ithaca after fighting in the *Trojan War*. His journey is prolonged due to the wrath of Poseidon, who is angered because Odysseus blinded his son, the Cyclops Polyphemus. Odysseus's voyage is filled with supernatural challenges. He must contend with the enchantress Circe, who turns his men into pigs; evade the Sirens, whose songs lure sailors to their deaths; and navigate the perilous waters between Scylla and Charybdis. He overcomes these obstacles with the help of the goddess Athena and the messenger god Hermes. He also descends to the *Underworld* to seek the advice of the seer Tiresias. Eventually, Odysseus is shipwrecked on the island of Ogygia, where the nymph Calypso keeps him captive for seven years. He is later shipwrecked again on the island of Scheria, home to the Phaeacians. There, he recounts his tales to King Alcinous and Queen Arete, who provide him with a ship to return to Ithaca. Meanwhile, in Ithaca, Odysseus's wife Penelope remains faithful to him despite the pressure, from the numerous suitors who have descended on her home in Odysseus's absence, to remarry. Odysseus's son Telemachus has grown into a young man and searches for news of his father. Upon returning to Ithaca, Odysseus, in disguise, evaluates the situation and plots to take revenge on the suitors. With the loyalty of Telemachus and a few of his own household, Odysseus slaughters the suitors and reunites with Penelope.

The Odyssey symbolizes the enduring human quest for identity. It explores perseverance, hospitality, loyalty, and the human desire for home and family. Its rich narrative depicts the ancient Greek world and its values, and it is considered a literary classic and an essential work in the Western canon.

Odyssey

10. Theogony (Hesiod, ca. 715 BCE)

"Love, who is most beautiful among the immortal gods,
the melter of limbs,
overwhelms in their hearts the intelligence
and wise counsel of all gods and all men."

— *Hesiod, Theogony*

Theogony recounts the origins of the universe, the birth of the gods, genealogies, and various myths surrounding the gods and mythical beings. It begins with Chaos, the *primordial state* or entity, and introduces the emergence of the sky god Uranus and the earth goddess Gaia. Uranus and Gaia give birth to various offspring, including the Titans and the Cyclopes. However, Uranus mistreats his children and keeps them imprisoned. In response, Gaia convinces her son Cronus to overthrow Uranus by castrating him. With Uranus defeated, Cronus assumes control and weds his sister Rhea. They bear six children, among them Zeus, Poseidon, and Hades. Aware of a prophecy that his children will overthrow him, Cronus devours them, but Rhea manages to save Zeus by substituting a stone. Zeus liberates his siblings and prevails over Cronus. As the new sovereign of the universe after defeating the Titans, Zeus, along with his brothers Poseidon and Hades, divide the dominion of the cosmos among themselves. Zeus assumes control over the heavens and the sky, Poseidon is allotted the sea, and Hades is given the Underworld to rule. This division allows each deity to have authority over different aspects of the universe and helps establish the rule and power of the Olympian gods.

Theogony is one of the earliest surviving works of Greek literature, offering invaluable insights into ancient Greek religion, thought, and culture. Its exploration of creation myths provides a fascinating perspective on the Greeks' understanding of their place in the cosmos. Furthermore, Theogony's influence extends to subsequent works, such as Virgil's Aeneid, which draws heavily from Hesiod's depiction of the Greek gods, thus affirming its enduring impact on classical literature and mythology.

Theogony

11. Homeric Hymns (Unknown, ca. 700 BCE)

"The divine one walked behind them,
sorrowing in her heart, her head veiled, dark robe
eddying around her slender, sacred feet."

— *Unknown, Homeric Hymns*

Attributed to Homer in antiquity due to their stylistic similarity to his epics, *the Iliad* and *the Odyssey*, the Homeric Hymns are a collection of ancient Greek poems that celebrate various deities. Among the hymns, there is an invocation to Dionysus, the god of wine, and the collection includes longer narratives about other gods. The longest hymn is dedicated to Demeter, the goddess of the harvest, and it tells the poignant story of her search for her daughter Persephone, who was abducted by Hades, the god of the underworld. This hymn gives thanks for the seasons and agricultural bounty, and it also provides a detailed account of the establishment of her mystery cult at Eleusis. The third hymn celebrates Apollo, the god of prophecy, music, and healing. It provides an account of his birth, his establishment of the oracle at Delphi, and his slaying of the dragon Python. In the fourth hymn, the trickster god Hermes is born; and on the very day of his birth, he invents the lyre, steals Apollo's cattle, and becomes the messenger of the gods. The fifth hymn recounts how Aphrodite, the goddess of love and beauty, seduced the mortal Anchises and bore him a son Aeneas. The collection also includes shorter hymns to a variety of deities, including Poseidon, Athena, Artemis, and Hera, among others. Each hymn praises the individual god or goddess and often tells a story about their deeds and adventures.

The Homeric Hymns offer a rich, immersive glimpse into the ancient realm of Greek mythology and culture. Through these enchanting hymns, we encounter some of the earliest examples of epic poetry, which has served as a model for later literary works.

12. Fables (Aesop, 620-564 BCE)

"Once a wolf, always a wolf."

— *Aesop, Fables*

Aesop is traditionally thought to have lived in ancient Greece during the 6th century BCE, but the precise dates of his life and even his existence remain matters of debate among historians. Many believe Aesop was a real person, while others argue that he was a fictional figure and that the fables attributed to him were likely the work of many authors over centuries. Passed down through generations, these tales typically feature animals with human-like qualities as characters and impart moral lessons to readers. Among the most famous of Aesop's Fables is *The Ant and the Grasshopper*. It tells the tale of an ant diligently preparing for winter by storing food, while a carefree grasshopper sings and plays. When winter arrives, the grasshopper finds itself in need, but the ant refuses to share its provisions, highlighting the importance of foresight and planning for the future. Another well-known story is *The Tortoise and the Hare*, in which a hare challenges a tortoise to a race. Despite the hare's initial confidence, the persistent tortoise ultimately triumphs by maintaining a constant pace, teaching the moral that being slow and steady wins the race. *The Boy Who Cried Wolf* is yet another famous fable in which a shepherd boy repeatedly tricks villagers by falsely claiming a wolf is attacking the flock. When a real wolf appears, and the boy cries out for help, no one believes him, resulting in the loss of some of the flock. The moral of this story warns against lying and exaggeration, as it erodes trust.

Aesop's Fables have been utilized to teach children life lessons since ancient times, and they continue to inspire modern literature. The influence on subsequent works is undeniable, with references and adaptations found in Shakespeare. Similarly, George Orwell incorporated elements from Aesop's fable "The Wolf in Sheep's Clothing" in his novel Animal Farm.

13. Upanishads (Unknown, 1500-500 BCE)

> *"Beyond the senses are the objects,*
> *beyond the objects is the mind,*
> *beyond the mind is the intellect,*
> *beyond the intellect is the great Atman."*

> — *Unknown, Upanishads*

The Upanishads are vital texts within Hinduism, containing some of the religion's most profound spiritual and metaphysical teachings. These diverse texts consist of stories, dialogues, and teachings, which explore a wide array of topics from the nature of the universe and the *Self* to the divine and the human connection to it. Some texts commence with creation myths, depicting the universe as an emanation of a single-encompassing divine force known as *Brahman*, the source of all existence. Subsequently, the Upanishads delve into the true nature of the *Self* and its relationship with Brahman. They expound the concept of *Atman*, the *individual self*, and its inherent connection to the greater divine force. Through meditation, individuals can realize their divine nature and access spiritual enlightenment. *Karma*, the law of cause and effect, is also discussed, emphasizing that every action carries consequences that shape both the present and future. Furthermore, the Upanishads elucidate the notion of *Moksha*, liberation from the cycle of death and rebirth, leading to ultimate peace and unity with the divine. The Upanishads culminate with teachings on harmonious living with nature and the significance of spiritual knowledge and enlightenment.

The Upanishads are revered works of ancient Indian literature and are part of the more extensive Vedic literature, which forms the scriptures of Hinduism. While many Upanishads are composed in verse, some are written in prose. Regardless of their form, they use various poetic devices, including repetition, metaphors, personification, and parables, to effectively communicate complex philosophical ideas.

14. Ramayana (Valmiki, 700-200 BCE)

"You will find no rest for the long years of Eternity
For you killed a bird in love and unsuspecting."

— *Valmiki, Ramayana*

The Ramayana, attributed to the sage Valmiki, is a cherished ancient Indian epic that tells the remarkable story of Prince Rama of Ayodhya, an incarnation of the deity Vishnu, and his quest to rescue his beloved wife Sita. The tale begins with King Dasharatha of Ayodhya and his three wives: Kausalya, Kaikeyi, and Sumitra. Kausalya gives birth to Rama, Kaikeyi to Bharata, and Sumitra to the twins Lakshmana and Shatrughna. Rama is exiled due to a request made by his stepmother Kaikeyi, who asks King Dasharatha to fulfill two boons he had granted her years before, one of which she uses to demand that Rama be sent into exile. Joined by Sita and Lakshmana, Rama leaves for the forest, where they encounter the sage Vishwamitra. This leads them to Mithila, where Rama wins Sita's hand in marriage by bending Shiva's bow. They return to the forest and settle in Chitrakuta. During their time in the forest, Rama kills Maricha, who is disguised as a golden deer. This event leads to Sita's abduction by Ravana. Rama and Lakshmana, aided by the monkey king Hanuman and his army, wage a great battle against Ravana and successfully rescue Sita. Upon returning to Ayodhya, Rama assumes the throne. However, a false accusation against Sita results in her second banishment. To prove her purity, Sita calls upon the Earth (her mother) to take her back, disappearing into the ground and leaving the mortal world. The Ramayana concludes with Rama's reign over Ayodhya.

Valmiki skillfully creates vivid scenes that depict a wide range of emotions, paying meticulous attention to detail. Throughout the text, Valmiki employs poetic devices such as similes and metaphors, enriching each scene described, thus giving readers a nuanced and immersive experience of his epic narrative.

15. The Art of War (Sun Tzu, 512 BCE)

"The wise warrior avoids the battle."

— Sun Tzu, The Art of War

Written by a revered Chinese military general and strategist, the treatise begins by emphasizing the gravity of warfare and the necessity of thoughtful deliberation and meticulous planning. It underscores that war should not be taken lightly, and the stability of the state hangs in the balance. Sun Tzu examines what he calls the five virtues of a successful leader: wisdom, sincerity, benevolence, courage, and strictness. He explains how these virtues influence the five essential factors for success in warfare, which he identifies as the *Way* (moral influence), *Heaven* (weather and seasons), *Earth* (terrain advantages and disadvantages), the *General* (leadership qualities), and *Discipline* (the organization and control of military forces). Sun Tzu's strategic brilliance shines through as he proposes that the supreme art of war is to subdue the enemy without fighting. He explains the concept of *shi*, the *strategic advantage*, suggesting that an army's power derives not from its size but from its *energy* and *unity*. He stresses that understanding and influencing the enemy's plans is far more effective than directly attacking their forces. The book also explores the importance of *strategic positioning* in different types of terrain; the critical role of intelligence and espionage; the use of deceit and subterfuge; and the psychological dimensions of warfare, such as morale and momentum. The treatise also discusses the effective use of *unconventional tactics*, such as the strategic use of fire and various psychological strategies. In the final chapters, Sun Tzu provides a comprehensive guide to different military tactics, the proper use of spies, and the importance of adaptability.

The Art of War is a strategic primer applicable to various fields of life, from corporate leadership to personal development and conflict resolution.

The Art of War

16. Prometheus Bound (Aeschylus, 452 BCE)

"Time, as it grows old, teaches all things."

— *Aeschylus, Prometheus Bound*

Prometheus Bound is one of the most famous Greek tragedies traditionally attributed to the playwright Aeschylus, centering on the story of the Titan Prometheus, who faces dire punishment for granting humanity the gift of fire, a privilege reserved for the gods. Prometheus is found bound to a desolate mountain by the order of Zeus, the chief of the gods. The divine servants Kratos (Power), Bia (Force), and Hephaestus (the god of blacksmiths and fire) carry out Zeus's command by chaining Prometheus. Hephaestus, feeling a kinship with Prometheus as a fellow helper of humanity, is reluctant but complies to avoid Zeus's wrath. Despite his suffering, Prometheus remains resolute and refuses to submit to Zeus. Throughout the play, he receives several visitors, including the Chorus of Oceanids (sea nymphs), who sympathize with his plight, and their father Oceanus, who advises Prometheus to capitulate to Zeus. However, Prometheus refuses. The play introduces Io, a maiden turned into a cow by Zeus and tormented by a gadfly sent by his wife Hera. Prometheus foretells her future wanderings and eventual release from her affliction, which parallel Prometheus's dilemma. Hermes, the messenger of the gods, arrives to demand that Prometheus reveal the secret prophecy he holds concerning the potential downfall of Zeus. Prometheus, steadfast in his defiance, refuses to yield, and Hermes predicts an even harsher punishment. The play ends dramatically with Prometheus and the sympathetic Chorus being swallowed by the earth in a divine thunderstorm.

Prometheus Bound explores the rebellion against injustice, the suffering of the benefactor of humankind, the arrogance of power, and the consequences of defying divine authority. Despite the antiquity of the play, these themes resonate deeply, making it an enduring masterpiece in world literature.

17. Oresteia (Aeschylus, 452 BCE)

"There are times when fear is good.
It must keep its watchful place
at the heart's control.
There is an advantage
in the wisdom won from pain."

— *Aeschylus, Oresteia*

The Oresteia, a remarkable trilogy of Greek tragedies by Aeschylus, traces the harrowing narrative of the House of Atreus, ensnared in a self-perpetuating cycle of violence. In the first play *Agamemnon*, King Agamemnon returns victorious from the *Trojan War*, accompanied by Cassandra, a captured Trojan prophetess. However, his triumphant homecoming is marred by treachery when his wife Clytemnestra and her lover Aegisthus murder him, avenging the sacrificial death of their daughter Iphigenia. *Libation Bearers*, the second play in the trilogy, follows Agamemnon's son Orestes. Guided by his sister Electra, Orestes retaliates against Clytemnestra and Aegisthus, killing them to avenge his father's death. The matricide incites the wrath of the Furies, primordial deities of vengeance, setting the stage for the final play *The Eumenides*. Pursued by the Furies for his crime, Orestes seeks asylum at Apollo's sanctuary. Athena intervenes and convenes a trial with Athenian citizens as jurors. After an almost unanimous decision, Athena casts the deciding vote, and Orestes is acquitted. The Furies, calmed by Athena, transform into the Eumenides – benevolent protectors of Athens. The trilogy concludes with the celebration of the rule of law, democratic decision-making, and the cessation of the violent cycle tormenting the House of Atreus.

Oresteia examines how individuals can be both victims and perpetrators in a cycle of violence. The play has immensely influenced later literature, particularly in its exploration of the consequences of revenge and justice. Its themes have been echoed throughout history by writers such as Shakespeare, Sophocles, Euripides, Dante Alighieri, and many others.

18. Antigone (Sophocles, 441 BCE)

"No man shall say that I betrayed a brother."

—— *Sophocles, Antigone*

Antigone is a powerful Greek tragedy centering around the eponymous heroine and her principled defiance of King Creon's decree. As the daughter of Oedipus, Antigone has already endured her family's tragic fate. Her brothers Eteocles and Polynices have slain each other in a violent contest for the throne of Thebes, leaving their uncle Creon as the new king. Creon decrees that Eteocles will receive a hero's burial, while Polynices' body will be dishonored and left unburied as a grim spectacle. Driven by familial love and respect for divine laws, Antigone defies Creon's edict and performs burial rites for Polynices. This act of civil disobedience results in her arrest. Undeterred by the threat of death, she stands defiant when brought before Creon. Her sister Ismene courageously steps forward to share Antigone's guilt, but Creon remains resolute in his judgment – death for Antigone. Creon's son Haemon, betrothed to Antigone, pleads for his father's mercy. Yet, even when the seer Teiresias warns him of divine retribution, Creon's arrogance prevails. Creon's stubbornness incites the tragic climax: a messenger reports that Antigone has hanged herself, leading to Haemon's suicide in despair. Creon's wife Eurydice, also overcome with grief, takes her own life. With the death of his family, Creon realizes his grave errors and prays for forgiveness. He orders a dignified burial for Antigone, but it is too late to escape the devastating consequences of his actions.

Antigone is a profound exploration of individual conscience in conflict with the law and the moral complexities of civil disobedience. Its enduring relevance has inspired numerous adaptations, such as Jean Anouilh's version set against the backdrop of World War II; Bertolt Brecht's 1948 rendition responding to Nazi Germany; and Tony Kushner's 2003 adaptation set during the Iraq War.

Antigone

19. Medea (Euripides, 431 BCE)

> *"Gods often contradict our fondest expectations.*
> *What we anticipate does not come to pass.*
> *What we don't expect some god finds a way to make it happen.*
> *So with this story."*

— *Euripides, Medea*

The tragedy narrates the harrowing tale of a scorned woman, her all-consuming desire for vengeance, and the catastrophic repercussions. Medea, a sorceress from Colchis (which was considered by the Greeks to be as a land of barbarians), finds herself forsaken by her husband Jason, the hero who had once won the Golden Fleece with her help. Abandoned in Corinth, Medea is distraught when Jason decides to marry Glauce, the young daughter of King Creon, hoping to secure a prosperous future for himself and his sons. As the tragedy begins, Medea is consumed by a profound sense of betrayal, a deep longing for her lost home, and an overpowering desire to exact revenge. Creon, fearing Medea's wrath, decrees her exile, but she persuades him to allow her one more day in Corinth. With time running out, Medea concocts a devious plot. Under the pretense of reconciling with Jason and seeking the welfare of their children, Medea sends her sons with gifts – a robe and a crown – to Glauce. Unknown to everyone, the gifts are cursed, bringing death to Glauce and Creon as they succumb to the deadly poison. In a horrifying climax, Medea murders their two sons, inflicting the deepest wound on Jason and annihilating the lineage he hoped to preserve. The play culminates with Medea, seemingly triumphant in her revenge, escaping in a divine chariot provided by her grandfather, the sun god Helios. Jason is left bereft: his new life in ruins, his progeny lost, and cursed to die alone and unlamented.

Medea is a chilling exploration of passion's destructive power. Its profound influence is seen in works such as Shakespeare's 'Othello' and Toni Morrison's 'Beloved', which delve into similar matter.

20. Histories (Herodotus, circa 431-404 BCE)

> *"Human prosperity never abides long in the same place."*
>
> — *Herodotus, Histories*

Histories offers a comprehensive narrative of the genesis and growth of the Persian Empire and its consequential confrontations with Greece in the 5th century BCE. The work begins by shedding light on Cyrus the Great's ascension, leading to the formation of the Persian Empire. It illustrates the grandeur of the empire, the socio-political landscape of the *Greek city-states*, and the turbulent relationships between them. The narrative then intricately chronicles the *Ionian Revolt*, which sparked the first wave of the *Persian invasion of Greece* under the leadership of King Darius I. This phase culminates in the decisive *Battle of Marathon* in 490 BCE. Subsequently, the narrative shifts focus to Xerxes I, Darius' successor, and details his massive military campaign against Greece. The reader is taken through the renowned *battles of Thermopylae, Artemisium, Salamis,* and *Plataea,* vividly showcasing the Greek perseverance and strategic acumen, which successfully thwarted the colossal Persian forces. Herodotus expertly intersperses the central narrative with fascinating digressions covering ethnographic, geographical, and historical aspects. He offers detailed insights into the cultures and histories of various peoples and territories, ranging from Egypt and Scythia to Libya and India, thus painting a multi-faceted picture of the world during this period. The final chapters revisit the Persian Empire post the *Greco-Persian Wars,* tracing the reigns of Xerxes' successors and the persistent power struggles that marked this era. The narrative, however, ends unexpectedly amid a siege account, suggesting a possible intent by Herodotus to continue the work.

Dubbed the 'father of history,' Herodotus has left an indelible mark with his meticulous research, providing a dynamic and engrossing glimpse into the ancient world's cultural, political, and military dimensions.

21. Oedipus Rex (Sophocles, 429 BCE)

> *"Long, long ago; her thought was of that child*
> *By him begot the son by whom the sire*
> *Was murdered, and the mother left to breed*
> *With her seed, a monstrous progeny."*

> — *Sophocles, Oedipus Rex*

Sophocles' renowned tragedy unveils the devastating narrative of Oedipus, the King of Thebes, unknowingly ensnared in a harrowing prophecy. The tale commences amidst a catastrophic plague ravaging Thebes, with its desperate populace pleading for Oedipus's intervention. Oedipus, in turn, sends his brother-in-law Creon to the esteemed Oracle at Delphi to decipher the cause of their suffering. Creon returns with an unsettling revelation – the plague has been a consequence of the unpunished murder of former King Laius. Determined to alleviate his people's suffering, Oedipus vows to uncover and punish Laius' murderer. However, this well-intentioned pursuit of the truth leads him to a horrifying realization: he himself is the culprit, fulfilling a dreaded prophecy he had once sought to escape. As the truth dawns, a cascade of tragic events follow. His wife and, unknowingly, his mother Queen Jocasta, who is devastated by guilt and horror, takes her own life. Tormented by remorse and the unbearable weight of his actions, Oedipus blinds himself and, eventually, is exiled, leaving Thebes in despair.

Oedipus Rex is a masterstroke of tragic narrative; its characters and dialogues echo with profound emotions. Its influence transcends centuries, inspiring works such as Shakespeare's Hamlet and King Lear. Moreover, the tale's central theme found resonance in psychology, where Sigmund Freud articulated the 'Oedipus complex' theory, highlighting the narrative's timeless relevance. This gripping tragedy is a chilling reminder of fate's implacable nature and the devastating repercussions of inescapable truth.

22. Lysistrata (Aristophanes, 411 BCE)

> *"And yet you are fool enough, it seems,*
> *to dare to war with me,*
> *when for your faithful ally you might win me easily."*

— *Aristophanes, Lysistrata*

Set in Athens during the *Peloponnesian War*, the play Lysistrata depicts a strong-willed woman who leads a group of other women in a plan to end the fighting. The women of Athens are fed up with the conflict and the suffering it has caused their families. Lysistrata decides that the only way to end it is to convince the men of Athens to come to the negotiating table, proposing a plan to prevent them from having sex until they have decided to end the battle. The women gather at the Acropolis and agree to Lysistrata's plan to close the gates and barricade themselves inside. The men initially attempt to force their way into the Acropolis, but later they resort to trying to smoke the women out. Eventually, the men decide to negotiate with the women. The women already had their own plan, having smuggled food and wine to the Acropolis and organized a feast. The women publicly announce that they will not have relations with the men until they agree to end the hostilities. This causes a great stir among the men, who, after some further events and negotiations, agree to end the warfare. The play concludes in a festive manner with the participation of both men and women celebrating the end of the conflict.

Through its lighthearted yet poignant depiction of female empowerment, Lysistrata is a powerful commentary on gender dynamics within Ancient Greece. Beneath its comedic exterior lies a subversive critique of patriarchal authority structures and systems of governance based upon hierarchies. Having her female characters challenge such outdated customs through humor rather than violence or fear tactics was revolutionary in its time. Lysistrata stands out among classical comedies due to its sophisticated blend of wit and social criticism.

23. The Bacchae (Euripides, 405 BCE)

> *"Prepare yourselves for the roaring voice of the God of Joy!"*
>
> — *Euripides, The Bacchae*

Dionysus (the god of wine, fertility, ritual madness, theater, and religious ecstasy) finds himself at the center of a contentious plot: he is accused of not being a *true* god by some relatives of Pentheus, the king of Thebes, who insinuate that he was born out of an affair between his mother and an ordinary man, casting doubt on his true divine nature. The narrative evolves with Dionysus gathering a large group of female followers called *Bacchae* in *Mount Cytheron*, transforming himself into a bull, and leading a wild and ecstatic ritual dance. When Pentheus learns of what Dionysus has done, he orders his soldiers to capture and imprison the Bacchae. Despite his grandfather Cadmus's warning, Pentheus refuses to recognize Dionysus as a god and orders the Bacchae to be executed. In anger, Dionysus appears before Pentheus and tells him that he will have to answer for his actions. The god then sends Pentheus into a trance and orders him to dress in women's clothing and follow the Bacchae up the mountain. When Pentheus reaches the top of the mountain, he is horrified to find the Bacchae in a wild frenzy, intent on mauling animals and participating in ecstatic rituals. Pentheus is taken prisoner and brought before Dionysus. At this point, Dionysus reveals himself to Pentheus and orders the Bacchae to tear him apart. The tragedy ends with Agave, Pentheus' mother, returning to Thebes carrying her son's severed head, believing it to be the head of a lion. When she realizes the horror of what she has done, she is overcome with grief. Dionysus pronounces punishment on Agave and the other family members involved for not recognizing his divinity.

Euripides masterfully crafts an enthralling narrative punctuated with dramatic tension and human folly. Suspense deepens the narrative's impact, underscoring the tragic consequences of doubting divine power.

24. Tao Te Ching (Lao Tzu, ca. 400 BCE)

> *"Those who know do not speak.*
> *Those who speak do not know."*
>
> — *Lao Tzu, Tao Te Ching*

Comprising 81 thought-provoking verses, the Tao Te Ching by Lao Tzu is an illuminating guide to the Tao or *Way* of Life, a philosophic system espousing a harmony between the spiritual and physical realms. This treatise uncovers the path toward enlightenment, inviting us into a balanced life of wisdom, serenity, and fulfillment. The book opens with exploring the Tao itself – the ineffable *Way of Nature*. This transcendental force exists beyond the constructs of time and language, representing the boundless, ever-present origin of all things. The essence of the Tao evades definition and expression, but its profound influence permeates all facets of life and existence. The verses prescribe a lifestyle aligned with the Tao. They advocate for humility, simplicity, and detachment from material possessions, asserting that true power lies in understanding and embodying the Tao. Inner tranquility and self-awareness are emphasized through a keen consciousness of thoughts and emotions, patience, and an attitude free from judgment. Intricate elements of Taoist philosophy are then brought to light, particularly the concept of *Yin* and *Yang*, the interplay and co-existence of complementary opposites – the light in the darkness, the calm amidst chaos, and the life within death. It encapsulates the cyclic nature of existence, where each extreme inherently encompasses its counterpart. This ancient text subsequently underscores the necessity of equilibrium, urging readers to understand life's impermanent, cyclical nature and the interconnections of actions and their effects.

Lao Tzu highlights the principle of 'wu-wei', or 'non-action', a state of being unburdened by desires and attachments. The wisdom of the Tao Te Ching is imparted through concise yet profound language.

25. History of the Peloponnesian War (Thucydides, ca. 380 BCE)

> *"Men who are capable of real action first make their plans,*
> *and then go forward without hesitation*
> *while their enemies have still not made up their minds."*

> — Thucydides, *History of the Peloponnesian War*

Thucydides chronicles the intense conflict between the *Athenian Empire* and the *Peloponnesian League*, a coalition led by Sparta, in a war from 431 BCE to 404 BCE. A dispute between Corinth and Corcyra, a crucial trading ally of Athens, provided the catalyst for the war. Corinth desired to bring Corcyra under its control, putting it at odds with Athens and leading to the war's declaration in 431 BCE. This war stretched across land and sea, with the balance of power fluctuating between the two dominant city-states. The Spartans held the upper hand on land with their formidable hoplite infantry, while the Athenians dominated the seas with their impressive navy. The Athenians exploited their naval superiority to disrupt the Spartan trade and starve their adversary of crucial resources. In response, the Spartans garnered support from various allies and the Peloponnesian League, an alliance of states pledging support to Sparta. The war ebbed and flowed over decades, witnessing numerous victories and defeats on both sides. A decisive turning point came in 425 BCE when the Spartans invaded Attica and besieged Athens for two years. Athens finally capitulated in 404 BCE. This conflict left deep scars on Greek society, claiming thousands of lives and reducing cities to ruins.

Thucydides's account stands out for its lucidity and conciseness, skillfully avoiding extraneous diversions. He frequently employs speeches to underscore his points and offers analytical perspectives, lending his readers a holistic view of the events. His thorough report, encompassing both Hellenic and non-Hellenic viewpoints, provides an insightful portrayal of the tumultuous period, making it a crucial historical document.

History of the Peloponnesian War

26. Republic (Plato, ca. 380 BCE)

"The object of education is to teach us to love what is beautiful."

— *Plato, Republic*

Through a dialogue between the character of Socrates and various Athenian contemporaries, Plato examines the nature of justice and the blueprint of an ideal society. The dialogue commences with Athenian citizens debating justice and governance. Glaucon introduces a mental experiment, constructing the *Ring of Gyges* concept. This *invisible ring* symbolizes the potential to commit acts without consequences, underscoring the need for justice. Through the character of Socrates, Plato presents a vision of an optimal state where justice is both viable and sought-after. He partitions the ideal society into three groups: *guardians, auxiliaries,* and *producers*. Each group plays a distinct role. Guardians, composed of rulers and philosopher-kings, should exude wisdom and courage to uphold justice. Auxiliaries serve as warriors and protect the city. Producers include farmers, artisans, and other laborers for everyday needs. Socrates expounds on the proposed state's educational paradigm, beginning with the *noble lie*. According to him, this essential falsehood stirs citizens to embrace their societal roles. He advocates for a censorship mechanism, intending to shield the populace from immoral artistic influences. Socrates then navigates through the four cardinal virtues: *wisdom, courage, temperance,* and *justice*, which are integral to upholding justice in the optimal state. These virtues are presented as the cornerstones of a just and harmonious society, crucial to the prosperity of the ideal state.

The Republic has etched its mark in academic discourse. Plato's use of metaphor adds depth to his arguments while offering evocative imagery that aids memory retention. This technique encourages readers to ponder the concepts presented, engaging them in active critical thinking. It continues to offer valuable insights into governance, justice, and societal structure.

27. Anabasis (Xenophon, ca. 370 BCE)

"The thing is to get them to turn their thoughts to what they mean to do, instead of to what they are likely to suffer."

— *Xenophon, Anabasis*

The Anabasis recounts Xenophon's travels as part of an army of Greek mercenaries hired by Cyrus the Younger to aid him in his campaign against Artaxerxes II for control over Persia in 401 BC. After Cyrus' death on the battlefield at Cunaxa, near Babylon, his ten thousand Greek soldiers are stranded deep within the enemy territory, facing hostile forces far more numerous than their own. With no means to retreat through such hostile terrain or resources to sustain them if they stayed put, Xenophon takes on a leadership role among the commanders. He is instrumental in leading his men on a long journey through Mesopotamia (modern Iraq) and Anatolia (modern Turkey), which eventually brings them back home safely after two years of marching across thousands of miles with little food or water available along their route. Hence, both its title (*Anabasis*, meaning an *upward journey* or an *expedition from a coastline into the interior of a country*) and its fame as an epic tale describe a daring feat of survival. The soldiers' determination and courage stand out against seemingly insurmountable odds, as they have to rely on their own resourcefulness without any help from outside sources. They remain unyielding throughout their perilous trek across unknown lands, filled with dangerous threats lurking behind every corner. These threats, waiting to ambush them at any moment, should they let their guard down, add to the suspense of this grueling ordeal away from home.

Anabasis offers insight into the Ancient Near East's military, social, and cultural characteristics. Xenophon's detailed account of the geography, customs, and military operations provides valuable historical information. As a primary source, it offers a glimpse into the immense challenge of mobilizing an army in a foreign land.

28. Metaphysics (Aristotle, ca. 350 BCE)

> *"It is through the wonder that men now begin*
> *and originally began to philosophize;*
> *wondering in the first place at obvious perplexities,*
> *and then by gradual progression*
> *raising questions about the greater matters too."*

> — *Aristotle, Metaphysics*

This monumental work begins by exploring the nature of *being*, *identity*, and *change*, and it then examines the first principles that govern these concepts. Additionally, it examines the relationship between *substance* (or *essence*) and *accidents* (*individual properties* that are not essential to the substance). This leads to a discussion on *causation*, including an analysis of four possible types: *material cause* (what something is made of), *formal cause* (its form or structure), *efficient cause* (the process that brings it into existence), and *final cause* (its purpose or function). Aristotle also explores time, space, possibility and necessity, as well as causality and determinism. He applies his philosophical theories to traditional questions in metaphysics, such as whether motion is eternal or whether there is something eternal underlying all existence. The work concludes with a discussion on the nature of knowledge, specifically, how we can gain access to the truth about reality through concepts like language or reason. Aristotle argues that knowledge comes from experience but can only be understood through contemplation or reflection. In this way, he establishes the foundations for modern epistemology.

Metaphysics provides a comprehensive overview of the fundamental questions concerning being and knowledge, laying the groundwork for categories and 'ontological' structures that would influence philosophy for the following two thousand years. Aristotle's notion of potentiality versus actuality has also been widely adopted throughout history; this concept suggests that things exist in two forms: their 'potential' state before they come into being and their 'actual' state once they have been realized.

29. Nicomachean Ethics (Aristotle, ca. 350 BCE)

"With the truth, all given facts harmonize;
but with what is false,
the truth soon hits a wrong note."

— *Aristotle, Nicomachean Ethics*

Aristotle's Nicomachean Ethics consists of ten chapters, often referred to as *books*, that discuss various aspects of ethical theory and practice. The first book focuses on the nature of happiness and how it can be achieved through virtuous action. Aristotle argues that everyone seeks to attain happiness but often follows misguided paths in their attempt to do so. He posits that true contentment can only be found by living a virtuous or moral life. The second book examines pleasure and pain's roles in pursuing happiness and how they should be balanced with ethical action. In the third book, Aristotle outlines what he believes are the virtues required for a life of moral excellence and how these virtues must be attained if one is to achieve true happiness. The fourth book looks at justice, which Aristotle defines as *giving each one his due*; while the fifth and sixth books address friendship and courage. The seventh book examines other types of virtue, such as temperance and generosity; while the eighth examines intellectual qualities, such as wisdom and prudence. In the ninth book, Aristotle discusses happiness from a political perspective, arguing that a just society is necessary for individuals to lead contented lives. The tenth book contains reflections on human nature and an overall summary of Aristotle's views on ethics.

Aristotle's Nicomachean Ethics provides an influential account of ethical theory. It emphasizes that achieving true happiness requires living virtuously according to reason rather than pursuing pleasure or avoiding pain. It serves as an essential source text for those interested in understanding the foundations of moral philosophy and continues to inspire contemporary thought in ethics and personal development.

30. Zhuangzi (Chuang-Tzu "Zhuangzi", ca. 300 BCE)

*"I do not know whether
I was then a man dreaming I was a butterfly,
or whether I am now a butterfly, dreaming I am a man."*

— *Chuang-Tzu, Zhuangzi*

The Zhuangzi is an ancient Chinese philosophical text written during the *Warring States Period*. The text is written in a mix of prose, poetry, and stories that explore the concepts of *Taoism* (also spelled *Daoism*), popular during this period. The *Tao* (also *Dao*) is considered the guiding principle of the universe and the source of all things. It is seen as a natural force that the ordinary human mind cannot comprehend. The Zhuangzi explores how one can live in harmony with the Tao. The text is divided into three sections. The first section, known as the *Inner Chapters* (the only ones attributable with certainty to the author), contains the most famous stories of the Zhuangzi. It includes Zhuangzi's encounters with other wise men, as well as anecdotes, such as the one where he *dreams of being a butterfly* (which is often used to explain the concept of *non-dualism*), and his conversations with the ancient sage Laozi. These stories explore how one can use knowledge and wisdom to live harmoniously with the Tao. The second section, known as the *Outer Chapters*, contains more philosophical musings and debates. Here, Zhuangzi explores the idea of the *emptiness of being*, or *wu-wei*, and the concept of the *unity* of all things. He also discusses the nature of time and the importance of letting go of the past and embracing the present. The third section, known as the *Miscellaneous Chapters*, contains reflections on the nature of life and death and various other topics.

Zhuangzi has been praised for its witty humor, clever paradoxes, and profound insights into human nature. This philosophical work encourages individuals to seek spiritual liberation through awareness rather than material attainment. Its relevant topics are still discussed in modern Chinese philosophy.

31. Mahabharata (Vyasa, attributed, 400 BCE-400 CE)

*"Whatever actions are performed by a man
under whatever circumstances,
he gets the fruits of those actions
under whatever circumstances they may be performed."*

— *Vyasa, Mahabharata*

Mahabharata portrays the grand epic of two familial branches, the Kauravas and the Pandavas, both descendants of King Bharata. Within the context of the Mahabharata, the term *Kaurava* is specifically used to refer to the 100 sons of King Dhritarashtra, while the *Pandavas* are the sons of King Pandu and his two wives Kunti and Madri. After King Pandu's death, his sons the Pandavas are compelled to live in exile in the forest. During this period, they acquire martial arts and other skills under the tutelage of their mentor Drona. After spending several years in exile, they receive an invitation from their visually-impaired uncle King Dhritarashtra to return to the kingdom. The Pandavas and Kauravas are initially close, but differences in opinion and ambition soon cause a rift between them. This leads to a great war between the two sides, resulting in a Pandava victory. Much of the story includes thrilling battles, heroic acts, intrigues, and betrayals. Various gods and goddesses also play a critical role, aiding their favored sides and intervening for the righteous. The war eventually ends with the Pandavas emerging victorious but at a high cost due to numerous losses and tragedies.

The Mahabharata is one of India's most significant literary works for its length and complexity. Its memorable narrative provides moral lessons on resolving conflicts by applying principles such as truthfulness, non-violence, and compassion. Scholars regard the Mahabharata with great reverence because it gives insight into ancient Indian society during this period while simultaneously exploring universal questions about life's purpose through mythological tales. The characters in the Mahabharata have been adapted in works ranging from classical Sanskrit plays to modern films.

32. Kama Sutra (Vatsyayana, 300 BCE-200 BCE)

"Women are hardly ever known in their true light,
though they may love men,
or become indifferent toward them;
may give them delight, or abandon them;
or may extract from them
all the wealth that they may possess."

—— *Vatsyayana, Kama Sutra*

Kama Sutra is an ancient Indian treatise on love, relationships, and sexual behavior. Although it is often associated primarily with eroticism, the Kama Sutra covers many aspects of life, including virtuous living, prosperity, desire, and sexuality. Vatsyayana posits that passion and desire are essential for a fulfilling life and discusses different types of love, from romantic love between a man and a woman to familial love, such as that between brothers and sisters. He then examines the various forms of marriage and their benefits. Vatsyayana also talks about the duties and responsibilities of a husband and wife, explaining the different kinds of adultery and the consequences for those involved. After discussing marriage, Vatsyayana moves on to sexual positions and techniques. He explains the various positions and practices in detail and the different types of pleasure and satisfaction that can be derived from them. The Kama Sutra also contains advice on how to attract a partner, as well as how to maintain a happy relationship. Vatsyayana also talks about handling jealousy and other emotions in a relationship.

The Kama Sutra is an essential work of literature on sexuality, eroticism, and the art of living. It is still relevant today and can be a valuable guide for those looking to improve their relationships. Beyond its explicit content, the Kama Sutra promotes respect, intimacy, and understanding as vital components of a successful relationship, thereby enriching modern discussions on love and companionship.

33. Commentarii de Bello Gallico (Julius Caesar, 58-50 BCE)

"Without training, they lacked knowledge.
Without knowledge, they lacked confidence.
Without confidence, they lacked victory."

— *Julius Caesar, Commentarii de Bello Gallico*

Commentarii de Bello Gallico, or *Commentaries on the Gallic War*, is an insightful first-hand narrative written by Caesar himself, chronicling the *Gallic Wars* fought between 58 and 50 BCE. Caesar's text provides a detailed account of his military campaigns against various Gallic tribes, including the Helvetii, Belgae, Nervii, Aedui, Sequani, Suebi, and most prominently, the army led by the Gallic chieftain Vercingetorix. In this work, Caesar expertly captures the complexity of the Gallic tribes, painting vivid pictures of their diverse customs, social structures, and geographic territories. His expeditions to Britain, among the earliest documented in Roman history, are meticulously detailed, offering interesting insight into the then largely unknown world of the Celts. While the historical accuracy of Commentarii de Bello Gallico is occasionally questioned due to potential exaggerations intended to glorify Caesar and his achievements, it remains an unparalleled source of information about the Roman conquest of Gaul. Caesar's prose is unembellished yet potent, with its concise military accounts often veiling the political implications of his actions. These undertones suggest that the text was not merely a record but a deliberate piece of propaganda designed to influence his contemporaries.

The text's importance transcends its military chronicles. It serves as a looking glass into the mind of Julius Caesar, one of history's most influential figures. It offers lessons in leadership and showcases Roman military strategies, which continue to be studied in modern times. While not directly linked, the style and content of the Commentarii influenced Shakespeare's portrayal of Caesar.

34. Aeneid (Virgil, 29-19 BCE)

> *"But you, Roman, remember, rule with all your power*
> *the peoples of the Earth – these will be your arts:*
> *to put your stamp on the works and ways of peace,*
> *to spare the defeated, break the pride in war."*

— *Virgil, Aeneid*

The Aeneid, Virgil's *magnum opus*, centers on the hero Aeneas, a survivor of the fall of Troy. Following the city's destruction, Aeneas is guided by an unyielding sense of duty as he embarks on a perilous journey that is destined to culminate in the founding of a mighty nation – Rome. Throughout the narrative, Aeneas and his fellow travelers face numerous adversities, including tumultuous sea storms and combative encounters with formidable opponents such as Turnus, an aggressive warrior king. With divine intervention from deities such as Venus and Jupiter, Aeneas successfully reaches Latium, marries Lavinia, and lays the foundation for what will become the Roman Empire. However, the journey is not without its tribulations. The climax involves a brutal confrontation between Aeneas and Turnus, which results in heavy casualties. Despite the devastation, Aeneas' victory is bolstered by divine favor and highlights the duality of war – its glory and its tragedy. Virgil's masterpiece is not merely a celebration of Roman might; it also exposes the horrific consequences of war and offers a poignant critique of the *hubris* and recklessness often seen in conflict. It stresses the understanding that victory in war is often *pyrrhic*, with the irreplaceable cost of lives, regardless of the righteousness of the cause.

The Aeneid, through its richly crafted verses, provides an insight into Roman mythology, culture, and society. Moreover, it had a profound influence on subsequent literary works, including Dante's Divine Comedy, where Virgil assumes the role of Dante's guide through Hell and Purgatory. It continues to be an invaluable source of inspiration for contemporary writers and artists, captivated by its enduring themes and poetic excellence.

Aeneid

35. Metamorphoses (Ovid, 8 BCE)

> *"I am dragged along by a strange new force.*
> *Desire and reason are pulling in different directions.*
> *I see and approve the right way, but follow the wrong."*

— *Ovid, Metamorphoses*

Metamorphoses presents a compendium of enthralling tales depicting the creation and evolution of the universe through the *transformations* of gods and mortals. The narrative begins with the universe's inception, transformed from primordial Chaos into a harmonious order of heavenly bodies and elements. Following this, gods fashion the first humans from the earth, endowing them with boons such as fire and language that foster the development of civilizations. However, the trajectory of human progression is marked by various conflicts and challenges. The mortals' actions often incur divine wrath, leading to divine retribution or reward manifested through transformations. Memorable characters such as King Midas, cursed with the golden touch, and King Lycaon, transformed into a wolf, form an integral part of these narratives. Gods also give birth to fascinating creatures like the Centaurs and the Minotaur, which embody both chaos and aid for mortals. The lyricism of the tales is epitomized in incidents like Orpheus' ability to charm the gods with his lyre to gain access to the *Underworld*, and Daphne's transformation into a tree to evade Apollo's amorous advances. The triumphant procession of mortals and gods to *Mount Olympus* led by Bacchus offers a vibrant spectacle of celebration, concluding the epic on an exultant note.

Metamorphoses provides a compelling exploration of the dynamic interplay between gods and mortals, underscoring the omnipotence of gods and the consequent rewards and punishments meted out to mortals based on their deeds. It paints a rich tableau of mythological narratives and philosophical insights and continues to be revered for its poetic artistry and profound wisdom regarding the human condition.

36. Satyricon (Petronius, 61 CE)

> *"No man on Earth may look on forbidden things*
> *as you have done and escape punishment.*
> *Especially here, a land so infested with divinity*
> *that one might meet a god more easily than a man."*
>
> —— *Petronius, Satyricon*

Only fragments of the Satyricon survive, presenting a challenge to the reconstruction of its plot. The narrative is a satirical and picaresque account primarily following the adventures of Encolpius, Ascyltos, and Giton. Encolpius, the protagonist and former gladiator, embarks on various misadventures often accompanied by his friend Ascyltos and his young lover Giton. These misadventures involve comical and satirical episodes of lust, deception, and social commentary on Roman society. One of the most famous sections is *Cena Trimalchionis* or *Trimalchio's Dinner*, where the characters attend a lavish banquet hosted by Trimalchio, an ex-slave turned wealthy man. The feast is marked by Trimalchio's ostentatious display of wealth and the indecent behavior of his guests, portrayed with satirical flair. As the story progresses, Encolpius faces a curse rendering him impotent, which forces him to seek a cure through encounters with priests and practitioners of magic. In the latter part of the surviving text, Encolpius and his companions meet Eumolpus, an old poet who often composes verse. Together, they journey to the city of Croton, where Eumolpus concocts a scheme to exploit the local *will hunters* by pretending to be a dying, wealthy man.

The Satyricon's fragmentary text blends prose and poetry (referred to as 'Menippean satire') to satirize Roman society, highlighting its excesses and moral decay. Petronius employs various literary devices such as irony, parody, and obscenity, and skillfully utilizes rhetorical techniques such as 'ekphrasis' (detailed description) and 'enargeia' (vividness) to immerse readers in the narrative's complexity. This results in a striking critique that invites readers to reflect upon their own society's morals and values.

37. Letters from a Stoic (Lucius Annaeus Seneca, ca. 65 CE)

> *"For the only safe harbor in this life's tossing, troubled sea*
> *is to refuse to be bothered about what the future will bring*
> *and to stand ready and confident, squaring the breast to take*
> *without skulking or flinching whatever fortune hurls at us."*

> — *Lucius Annaeus Seneca, Letters from a Stoic*

Letters of a Stoic (also known as *Epistulae Morales ad Lucilium* or *Moral Letters to Lucilius*) is a collection of letters to his friend Lucilius and follows Seneca's intention to live his life according to Stoic principles. He often draws upon history, myth, and contemporary events to provide concrete examples of the principles he discusses. Throughout his letters, he shares advice on practicing self-control and detachment from material things, being content with one's lot in life, and accepting death as part of the natural order of things. A key topic is that one should strive for knowledge and understanding rather than accumulating wealth or possessions. Seneca also provides examples of how Stoicism can be applied to everyday life through stories about people who have achieved greatness by following their passions; not worrying about what others think; being open-minded when faced with difficult situations; and learning to appreciate beauty in all aspects of life. Ultimately, Seneca has become more enlightened having followed this path. He encourages readers to take the same course, arguing that although it may require hard work and dedication, it will bring peace and joy into their lives.

Letters from a Stoic provide practical advice on self-control, courage, and resilience in adversity. Seneca also emphasizes the importance of integrity and cultivating relationships with others. His writings greatly influenced later literature, particularly in the Renaissance period when his works were rediscovered and widely read. Writers, such as Montaigne and Bacon, drew inspiration from Seneca's philosophy of Stoicism. Letters from a Stoic remains relevant today due to its immortal messages about leading an ethical life focused on personal growth and development.

38. The New Testament (Matthew, Mark, Luke, John, 65-100 CE)

> *"I am the way and the truth and the life.*
> *No one comes to the Father except through me.*
>
> — *The New Testament (John 14:6)*

The New Testament is central to Christianity, providing an understanding of Jesus Christ's mission, his teachings, and the formation of early Christian communities. The *Gospel of Matthew*, believed to have been written around 70 CE, covers events leading up to Jesus's birth, the visit of the Magi, and Herod's massacre of the innocents. It follows Jesus during his ministry in Galilee, preaching and performing miracles, and his final journey to Jerusalem. Matthew emphasizes Jesus as the fulfillment of Old Testament prophecies. The *Gospel of Mark*, written around 65-70 CE, portrays Jesus performing miracles, demonstrating his power over nature, and preaching *parables* about the Kingdom of God. Mark also narrates Jesus's crucifixion and resurrection. The *Gospel of Luke*, likely written between 80-90 CE, is attributed to an anonymous author, often thought to be a physician who accompanied Paul on missionary journeys. Luke includes several parables unique to this Gospel, such as *The Good Samaritan* and *The Prodigal Son*. The *Gospel of John*, likely composed between 90-100 CE, is one of the later books in the New Testament. It focuses on *theological subjects*, such as *light overcoming darkness* and *eternal life*. The New Testament also contains the *Acts of the Apostles*, which describes the early Christian community's history and the spread of Christianity. This is followed by the *Epistles*, which are letters written by early Christian leaders to various communities, and the *Book of Revelation*, a prophetic and apocalyptic text.

The Gospels particularly highlight how the 'law of love' subverts the ethics and religious views of the time. The teachings of Jesus convey a universal message of love, compassion, and salvation.

39. Discourses (Epictetus, 108 CE)

"Freedom is not achieved by satisfying desire, but by eliminating it."

— *Epictetus, Discourses*

Discourses is a collection of philosophical teachings of Epictetus, a *Stoic* philosopher. Epictetus was a former slave, and this background plays a role in the formation of his philosophy, particularly his emphasis on inner freedom and self-control, which is often viewed in light of his personal experience of physical enslavement. It is important to note that Discourses was not written by Epictetus himself, but instead was recorded by his student Arrian. In Discourses, Epictetus discusses the importance of understanding and accepting one's mortality, and the necessity of living purposefully. He encourages his followers to understand the nature of things, distinguish between what is in our control and what is not, and recognize the importance of virtue. He emphasizes that it is not external circumstances that dictate the quality of our lives but our choices and attitudes. Building upon these principles, Epictetus provides practical advice on how to live a virtuous life. He encourages individuals to cultivate inner peace and tranquility by focusing on the present moment and developing detachment from external concerns. He asserts that true freedom is internal and that one can be free from external influences such as fear and anxiety by learning to accept and manage emotions. Furthermore, Epictetus focuses on the importance of self-discipline and inner strength as essential components in achieving a meaningful life.

Based on Stoic philosophy, Discourses emphasizes living in accordance with reason and nature, cultivating inner peace through self-discipline. This work has been influential throughout history, inspiring many later philosophical writings, including Marcus Aurelius' Meditations. Modern authors such as Ryan Holiday have drawn upon the teachings of Epictetus in their works.

40. Parallel Lives (Plutarch, 110 CE)

> *"Perseverance is more prevailing than violence;*
> *and many things which cannot be overcome*
> *when they are together,*
> *they yield themselves up*
> *when taken little by little."*

> — *Plutarch, Parallel Lives*

Parallel Lives, written by the ancient Greek historian and biographer Plutarch, is a collection of biographies of famous Greek and Roman figures. The work comprises 23 pairs of biographies, with each pair consisting of one Greek and one Roman figure, along with four unpaired biographies. However, only 22 pairs survive in all. Plutarch intended to draw moral and ethical parallels between the lives of the individuals he chose. After each pair, there is usually a comparison (*synkrisis*) where Plutarch explicitly analyzes the two figures. Among the biographies included are those of prominent Greek statesmen such as Pericles and Solon, and military leaders like Themistocles and Alexander the Great. The Roman biographies include notable figures such as the orator Cicero, statesmen Pompey and Julius Caesar, and generals Marius and Sulla. Rather than focusing on a detailed historical account, Plutarch's biographies contain anecdotes and insights into the characteristics and virtues of the subjects and also serve as moral examples. He was interested in the personalities of his subjects and in how their traits molded their actions and, ultimately, the course of history. Additionally, Plutarch was not hesitant to include his own judgments and opinions.

Parallel Lives by Plutarch is not just a historical account but also a work of moral philosophy. Through the biographies, Plutarch offers an analysis of character and conduct, and subtly critiques the political and societal norms of his own time. The work is invaluable for the insights it offers into Greek and Roman history and culture, and its influence on literature and thought has been profound through the centuries.

41. Meditations (Marcus Aurelius, 175 CE)

"The happiness of your life
depends upon the quality
of your thoughts."

— *Marcus Aurelius, Meditations*

The Meditations of Marcus Aurelius is a collection of personal notes and reflections that the Roman Emperor Marcus Aurelius wrote to himself. It is a source of *Stoic* philosophy and offers guidance on how to live a life of virtue, wisdom, and inner peace. Marcus Aurelius expresses his reflections and thoughts on Stoic philosophy. He then focuses on topics such as reason, duty, death, justice, love, courage, and temperance. Throughout the work, he emphasizes the importance of keeping oneself free from negative emotions like anger and resentment. Instead, he focuses on cultivating inner peace by remaining mindful of one's mortality and appreciating what one has in life. Marcus Aurelius also discusses friendship, politics, war, and leadership, among many other things. At various points throughout the work, he encourages readers to contemplate deeply their own lives while reflecting upon the values they possess. In addition, he encourages readers to remain focused on living their lives according to the teachings of Stoicism by thinking critically about their actions and decisions rather than following societal norms blindly. The Meditations concludes with a reflection on fleeting life and how important it is for us all to use our time wisely by striving for a life filled with virtue and wisdom.

Marcus Aurelius reminds us that developing our character through reflection and introspection can help us lead meaningful lives regardless of circumstances or external pressures. With their profound yet simple musings, his writings offer timeless advice for readers seeking clarity amidst chaos, serving as a beacon of resilience, mindfulness, and inner strength.

Meditations (Marcus Aurelius)

42. Confessions (Augustine of Hippo, 398 CE)

"All who know the truth know this Light,
and all who know this Light know eternity."

— *Augustine of Hippo, Confessions*

The Confessions is an intimate prayer and reflective account of Augustine of Hippo, providing valuable insights into the life of the *early Christian Church*. The book opens with an exploration of his childhood: detailing his formative years in Thagaste, the pivotal role of his devout mother St. Monica, and the critical events that culminated in his conversion to Christianity. Augustine candidly acknowledges and repents his past sins, including pride, worldly ambitions, and carnal desires. The narrative unveils Augustine's intellectual and spiritual evolution, casting light on his upbringing and initial attraction to *Manichaeism* – a syncretic religion blending aspects of *Zoroastrianism*, *Gnosticism*, and Christianity. Overflowing with gratitude, Augustine's prayers articulate his liberation from the confines of Manichaean doctrine and his wholehearted embrace of Christian tenets. He proceeds by describing his intellectual journey through *Neoplatonism*, an ancient philosophical paradigm, and recounts his interactions with Ambrose, the esteemed fourth-century Bishop of Milan. His mind acutely explores theological concepts, including the *nature of God* and the *Holy Trinity*, followed by reflections on the *subjective* nature of time. Confessions culminates with heartfelt prayers directed toward the Church, as well as supplications for the souls that have passed on. It concludes with contemplative reflections on the ephemeral nature of earthly existence and its significance within the scope of eternity.

Confessions is a chronicle of Augustine's spiritual journey. It profoundly impacted later literary and theological writings, including Dante Alighieri's Divine Comedy and John Bunyan's Pilgrim's Progress, both exhibiting thematic parallels and drawing inspiration from Augustine's insights into salvation through faith.

43. Yoga Sutras (Patanjali, ca. 400 CE)

> *"This Union (or Yoga)*
> *is achieved through the subjugation*
> *of the psychic nature,*
> *and the restraint of the chitta (or mind)."*

— *Patanjali, Yoga Sutras*

The Yoga Sutras set forth the philosophical teachings of yoga and outline a systematic path to spiritual enlightenment. They consist of 196 *sutras*, or aphorisms, divided into four chapters. The first chapter, *Samadhi Pada*, illustrates the purpose and process of yoga and explains the goal of yoga practice as the attainment of *Samadhi* or a state of union with the Divine. The first two sutras of this chapter define yoga: "Yoga is the cessation of the modifications of the mind" and "When that is attained, one is established in his true nature." The second chapter, *Sadhana Pada*, describes the practices of yoga, including the five *yamas*, ethical guidelines, and the five *niyamas*, personal observances. It also outlines the eight limbs of yoga, or *Ashtanga yoga*: yama, niyama, asana, pranayama, pratyahara, dharana, dhyana, and samadhi. The third chapter, *Vibhuti Pada*, explains in detail the various powers experienced by a yogi who has achieved mastery over yoga practices. These powers, known as *siddhis*, are said to be supernatural abilities gained through yogic practice. The fourth chapter, *Kaivalya Pada*, describes the process of liberation and the stages of realization that a practitioner may experience on the path to spiritual enlightenment.

With its roots in ancient Indian philosophy, the text offers an array of teachings on physical and mental practices and ethical guidelines to help practitioners reach spiritual enlightenment. Even today, it is still an integral part of the yoga tradition and a reference for all those who want to practice it.

44. Tirukkuṛaḷ (Thiruvalluvar, 450-500 CE)

"It is compassion,
the most gracious of virtues,
Which moves the world."

— *Thiruvalluvar, Tirukkuṛaḷ*

The Tirukkural, or *The Kural*, is a renowned Tamil literary work comprising 1,330 couplets divided into 133 chapters, each containing 10 couplets (or *kurals*). This profound text follows a consistent structure and language throughout, leading scholars to believe it is a single author's work. It is often attributed to the sage and poet Thiruvalluvar. The Kural is divided into three books, each addressing different aspects of life. The first book, *Aṛam* (Virtue), serves as a guide to moral values and virtues that individuals should uphold. It delves into righteousness, honesty, compassion, and self-discipline. *Aṛam* includes essential teachings of yoga philosophy, emphasizing the importance of self-realization and the path to spiritual enlightenment. *Poruḷ* (Wealth) focuses on socio-economic values, governance, society, and administration. It provides insights into good governance, just rule, economic prosperity, and the responsibilities of leaders. *Inbam* (Love) explores psychological values and the concept of love. It explores various dimensions of love: romantic, familial, and universal. The Kural is renowned not only for its content but also for its unique poetic form. Each couplet consists of exactly seven words in two lines, known as *cirs*. Alongside the *Bhagavad Gita*, the Tirukkural is one of the earliest systems of Indian epistemology and metaphysics. It reflects the ancient Indian aims in life, known as *Puruṣārtha*, which encompass virtue (*dharma*), wealth (*artha*), love (*kama*), and salvation (*moksha*), the ultimate goal.

The Tirukkural serves as a timeless guide for righteous living, offering invaluable wisdom and practical guidance on various aspects of life. It emphasizes the importance of moral values, ethical behavior, harmonious relationships, and effective governance.

45.   Kadambari, (Bana Bhatt, ca. 625 CE)

> *"Like a dream, the desires of the young take forms that are not real.*
> *Like the feather brush of the magician*
> *the young mind creates impossible apparitions of hope."*

— *Bana Bhatt, Kadambari*

Kadambari holds the prestige of being one of the earliest novels in Sanskrit literature. Bana Bhatt weaves a captivating tale of romance, reincarnation, and divine beings. The narrative revolves around two celestial romances: Prince Chandrapeeda and Apsara Mahashweta and the Gandharva Pundarika with Apsara Kadambari. The story begins with a mystical parrot's arrival at King Shudraka's court. As the novel develops, the parrot narrates the entangled love stories of the two celestial couples. This complex plot, riddled with reincarnation, supposed deaths, and prolonged separation, fascinates readers as the characters' destinies play out amidst despair and longing for unattainable love. Frequently, the account ponders over profound metaphysical reflections and philosophical contemplations. Time, an omnipresent motif in the novel, mystifies the unfolding events and the characters' fates. The story contains a rich landscape of detailed descriptions and poetic expressions, indicative of the grandeur of Bana Bhatt's writing style. Its narration ends abruptly, suggesting that the author left it incomplete. Bhushanbhatt, Bana Bhatt's son, is believed to have concluded the remaining part of the novel.

The novel's uniqueness lies in its imaginative storytelling, enriched by the bright portrayal of celestial and human experiences, thereby offering readers an immersive dive into a world where divine and human emotions intermingle. Its intricate narrative and grand literary style secure Kadambari a well-deserved place in the annals of classical literature. Despite the centuries since its composition, Kadambari continues to intrigue scholars and literature enthusiasts with its profound philosophical insights, compelling narrative structure, and poetic beauty.

46. Qur'ān (Prophet Muhammad, "revealed to", ca. 650 CE)

> *"He is Who sent down tranquility into the hearts of the believers,*
> *that they might add faith to their faith;*
> *for Allah's are the forces of heaven and earth;*
> *and Allah is All-Knowing, Wise."*
> *(Qur'ān 48:4)*

— Prophet Muhammad, "revealed to", Qur'ān

The Qur'ān (Arabic for *Recitation*) is the holy scripture of Islam. It was revealed over a period of 23 years to *Prophet Muhammad* and compiled into one book under the first caliph Abu Bakr, and further standardized under the third caliph Uthman ibn Affan, after the death of Prophet Muhammad. The Qur'ān is considered the *literal* word of God (*Allah*), as conveyed through the *angel Gabriel* to the Prophet Muhammad in the Arabian cities of Mecca and Medina from 610 until Muhammad death in 632 CE. It is divided into 114 units called *sūrahs*, a word used within the Qur'ān to designate *revelatory passages*. The *sūrahs* are divided into verses called *āyāt* (singular *āyah*), a term that literally means *sign*. The central subject throughout the Qur'ān is submission to God's will through various actions: following His commands, believing in His messengers sent from time to time throughout history, living according to Islamic principles such as charity and justice, seeking knowledge through study or contemplation, and maintaining faith even when faced with adversity. Other points include warnings about disobedience to Allah's laws. There are reminders that all people are equal before Him and descriptions of paradise for those who follow Him faithfully. The holy text includes stories about past prophets like Abraham or Moses, who were tasked with delivering messages from God directly to humanity. There are also explanations regarding why specific punishments are necessary under Islamic law.

The Qur'ān encourages people to strive towards justice and fairness while showing mercy towards those less fortunate. It is the essential foundation of Islamic religion and laws.

47. Táin Bó Cúailnge (Unknown, ca. 750 CE)

> *"I am alone against hordes*
> *I cannot stop nor let go*
> *I stand here*
> *in the long cold hours*
> *alone against every foe."*

— *Unknown, Táin Bó Cúailnge*

Táin Bó Cúailnge, often known as *The Cattle Raid of Cooley*, is one of the earliest tales of the Ulster Cycle, a collection of ancient Irish legends and sagas. The epic tells the story of a great cattle raid and war waged by Queen Medb of Connacht to acquire the Brown Bull of Cooley, allowing her to attain the equivalent of her husband King Ailill's wealth. The kingdom of Ulster, in defending the bull, is led by the youthful warrior hero Cú Chulainn. As a result of an ancient curse, the warriors of Ulster are weakened, leaving Cú Chulainn to defend against the invading armies of Connacht single-handedly. He challenges and defeats a succession of champions in single combat, using various weapons and displaying incredible feats of strength. Throughout the tale, Cú Chulainn encounters mythological figures like the Morrigan and fights epic duels like the one with his friend and foster brother Ferdiad. Eventually, the warriors of Ulster join the battle, and the raid ends inconclusively with the mystical bulls fighting each other and Medb retreating.

Táin Bó Cúailnge is an epic tale of warfare and heroism and a reflection of early Irish society's values and beliefs. The story has had a lasting influence on Irish literature and culture and has inspired works beyond Ireland, including elements in J.R.R. Tolkien's Middle-Earth legendarium. It remains a quintessential tale of honor and valor, standing as a testament to the enduring allure of myth and legend.

48. Bhagavata Purana (Veda Vyasa, ca. 800 CE)

"By practicing yoga and knowledge of reality,
a person becomes fit to realize the supreme truth."

— *Veda Vyasa, Bhagavata Purana (6:12:15)*

The Bhagavata Purana, also known as the *Śrīmad Bhāgavatam*, is a monumental *Hindu* scripture; a treasure trove of mythological tales, devotional teachings, and philosophical reflections; centered on *Lord Vishnu* and *his incarnations*; with a particular focus on *Krishna*. The scripture comprises twelve books, known as *skandhas*, encompassing over 18,000 verses. It begins with a dialogue between the sage Shuka and King Parikshit, who seeks guidance on living his remaining days before meeting his foretold demise. This frames the narration of the Bhagavata Purana, which delves into the creation of the universe, the manifold *avatars* of Vishnu, the principles of *dharma (righteousness)*, and the significance of *bhakti (devotion)*. A central part of the Bhagavata Purana is *the tenth skandha,* which is devoted to the life and divine exploits of Lord Krishna. Born to Devaki and Vasudeva but swiftly taken to Gokul to be raised by Yashoda and Nanda, Krishna's childhood is depicted as both delightful and miraculous. Krishna's divine role becomes more evident as he matures. His participation in the *Mahabharata*, especially his discourse in the *Bhagavad Gita*, epitomizes his spiritual teaching. Krishna provides a comprehensive guide on life and spirituality to Arjuna on the *battlefield of Kurukshetra*, which has left an indelible impact on Hindu philosophy. After the life of Krishna, the scripture discusses the nature of time, the different *ages* of the world, and the characteristics of *Kali Yuga*, the current era.

The Bhagavata Purana serves as a narrative and a profound philosophical and devotional text. Its stories are replete with moral lessons, and its discourses range from metaphysics to practical ethics. It calls for devotion to the Supreme Being as the surest path to spiritual liberation (moksha).

Bhagavata Purana

The Library of Humanity

THE MIDDLE AGES

THE MIDDLE AGES

Medieval literature flourished within feudal courts and monastic environments, reflecting the values and structure of the time. It celebrated heroism, loyalty, and courage, often within the context of the Christian faith. However, it diverged from classical literature due to the political and religious turmoil of the era. As the *Roman Empire* declined, Europe experienced significant cultural transformations with the spread of Christianity. The emergence of the *middle class* and the rise of cities, particularly in Italy during the 12th century, challenged feudal power and the authority of the Christian Church. This led to the introduction of more nuanced narratives that explored issues related to faith and morality, as seen in works like Dante's *Divine Comedy* and Chaucer's *Canterbury Tales*.

Medieval writers employed allegory to explore topics such as love, loyalty, and courage while conveying ethical messages about good versus evil and right versus wrong. There was a diversity in the protagonists of medieval literature, with ordinary people facing daily life challenges and heroic figures battling supernatural forces. Characters also utilized regional dialects, adding authenticity and exposure to the diverse cultures of the time.

Recognizing the diversity of medieval works, which spans many centuries and regions, is crucial. This period saw many subjects and included works in Latin and vernacular languages. Besides Christian texts, there was a significant body of Jewish and Islamic literature during the Middle Ages, especially in places like Spain.

The importance of manuscript culture in the Middle Ages cannot be overlooked, and the invention of the printing press in the 15th century played a significant role in the dissemination and preservation of medieval texts.

The influence of the Middle Ages endures in the modern world, leaving a lasting impact on the literary landscape. Contemporary authors draw inspiration from this period, crafting tales that transport readers to an era of chivalry, quests, and mythical landscapes. J.R.R. Tolkien is a prominent example, with his renowned *Lord of the Rings* trilogy. Tolkien's imaginative storytelling and meticulous world-building bear the unmistakable imprint of medieval literature, showcasing the ever-lasting legacy of this rich and diverse tradition.

49. Beowulf (Unknown, ca. 850 CE)

> *"Do not grieve, wise warrior!*
> *It is better for each man to avenge his friend*
> *than to mourn him much.*
> *Each of us must accept the end of life here in this world*
> *so we must work while we can to earn fame before death."*

> — *Unknown, Beowulf*

Beowulf is an epic poem written in Old English, and it sets forth the story of a brave warrior named Beowulf, a *Geat* from what is now modern-day Sweden (*Götaland*). He comes to the aid of the Danes, whose realm is under attack by a powerful monster called Grendel. Grendel, believed to be a descendant of Cain, is portrayed as a sinister colossal monster who has been terrorizing the kingdom for twelve years, killing and consuming anyone who crosses his path. Beowulf hears of the kingdom's plight and travels to Denmark to help. He challenges Grendel in an epic battle and, despite Grendel's strength and size, manages to defeat him. After his victory over Grendel, Beowulf is celebrated by the Danes and rewarded with great riches. However, Grendel's mother soon seeks revenge for her son's death, and Beowulf confronts her in a second battle. Beowulf emerges victorious once more and returns to his homeland, where he eventually becomes king. Late in life, Beowulf sustains mortal wounds while facing his final challenge to protect his kingdom from a dragon. He is laid to rest with great honor after his death. The poem ends with a funeral where Beowulf's people mourn him and honor his memory as a great warrior and a symbol of strength and courage.

Beowulf is one of the oldest surviving pieces of literature in the English language, and its influence on subsequent works has been immense. Its epic structure has been a template for many stories since it was written.

50. The Tale of the Bamboo Cutter (Unknown, ca. 900 CE)

> *"He thought to himself that it looked like she was Kaguya-Hime going back to the moon as she said that, before passing out."*

> —— *Unknown, The Tale of the Bamboo Cutter*

In this enchanting tale from Japan's *Heian period* (794 to 1185), a humble bamboo cutter discovers a tiny, radiant princess inside a bamboo stalk. The bamboo cutter and his wife, previously childless, embrace this little miracle as their own, naming her *Kaguya-hime*. She experiences rapid growth and blossoms into an enigmatic beauty. Kaguya-hime's allure does not remain hidden for long, drawing the attention of five noble princes and even the emperor, each expressing a desire to marry her. However, Kaguya-hime sets impossible tasks for the princes and rejects all proposals, including a marriage proposal from the emperor, delicately insisting she does not possess royal lineage. Amid these happenings, an unexpected visit from a lunar envoy reveals a stunning truth – Kaguya-hime is of lunar origin, and she must return to her celestial home during the next full moon. Faced with this revelation, Kaguya-hime is initially saddened by the prospect of leaving her earthly home but accepts her fate with excitement for her true home. As the night of the full moon arrives, a celestial carriage descends to escort Kaguya-hime to the moon. The sight of her departure leaves the emperor and his court in despair, yet they understand her obligation to honor her lunar heritage. The tale concludes with Kaguya-hime's lunar family extending their gratitude to the bamboo cutter in a comforting letter, reassuring him of his adopted daughter's safety and happiness.

The Tale of the Bamboo Cutter captures the cultural milieu and ethos of Japan's classical Heian period. Adapted in various forms over centuries, it remains a testament to Japan's enduring literary heritage.

The Tale of the Bamboo Cutter

51. One Thousand and One Nights (Unknown, ca. 950 CE)

"Long, long have I bewailed the sev'rance of our loves,
With tears that from my lids streamed down like burning rain
And vowed that, if the days deign reunite us two,
My lips should never speak of severance again."

—— *Unknown, One Thousand and One Nights*

One Thousand and One Nights is a collection of folk tales that were compiled over several centuries, with some dating back to the *Islamic Golden Age* (ca. 750–1250). It recounts the story of a Persian king, Shahryar, and his wife Scheherazade. After discovering his first wife's infidelity, the king decides to marry a new wife each night and have her executed the following morning to ensure they remain faithful. Scheherazade, the *vizier*'s intelligent daughter, marries the king and devises a plan to save herself and future brides. She begins to recite a story to the king each night and stops at a cliffhanger, leaving the king eager to hear the next part. This way she can extend her life for *one thousand and one nights* until the king finally changes his ways. The stories introduce readers to various characters, including powerful *djinns* (genies), talking animals, and brave heroes. Many tales follow a similar structure, with a protagonist facing a difficult challenge and finding a clever solution. Some of the most popular stories in the collection include *Aladdin and the Magic Lamp*, *The Seven Voyages of Sinbad the Sailor*, and *The Tale of Ali Baba and the Forty Thieves*.

This collection is famous for its exotic adventures featuring magical creatures, daring heroes, and fantastical settings. It has inspired history's greatest authors, such as William Shakespeare, Charles Dickens, Edgar Allan Poe, and J.R.R Tolkien. The book is also praised for its unique structure, consisting of multiple interwoven narratives told by various characters over 1001 nights. This structure allows each storyteller to build upon previous narrators' stories while introducing new elements into the narrative arc, resulting in alluring plotlines full of suspenseful twists that keep readers engaged until the end.

One Thousand and One Nights

52. Shahnameh (Ferdowsi, between 977 and 1010 CE)

"Our lives pass from us like the wind,
and what would wise men grieve
to know that they must die?"

—— *Ferdowsi, Shahnameh*

The Shahnameh, known as the *Book of Kings*, is the national epic of Iran. It is a monumental work that recounts the mythical and historical past of Persia (modern-day Iran) from the creation of the world up until the *Islamic conquest of Persia* in the 7th century. The Shahnameh begins with the story of the first man Keyumars and the origins of the *Persian Empire*. It includes the stories of legendary kings and heroes such as Jamshid, credited with founding Persian civilization; Zahhak, a tyrannical king; and Fereydun, a hero who defeats Zahhak. The story of Rostam, one of Iran's greatest heroes, is a central part of the Shahnameh. His adventures, valor, and conflicts with several adversaries, including his son Sohrab, are some of the most notable aspects of the epic. The Shahnameh also covers the Sassanian dynasty's historical kings and the Persian Empire's eventual fall to the Arabs during the Islamic conquest. This includes the tragic story of the last Sassanian King Yazdegerd III and the battles fought by his loyal general Rostam Farrokhzad. Ferdowsi's epic is notable for its blend of myth and history and for preserving the great legends of Persia. It is written in classical Persian, and Ferdowsi is credited with revitalizing the Persian language and saving it from extinction due to the dominant use of Arabic at the time. The Shahnameh remains important in Persian literature and culture, and its stories and characters have influenced numerous literary works and cultural productions.

The Shahnameh is an epic poem narrating ancient Persia's history and myths. Ferdowsi's immense contribution through the Shahnameh is in the realm of literature and in the preservation of the Persian language and cultural heritage.

53. The Pillow Book (Sei Shōnagon, 1002)

> *"Lighting some fine incense and then lying down alone to sleep.*
> *Looking into a Chinese mirror that's a little clouded."*

— *Sei Shōnagon, The Pillow Book*

The Pillow Book, composed in *Japanese hiragana* during *Japan's Heian* period (794-1185 CE), is a collection of essays, anecdotes, poems, and observations made by the author during her time as a lady-in-waiting in the court of *Empress Consort Teishi*. Shōnagon was known for her wit, intelligence, and literary talent. The Pillow Book gets its name because it was written as if it were notes or musings that one might keep close by, such as under a pillow. Through her writings, Sei Shōnagon paints a vivid picture of life in the Heian court, reflecting the tastes, aesthetics, and daily affairs of the aristocracy of that time. Shōnagon's writing is celebrated for its eloquence and sharp observations. She also displays a profound sensitivity to beauty, particularly the natural world. The work includes various lists observed for their poetic consciousness, such as *Things That Make the Heart Beat Faster* or *Things That Arouse a Fond Memory of the Past*, and showcases her lyrical and evocative style. Unlike a continuous narrative or story, The Pillow Book is more akin to a journal or diary, containing personal reflections, court gossip, descriptions of natural scenes, and commentary on the manners of court life.

Shōnagon offers an intimate glimpse into the courtly culture and everyday life at the time. Her writing style is poetic yet concise. She also demonstrates a deep appreciation for nature. For example, she describes the beauty of snow falling on a moonlit night or the scattering of cherry blossoms across fields, likening them to tiny stars. Her observations demonstrate an awareness of beauty in even mundane moments, reminding us to cherish each moment we experience.

54. The Tale of Genji (Murasaki Shikibu, ca. 1010)

> *"Why do you grieve so uselessly?*
> *Every uncertainty is the result of certainty.*
> *There is nothing in this world really to be lamented."*
>
> — *Murasaki Shikibu, The Tale of Genji*

The Tale of Genji is often considered the world's first novel. The original manuscript was crafted in the *orihon style*, which involves adhering several sheets of paper together and then folding them in an accordion-like manner, alternating the direction of the folds. The novel narrates the life of *Hikaru Genji*, an imperial prince known as the *Shining Prince*. The novel opens with Genji's birth and childhood as the son of an emperor and a low-ranking concubine. Despite his low rank, Genji's charm and good looks quickly make him the emperor's favorite. Genji loses his mother at a young age and is then cared for and raised by his father and various stepmothers. Upon reaching adolescence, he receives education from renowned scholars, making him a perceptive scholar and poet. Genji's romantic escapades are central to the story as he engages in numerous courtly love affairs. He is eventually appointed as the *Minister of the Left*, or *Sadaijin*, a high-ranking court position. Throughout his life, Genji has several wives, including the refined Lady Murasaki, who becomes both a companion and a confidante. The Tale of Genji does not conclude with his death but continues to portray the lives of his descendants and acquaintances.

The Tale of Genji is celebrated for its complex and multidimensional characters, distinctively portraying the aristocracy during Japan's Heian period. The novel is especially noteworthy for its keen insights into human emotions, the complex web of relationships, and the elaborate court rituals of the time. Furthermore, as a female author, Murasaki Shikibu offers a unique perspective on the lives and psychologies of women in a historical context dominated by narratives written by male counterparts.

55. Lebor Gabála Érenn (Unknown, ca. 1050)

> *"Who is its king? I said.*
> *They answered: Mac Cuill, Mac Cecht, and Mac Greine*
> *are the names of the three kings that are over it."*

— *Unknown, Lebor Gabála Érenn*

The Lebor Gabála Érenn (*The Book of Invasions*) is an Irish mythological text. The Bible did not specifically mention Ireland; therefore, the unknown author created an epic narration to incorporate the Irish into *biblical world history*. It recounts the successive invasions of the island by various peoples and tribes. The book begins with the story of *Partholón*, a leader from Greece who, along with his followers, arrives on the island and begins to settle it. He and his people eventually die of the plague, and his memory is forgotten. The second invasion is by the *Nemedians*, a race of seafarers who settle in the north of the island. They are driven out by the *Fomorians*, a tribe of sea-dwellers who ruled for a time. The Fomorians are eventually overthrown by the *Tuatha Dé Danann*, a race of superhuman beings led by their leader *Dagda*. The Tuatha Dé Danann are then challenged by the sons of *Míl Espáine* (*mīles Hispaniae*), a *Scythian* prince. After a conflict, the Tuatha Dé Danann are defeated and driven underground. The sons of Míl Espáine take control of the island and are considered the ancestors of the modern Irish. The book then recounts the island's history up to the time of *St. Patrick* and the coming of Christianity.

Lebor Gabála Érenn is a fundamental source for understanding early Irish literature. It combines narrative techniques like repetition or parallelism to create dramatic images while providing information on mythological events. Additionally, it extensively uses alliteration – a common feature in Old Irish poetry – which helps highlight important points throughout its passages while creating a lyrical rhythm that adds to its poetic quality.

56. The Song of Roland (Turold, 1078)

> *"High are the hills, the valleys dark and deep,*
> *Grisly the rocks, and wondrous grim the steeps.*
> *The French pass through that day with pain and grief;*
> *The bruit of them was heard full fifteen leagues."*

— *Turold, The Song of Roland*

The Song of Roland is one of the earliest and most renowned *Chansons de Geste*, medieval narratives in the form of epic poems recounting heroic deeds. The poem's authorship is traditionally attributed to a Norman poet named Turold, though this attribution is uncertain. The song tells the story of the valiant knight Roland, Charlemagne's nephew, and one of his most loyal warriors. The poem is a fictionalized account of the *Battle of Roncevaux Pass*, portraying it as a conflict between the *Christian Franks* and *Muslim Saracens*, though historically, it was an ambush by Basques. In the poem, Roland is appointed to command the rear guard of Charlemagne's army. As they are attacked by the enemy, Roland is urged to blow his horn, the Oliphant, to call for aid from Charlemagne. Initially reluctant, Roland eventually blows his horn, but help arrives too late to save him and his men. The Franks defeat the Saracens, but Roland is mortally wounded in the battle. He dies, but his bravery and loyalty to Charlemagne are remembered and celebrated. The poem ends with a lament for Roland and his death and celebrates his heroic deeds and devotion.

The Song of Roland is one of the earliest surviving examples of French literature and is a cornerstone of the chivalric tradition of the medieval knight. It is a powerful story of loyalty, heroism, and courage, inspiring readers for centuries. Moreover, although historically imprecise, it offers insights into medieval Europe's political and cultural landscape during the time of Charlemagne. It had an enduring influence on the genre of epic poetry and in solidifying the image of the heroic knight in all subsequent European literature.

The Song of Roland

57. Hayy ibn Yaqdhan (Ibn Tufail, ca. 1125)

> *"Never allowing himself to see any plant or animal*
> *hurt, sick, encumbered, or in need*
> *without helping it if he could."*

> — *Ibn Tufail, Hayy ibn Yaqdhan*

The narrative of Hayy ibn Yaqdhan centers on Hayy, who grows up alone on a deserted island in the Indies, having been raised by a gazelle. Unaware of human society, Hayy evolves into a reflective and self-taught individual, often referred to as *The Solitary*. Hayy engages in natural science, astrology, philosophical contemplation, and religion as he matures, ultimately attaining a *spiritual realization* about God and the unity of creation. Upon reaching adulthood, Hayy encounters Absal, a religious hermit who has come to the island seeking solitude for his devotion. Through Absal, Hayy learns about human society and formal religious beliefs. Intrigued by this new knowledge, Hayy decides to accompany Absal to his homeland to share his philosophical insights and guide people to a purer understanding of God. However, once in the populated land, Hayy finds that the people are entrenched in ritual and not open to his philosophical interpretations. Despite gaining respect for his wisdom, Hayy becomes disillusioned with society's unwillingness to obtain deeper spiritual understanding. He decides to return to his island to live out his days in contemplation and unity with nature.

Tufail tackles three central questions of his time. Firstly, he contends that by solely observing and reflecting upon nature, humans have the innate capability to attain the state of al-Insān al-Kāmil, or the Perfect Human, without formal education. Secondly, he makes a case for the consonance between religion, philosophy, and science, asserting that information gleaned from observation, experimentation, and reasoning does not clash with divine revelation. Lastly, he underlines the individualistic quest for absolute knowledge, maintaining that any human being can achieve enlightenment.

58. Layla and Majnun (Nizami Ganjavi, ca. 1150 CE)

"Whatever befalls us has its meaning, though it is often hard to grasp.
In the Book of Life, every page has two sides.
On the upper one, we inscribe our plans, dreams, and hopes;
the reverse is filled by providence, whose verdicts rarely match our desire."

— *Nizami Ganjavi, Layla and Majnun*

Set in ancient Arabia, the tale revolves around Layla and Majnun, two young lovers who are deeply enamored with each other. However, societal and familial barriers prevent them from being together as they wish. Forced to keep their love a secret, they cherish stolen moments and yearn for a future in which their love can flourish. When Layla's father discovers their relationship, he arranges her marriage to another man, shattering their dreams. Majnun, devastated by the loss, descends into madness. He roams the desert, pouring his heartache into love songs and poems dedicated to Layla. Meanwhile, Layla is trapped in an unhappy marriage, and she has to deal with her husband's suspicions. Eventually, Layla confesses her love for Majnun, leading to her divorce and abandonment by her family. Determined to be reunited, Layla journeys to the desert where Majnun resides. Their passion is rekindled, but their families continue to oppose their union. Desperate to escape, they are captured and separated once again. Majnun is imprisoned, and Layla is labeled as an adulteress. Layla's heart cannot withstand the overwhelming grief, and this leads her to death. Majnun, consumed by sorrow and guilt, is eventually released from prison. He becomes a wandering poet, continuing to express his love for Layla through his verses. As Majnun reaches the end of his life, he experiences a vision in which he is reunited with Layla. During this transcendent moment, he peacefully dies.

The story explores the power of love in the face of societal constraints. Its emotional depth and lyrical beauty have inspired numerous adaptations.

59. Epic of King Gesar (Unknown, ca. 1150)

"No one can block previous karma with their hand."

— *Unknown, Epic of King Gesar*

The Epic of King Gesar is a legendary tale from the ancient kingdom of Ling in eastern Tibet. It revolves around the heroic figure of King Gesar, who possesses extraordinary qualities and is destined to protect his kingdom from evil forces. Born of a divine union between a human mother and a heavenly father, Gesar displays exceptional strength, bravery, and skill in archery and swordsmanship from a young age. When the previous king of Ling dies without an heir, Gesar is chosen as his successor. With his innate abilities and charismatic leadership, Gesar engages in a series of victorious military campaigns, expanding his empire and establishing peace within his realm. However, Gesar's true test comes when he confronts the malevolent kingdom of Trong, which has long been a source of terror for the people of Ling. With his army of loyal warriors, Gesar engages in a fierce battle against the forces of Trong, at last triumphing over them and liberating his kingdom from their tyranny. Having secured the safety of his people, Gesar turns his attention to improving their lives. He institutes measures to promote education and healthcare, enhances infrastructure, and implements welfare programs to support the less fortunate. Additionally, Gesar builds a magnificent temple for worship and communication with the gods. It is believed that Gesar possesses a direct line of contact with the divine, seeking their guidance and receiving miraculous powers to aid his quest for the betterment of his kingdom.

The epic is an integral part of Tibetan culture, contributing to shaping Tibetan identity. Passed down through generations, it continues to be told and cherished in Tibetan villages, preserving the history and traditions of the region.

60. Cantar de mio Cid (Unknown, ca. 1170)

> *"Men and women came out when they appeared;*
> *Merchants and their wives leaned from their windows, staring,*
> *Weeping, overcome with sorrow.*
> *And from their lips,*
> *all of them fell the same prayer:*
> *O God, what a wonderful servant*
> *if only he had a decent master!"*

> — *Unknown, Cantar de mio Cid*

The Cantar de Mio Cid, also known as *Poema de Mio Cid*, is a Castilian epic poem that combines historical events with fictional elements portraying the legendary exploits of a nobleman and military leader, Rodrigo Díaz de Vivar, known as *El Cid*. The poem narrates El Cid's unjust exile by King Alfonso VI and his subsequent campaigns in Castile and Aragon. Throughout the poem, El Cid is depicted as heroic, exemplifying bravery and chivalry as he fights against the Moors and seeks to restore his honor. One of El Cid's notable triumphs includes defeating the Moorish king Al-Mutamid at the *Battle of Cabra*, leading to the capture of Valencia. Additionally, the poem encompasses his endeavors to regain favor with King Alfonso and reinstate his family's honor, which had been tarnished due to his exile. This is achieved not only through his military victories but also through clever diplomacy and unwavering loyalty to the king.

Cantar de Mio Cid is an essential piece of Spanish literature, reflecting medieval Spain's social and political fabric. Moreover, it is instrumental in understanding the development of the Spanish language and is celebrated as the national epic of Spain. The poem's blend of historical and literary elements has made it an enduring classic, extensively studied and revered in educational settings and beyond.

61. Lais of Marie de France (Unknown "Marie de France", ca. 1170)

"Love is not honorable unless it is based on equality."

— *Unknown "Marie de France", Lais of Marie de France*

Lais of Marie de France is a collection of French poems focusing on the tribulations of chivalric love. In the initial story of Yonec, a woman is locked in a tower by her jealous husband. She falls in love with a shape-shifting knight who visits her in the form of a hawk. Together, they have a son named Yonec. The second is the story of Eliduc, a knight in love with two women: his wife and a maiden. After much internal struggle, Eliduc chooses his wife, but the girl is so hurt that she takes her own life. Overcome with intense grief, Eliduc becomes a hermit. The third is the story of Bisclavret, a werewolf who loses the ability to change back into human form due to his wife's betrayal. After years of living in the forest, he is eventually found by a knight who helps him regain his human form. Bisclavret attacks his wife as revenge for her betrayal. The fourth is the story of Lanval, a knight courted by a beautiful fairy. The fifth is the story of Guigemar, a knight cursed with a broken heart. The sixth is the story of Chievrefoil, which tells of two lovers who are separated by their families but then find a way to reunite. The seventh is the story of The Knight of the Lion, who must complete a quest to prove his worthiness.

Marie de France, an appellation that hides the true identity of this influential poet, has long remained a figure shrouded in mystery. Despite this, her impact on French literature is unequivocal, as she is credited to be the first known woman to compose in the French language. The style is characterized by its lyrical elegance full of symbolism through innovative rhyme schemes and assonance.

62. Nibelungenlied (Unknown, ca. 1200)

> *"Whatever I fail to get from them*
> *by friendly requests,*
> *I shall take by my own valour."*
>
> — *Unknown, Nibelungenlied*

This *Middle High German* literature masterpiece recounts the saga of Siegfried, a dashing prince renowned for his valor and nobility. Siegfried falls in love with and marries Kriemhild, a breathtakingly beautiful princess. Their union paves the path for an intricate storyline in the royal court of King Gunther of Burgundy. Siegfried aids Gunther in winning the heart and hand of Brunhild, a fierce warrior queen, through an impressive display of heroism. He receives the Nibelungen hoard as a reward, a symbol of power and wealth. A disagreement between Kriemhild and Brunhild ignites a chain of unfortunate events. Gunther's trusted counselor Hagen deceives Siegfried and murders him to seize the Nibelungen hoard. In the face of her husband's cruel and untimely demise and overcome with grief, Kriemhild seeks revenge against Hagen and her kin. She marries Etzel, the formidable King of the Huns, and cunningly lures Gunther, Hagen, and their retinue to her new kingdom under the guise of reconciliation. Kriemhild's insatiable desire for vengeance leads to a horrifying slaughter at Etzel's court, resulting in the death of her relatives and former allies. She confronts Hagen, slaying him herself, to avenge Siegfried's death. However, her victory is short-lived, as she is killed by Hildebrand, Etzel's legendary warrior and ally.

The Nibelungenlied weaves a tale of love, betrayal, ambition, and revenge, which has resonated with audiences for centuries. The story has inspired many cultural adaptations, including Richard Wagner's celebrated opera cycle Der Ring des Nibelungen.

63. Parzival (Wolfram Eschenbach, 1210)

"Tear-filled eyes make sweet lips."

—— *Wolfram Eschenbach, Parzival*

Parzival is a medieval German romance that focuses on the *Arthurian hero* Parzival and his long quest for the *Holy Grail*. Parzival, initially portrayed as a naïve and innocent youth, is the son of the noble knight Gahmuret and Queen Herzeloyde. Raised in isolation in the forests by his overprotective mother, he is sheltered from the chivalric world and its customs. When Parzival encounters a group of knights, he is fascinated and decides to seek King Arthur's court to become a knight. The impetuous young Parzival takes on a Red Knight and gains his armor and weapons. At Arthur's court, he is dubbed a knight but is still unaware of the many customs and courtesies expected of a knight. One day, Parzival comes across the mystical *Grail Castle*, where he meets the suffering Fisher King Anfortas, who guards the Holy Grail. Parzival fails to ask the crucial question about Anfortas's pain, which would have healed the king, because a fellow knight advised him against talking too much. This failure casts him into a prolonged quest for redemption and self-discovery. Along the way, he marries the beautiful Condwiramurs, encounters mythical beings, faces formidable adversaries, and experiences deep introspection. His path is laden with moral dilemmas and intense combats, ultimately shaping his character. Years later, a mature and enlightened Parzival returns to the Grail Castle. This time, with compassion and understanding, he asks the question that heals the Fisher King's suffering, and is crowned as the Grail King, taking up the mantle of a guardian of the Holy Grail.

Parzival significantly influenced medieval literature, casting ripples that can be traced in subsequent works of prominent authors like Dante and Spenser. The narrative has found a new lease of life in various media, the most notable being Richard Wagner's opera Parsifal.

64. Carmina Burana (Unknown, 1230-1235)

> *"Fate, as vicious as capricious, you're a wheel whirling around.*
> *Evil doings, worthless wooings, crumble away to the ground.*
> *Darkly stealing, unrevealing, working against me, you go.*
> *For your measure of foul pleasure bare-backed,*
> *I bow to your blow."*

— *Unknown, Carmina Burana*

The Carmina Burana is a fascinating manuscript of medieval poems and dramatic texts that gained scholarly attention in the early 19th century. It is preserved in the Benedictine monastery of Benediktbeuern in Bavaria, Germany. This remarkable collection comprises over 200 Latin, Middle High German, and Old French pieces. Its exceptional diversity makes the Carmina Burana truly unique for its time. The works included in the collection were authored by individuals from various regions and social strata, including clerics, *Goliards* (wandering scholars), and possibly students. The topics explored in the poems cover a wide spectrum. Love and drinking songs, moral and satirical poems, and religious hymns all find their place within the manuscript. The poems exhibit a remarkable sense of humor, irreverence, and candidness, offering a glimpse into people's everyday lives and experiences during that time. The poems present frank depictions of carnal desire and revel in the joys of love, romance, and sensual experiences. This juxtaposition of the secular and the religious is notable, with hymns and moralistic texts coexisting alongside the more worldly and pleasure-seeking pieces.

Carmina Burana has significantly influenced subsequent literature, mainly through its innovative use of poetic devices such as alliteration and assonance. Its influence can be observed in works ranging from those of Shakespeare to modern-day poetry. The 20th-century composer Carl Orff famously adapted 24 of the poems from Carmina Burana into a cantata, also titled "Carmina Burana," which has since become a staple in classical music and widely recognized in popular culture.

Masnavi

65. Masnavi (Rumi, 1247)

> *"Out beyond ideas of wrongdoing and rightdoing there is a field.*
> *I'll meet you there. When the soul lies down in that grass*
> *the world is too full to talk about."*

— *Rumi, Masnavi*

The Masnavi (also known as *Mathnawi* or *Mathnavi*), considered one of the most outstanding achievements in the evolution of *Sufi* poetry and thought, is a spiritual and poetic epic comprising six books of poetry that amount to around 25,000 verses or 50,000 lines. It consists of a series of allegorical tales and stories, meant to guide seekers of spiritual wisdom on the path toward union with the Divine, repleting with profound spiritual teachings and immersing the reader in a world rich with mystical insights. One of the central messages of the Masnavi is the concept of *tawhid*, or the *oneness* of God, and the interconnectedness of creation. Rumi encourages the reader to transcend the physical bounds of the world to see the spiritual reality that lies within. He also emphasizes the importance of love as a force that pierces through the illusions of the material world. In the Masnavi, Rumi explores the various facets of Sufism, an esoteric school of *Islamic mysticism*. His poetic narrative journeys through spiritual evolution stages, such as the purification of the soul, overcoming ego, and attaining higher consciousness. Rumi often employs fascinating stories to convey complex metaphysical concepts, making them more accessible and resonant with a broad audience.

Masnavi is an essential work in Persian and Sufi literature that continues to enlighten and inspire. Its influence has been wide-reaching, inspiring literary figures across Eastern and Western cultures. Writers like Goethe, Ralph Waldo Emerson, and Jorge Luis Borges have acknowledged Rumi's influence. In contemporary times, Rumi's poetry, including excerpts from the Masnavi, continues to be widely read, resonating with modern readers who find inspiration and solace in his words.

66. Mabinogion (Unknown, ca. 1250)

> *"So they took the blossoms of the oak,*
> *and the blossoms of the broom,*
> *and the blossoms of the meadow-sweet,*
> *and produced from them a maiden,*
> *the fairest and most graceful that man ever saw.*
> *And they baptized her,*
> *and gave her the name of Blodeuwedd."*

> — *Unknown, Mabinogion*

The Mabinogion, one of the earliest examples of British prose, is an enthralling anthology of Welsh myths and legends. Its stories interlace adventure, magic, and extraordinary feats, providing unique insights into Celtic mythology and ancient societal values. Centered on notable characters, these narratives traverse heroism, tragedy, wisdom, and revenge themes. The following key figures are intricately portrayed: Pwyll, the hero who falls prey to divine deception; Branwen, the tragic princess caught in a cataclysmic conflict; Manawydan, who grapples with a curse inflicted by a malevolent sorcerer; and Gwydion, entangled in familial power struggles. The tales also depict the adventures of the prophet-bard Taliesin and the undeterred Culhwch in his quest for Olwen's hand. Other stories narrate magical duels, as in the tale of Lludd and Llefelys, the king brothers of Britain and France; while some recount heroic quests, as in the journeys of the valiant warrior Peredur. These narratives, marked by their distinct plotlines and unpredictable turns, vividly depict ancient Celtic life and morality.

The Mabinogion's enduring allure lies in its seamless blend of the fantastical and the ordinary: capturing the essence of adventure, the complexities of power and conflict, and the timeless pursuit of knowledge and wisdom. Through its richness and diversity, this significant literary work continues to reflect Wales's cultural and historical roots, casting a lasting impact on mythology and folklore.

67. Poetic Edda (Unknown, ca. 1250)

"I have traveled so much,
I have tried much,
and I have often tested the mighty.
How will there still be a Sun
when the wolf has eaten
the one that now flies in heaven?"

— *Unknown, Poetic Edda*

The Poetic Edda is an invaluable source of *Norse mythology* and a significant part of *Viking Age* literature. These tales chronicle the adventures of gods like Odin, Thor, Freya, and Loki, illustrating their confrontations with giants and monsters. The Edda begins with the story of creation, depicting how Odin fashioned the world from the void and blessed humans and animals with life and gifts like poetry and music. Subsequent tales center on Thor, Odin's warrior-god son, and his endeavors to safeguard Asgard. It also introduces a pantheon of gods such as Loki, Baldur, Heimdallr, Bragi, and Freyja. The work concludes with Ragnarok, describing the prophecy of the world's end and the cataclysmic battle between gods and giants. In addition to the more protracted sagas and epics, several shorter poems offer a glimpse into Norse society during the period in which they were recorded. These works touch on various topics, including love, friendship, wisdom, and the virtues of courage and honor. They also explore the joys and sorrows of life, the workings of fate, the beauty of the natural world, and the mysteries of magic.

These poems give us an invaluable glimpse into the Viking Age. Its influence can be seen in later works such as Richard Wagner's Der Ring des Nibelungen (1876). The Poetic Edda is unique among ancient texts from this period because it uses alliterative verse forms like kennings (metaphorical phrases) or skaldic stanzas (longer narrative passages). Ancient bards used these techniques to create memorable and evocative verses endowed with musicality.

68. Summa Theologica (Thomas Aquinas, 1250)

"To be united to God in the unity of person
was not fitting to human flesh,
according to its natural endowments,
since it was above his dignity;
nevertheless, it was provided that God,
because of his infinite goodness,
should unite it to himself for human salvation."

— *Thomas Aquinas, Summa Theologica*

Summa Theologica is a masterful synthesis of Christian theology and philosophy, extending from the existence and attributes of God to the nature of the soul, the problem of evil, and the intricacies of moral life. Drawing on the Aristotelian tradition, Christian theology, and the wisdom of the Church Fathers, Aquinas creates a comprehensive vision of the truth about God and the world. For Aquinas, philosophy and theology are not opposed but complementary since both aim at the same ultimate goal: to understand the truth about God and the world. The work is structured into three sections mirroring Aquinas's systematic approach: the first explores God and creation, addressing God's existence, simplicity, perfection, infinity, and the problem of evil; the second delves into the moral life of humans, discussing human happiness, virtues, vices, and the interplay of law, justice, and grace; the third centers on Christ and the sacraments, elaborating on incarnation, redemption, and the Church's sacramental life.

Considered a cornerstone of Christian thought, Summa Theologica demonstrates a powerful fusion of reason and faith. Its enduring relevance lies in its profound influence on Christian theology and philosophical education, making it an indispensable resource for understanding the intellectual underpinnings of Christian belief. Moreover, its systematic exploration of ethical questions provides a comprehensive framework for moral reasoning, extending its significance beyond religious discourse.

69. Sumer is Icumen in (Unknown, 1263)

> *"Sumer is icumen in, Lhude sing cuccu!*
> *The seed grows, and the meadow blooms*
> *And the wood springs anew, sing, cuccu!"*
>
> — *Unknown, Sumer is Icumen in*

This medieval English song provides a joyous proclamation of summer's arrival and nature's resurgence, encapsulating the awe and exhilaration of witnessing the rejuvenation of life during the vibrant season. It is an ode to the pulsating vitality of life and the invigorating experience of being surrounded by such rich natural beauty. The song is structured as a scenic journey, leading us through an enchanting landscape alive with summer's sounds, sights, and sensations. The listeners are invited to partake in a shared experience: walking through a meadow teeming with wildflowers, feeling the cooling spray of a river with crystal clear waters, and taking in the beauty of the serene countryside. The ode celebrates these simple joys of life, painting an idyllic picture of summertime pleasures. As the day gives way to night, the distant sound of church bells wafts through the air, echoing the jubilant motif of the song and welcoming the arrival of summer. This melodic symbol of joy harmonizes perfectly with the song's optimistic message: "Summer has arrived – let's indulge in its beauty!"

"Sumer is Icumen in" holds historical importance as it is one of England's oldest-known secular songs. It is an example of a rota (round), a musical composition where voices sing the same melody but start at different times, creating an enthralling call-and-response pattern. In this song, one voice initiates with "sumer," and the other echoes with "icumen." This piece incorporates a fascinating blend of traditional musical practices, employing modal scales and melodic patterns known as "cantus firmi." Its enduring charm and musical complexity showcase the sophistication of medieval music, offering unique insights into the artistic expression of that era.

70. Roman de la Rose (Guillaume de Lorris; Jean de Meun, 1275)

"Many a man holds dreams to be but lies,
All fabulous, but there have been some dreams
No whit deceptive, as was later found."

— *Guillaume de Lorris; Jean de Meun, Roman de la Rose*

Roman de la Rose is a profound medieval French poem exploring the intricacies and paradoxes of *courtly love*. It unwinds as an allegorical dream journey to achieve an object of desire – *the Rose*, representing an *ideal woman*. Guillaume de Lorris commences the narrative with the protagonist, an unseasoned lover, accidentally discovering a charming walled garden, symbolic of the *feminine mystique*. In this enchanted domain, he encounters a beautiful rose, the embodiment of idealized love. As he attempts to pluck the rose, he is pricked by its thorns, and this pain leads him to become a servant of the *God of Love*. His service to the *God of Love* sets him on an arduous quest to attain the rose, representing the pursuit of love. In Jean de Meun's continuation, the journey veers towards a more philosophical and satirical exploration. The lover's quest becomes a complex labyrinth populated by various allegorical figures, each representing aspects of medieval thought on love, religion, and philosophy. These include notable personifications like *Jealousy*, *Envy*, and a wise old woman named *La Vieille*. These encounters illuminate various facets of human existence, prompting introspection and enlightenment in the process. Through trial, tribulation, and wisdom, the lover finally reunites with his rose, signifying the attainment of love amidst life's complexities.

Roman de la Rose is a canvas reflecting medieval society's intellectual and moral norms. This sophisticated work of literature blends intricate allegory with rich lyrical eloquence, underscored by poetic devices such as alliteration and assonance. Its influential legacy impacted later literary works, including Geoffrey Chaucer's "Canterbury Tales."

71. Njáls Saga (Unknown, ca. 1270-1290)

> *"You will be paid for like any other free man.*
> *You will be paid for in blood."*
>
> — *Unknown, Njáls Saga*

Njáls Saga is an epic tale from the *Icelandic Commonwealth* period, centering around Njáll Þorgeirsson, a respected lawyer known for his wisdom and fairness. Njáll shares a deep friendship with Gunnar Hámundarson, a noble warrior known for his bravery and impeccable character. The saga's narrative weaves a complex fabric of feuds and alliances sparked not by the principal characters but by their wives Bergthora and Hallgerd, respectively. In an escalating cycle of retaliation, these women instigate a series of bloody acts of revenge that entangle their husbands and sons, pulling them into a vortex of violence that spirals out of control. Caught in the web of these conflicts, Gunnar earns the wrath of his community, leading to his outlawry. During an attack on his home, Gunnar fights valiantly but is ultimately unwilling to kill a man he recognizes as his kinsman, and this seals his fate. His death leaves a void in Njáll's life. This void is further deepened when Njáll's sons, under the influence of an ill-omened marriage alliance, transgress societal norms and invoke the wrath of their peers. As the feuds intensify, they culminate in a tragic event – the burning of Njáll's house. Njáll willingly stays in the burning house with his wife, while his sons are killed – an episode of chilling brutality. Finally, Njáll's foster son Kári confronts those responsible for the bloodshed and brings an end to the long-standing feuds.

Njáls Saga is a striking exploration of friendship, honor, and fate set against the harsh and law-driven backdrop of 10th and 11th-century Iceland. It masterfully weaves personal narratives with significant societal complexities and keeps readers engrossed until the tragic end.

72. The Travels of Marco Polo (Marco Polo, 1298-1300)

"If you put together all the Christians in the world,
with their Emperors and their Kings, the whole of these Christians
— aye, and throw in the Saracens to boot —
would not have such power or be able to do so much as this Kublai."

— *Marco Polo, The Travels of Marco Polo*

The book is the account of the Venetian explorer Marco Polo's famous journey to the Far East. It was written by Rustichello da Pisa, who transcribed Marco Polo's memoirs under dictation while the two were imprisoned in Genoa. In 1271, Marco, his father Nicolo, and his uncle Maffeo set out from Venice on their journey east. They traveled overland through Anatolia and Persia and eventually arrived at the court of Kublai Khan in China. The Khan was extremely impressed by Marco's knowledge of the world, and he placed him in high favor at his court. Marco spent the next several years traveling throughout the Khan's empire, gathering information and learning about the customs and cultures of the people he encountered. On his return trip to Venice, Marco stopped in many cities along the way. He wrote about the beautiful places he had seen, the exotic foods he had tasted, and the people he had met. When he finally returned to Venice in 1295, he brought a wealth of information about the Far East. Sometime after his return, Marco was captured and imprisoned during the conflict with Genoa, where he met Rustichello da Pisa.

The book was an instant success and was widely read across Europe. It sparked a renewed interest in exploration and travel and inspired many Europeans to set out and explore the world. The Travels of Marco Polo is considered one of the first detailed accounts of the Far East and Central Asia. It contains geographical descriptions and practical advice for travelers. The book's narrative style is highly engaging, and its contents are wide-ranging, covering various topics about Asia, including geography, politics, economics, customs, and culture.

73. Codex Runicus (Unknown, ca. 1300)

"I dreamed a dream last night
Of silk and fine fur
Of right and honest play."

— *Unknown, Codex Runicus*

The Codex is an invaluable treasure trove for understanding medieval Scandinavian society's social, legal, and cultural facets. Comprising around 202 pages, it is distinctively written in the medieval *runic alphabet*, known as *futhark*, and primarily contains the *Scanian Law* (*Skånske lov*), one of the earliest provincial laws of Denmark. The Scanian Law encompasses a broad spectrum of legal issues and regulations by offering intricate insights into the societal norms and practices in the region of Scania, which was part of Denmark during the 13th century but now part of modern-day Sweden. These include, but are not limited to, laws on marriage, inheritance, property rights, penalties for various crimes, and societal obligations. One of the intriguing aspects of the Codex Runicus is its use of runes, an ancient script that predates the adoption of the Latin alphabet in Northern Europe. Runes have an air of mystique and are often associated with magic and divination in popular culture. Additionally, the Codex Runicus contains a *runic calendar* at the end of the manuscript. This calendar is an intriguing fusion of ancient pagan and Christian traditions, with notations of Christian feast days along with astronomical events, which would have been significant in the agrarian society of the time. Codex Runicus is an essential resource for studying the Old Norse language and the evolution of runic scripts.

In contemporary culture, the allure of runes and the Viking Age continues to stimulate imaginations. Codex Runicus is an inspiration and a resource for authors, researchers, and enthusiasts who seek to explore and portray the rich tapestry of Scandinavian history and myth.

74. The Divine Comedy (Dante Alighieri, 1306-1321)

"In the midway of our mortal life,
I found myself in a gloomy wood, astray"

— Dante Alighieri, The Divine Comedy

Dante's journey is both a search for his beloved Beatrice and a profound exploration of the progression of the human soul toward salvation, passing through a moral reflection on the concepts of sin, virtue, punishment, and redemption. The Divine Comedy comprises three sections, referred to as *cantiche* in Italian (singular *cantica*). These sections are *Inferno* (Hell), *Purgatorio* (Purgatory), and *Paradiso* (Paradise). Each section contains 33 *canti* (singular *canto*) plus an additional introductory *canto*. Inferno begins with Dante lost in a dark forest and attacked by three wild beasts. He is rescued by the Roman poet Virgil, who guides him through the *nine circles of Hell*. Dante encounters various sinners in each circle, ranging from the violent and lustful to the treacherous and fraudulent. Dante and Virgil eventually reach the center of Hell, where they encounter Satan, imprisoned in ice. Dante then ascends *Mount Purgatory* and cleanses himself of the sins he discovered in Hell, meeting other souls who seek to redeem and purify themselves through prayer and by listening to examples of punished sins mixed with rewarded virtues. In the final cantos of Purgatorio, Dante finds Beatrice, and she guides him to Heaven. Dante encounters the *nine celestial spheres* representing the *nine circles of Heaven*, and here he meets various saints, angels, and prophets, each one providing him with divine knowledge. He meets Beatrice again, and together, they reach the ultimate goal of the journey: the presence of God. Dante is granted the power to write and share his experience with the world.

The Divine Comedy is a universally recognized masterpiece and one of the first examples of an epic poem written in Italian rather than Latin, thus paving the way for a new era in Italian language and culture.

The Divine Comedy

75. Tsurezuregusa (Yoshida Kenko, 1330-1332)

> *"It is an admirable thing in a man*
> *to keep his mind on the world to come,*
> *and remain heedful of the Buddhist path."*
>
> — *Yoshida Kenko, Tsurezuregusa*

Tsurezuregusa, or *Essays in Idleness*, is a collection of 243 musings by Yoshida Kenko, a Buddhist monk. His essays encompass a variety of topics, reflecting on religion, the transitory nature of life, and the essence of existence. Though appearing random and unrelated, the essays coalesce into an intriguing exploration of medieval Japanese philosophy. Kenko's contemplations reveal a deep understanding of Buddhism and its teachings. He underlines the significance of mindfulness and spiritual connection, drawing parallels with life and death and our pursuit of meaningful existence. Another recurrent thought is the impermanence of the world. Kenko's reflections promote acceptance of change and the ephemeral nature of reality. Moreover, Kenko explores the human condition by encouraging his readers to live authentically, cognizant of our mortality. His reflections exhort us to appreciate life's fleeting beauty and extract joy from every moment, shining light upon the essence of existence. Despite its seemingly haphazard structure, Kenko's Tsurezuregusa is a philosophical work that offers profound insights into life, spirituality, and our transient world. The work's lyrical style has influenced writers to adopt its eloquent and expressive language.

This influential collection provides an invaluable look into medieval Japan's mindset; contributing significantly to Japanese literature and philosophy; with its impact resonating through subsequent literature due to its lyrical style and evocative language. Kenko's work inspires readers by illuminating their path toward a mindful and fulfilling life.

76. Il Canzoniere (Francesco Petrarca, 1336-1374)

> *"You who hear in scattered rhymes the sound of those sighs*
> *with which I nourished my heart during my first youthful error*
> *when I was in part another man from what I am now."*

— *Francesco Petrarca, Il Canzoniere*

Il Canzoniere, also known as *Rime Sparse* or *Scattered Rhymes*, is an exquisite collection of 366 poems exploring themes of unrequited love, spirituality, and the fugitive nature of life. Petrarch's verses are characterized by their innovative structures, skillful blending of classical forms, and expressive lyricism, cementing his status as one of the greatest Italian poets ever. The collection is traditionally divided into two main sections: *In Vita di Madonna Laura* and *In Morte di Madonna Laura*. These sections distinguish the poems Petrarch wrote during Laura's lifetime from those written after her death. Laura, an elusive figure believed to be based on a woman Petrarch met in 1327, serves as the focal point of Petrarch's impassioned verses. The intensity of his emotions is poignantly articulated, rendering his unrequited love in relatable, universal terms. In addition to the problem of unattainable love, Petrarch's poetry navigates the complex terrain of spirituality and the human quest for salvation. His relationship with Laura is an allegory for his spiritual journey, with his unwavering faith mirroring his passionate but unfulfilled pursuit of love. The collection is also imbued with a palpable sense of the evanescent nature of life. Petrarch's reflections on mortality and the transient nature of existence lend a melancholic tone to his poems, resonating with the universal human condition.

Il Canzoniere is a masterpiece of lyric poetry. Petrarch's exploration of love, spirituality, and mortality within his poetry provides profound insights into the human experience, leaving an indelible mark on the literary landscape. His work has significantly influenced European literature and continues to inspire writers and poets today.

77. Romance of the Three Kingdoms (Luo Guanzhong, ca. 1350)

> *"The long-divided empire must unite;*
> *long united must divide."*
>
> — *Luo Guanzhong,* Romance of the Three Kingdoms

The Romance of the Three Kingdoms is a classic Chinese novel set during the tumultuous *period of the kingdoms* in the 2nd and 3rd centuries. The book explores the power struggles and conflicts between the three main kingdoms: Wei, Shu, and Wu, as they vie for control over ancient China. The story begins with the decline and fall of the Han Dynasty, leading to the empire's fragmentation into three kingdoms. The central characters of the novel are the warlords Cao Cao, Liu Bei, and Sun Quan, each representing one of the three kingdoms. Cao Cao, known for his cunning and ambition, quickly rises to prominence and seeks to conquer his rivals. On the other hand, Liu Bei and Sun Quan form a coalition to resist Cao Cao's advances. The novel follows the epic battles, political maneuverings, and personal relationships between the warlords and their generals. It highlights the military strategies of renowned figures such as Zhuge Liang and the valor and loyalty of famous warriors like Guan Yu and Zhang Fei. One of the most significant events depicted in the novel is the Battle of Red Cliff, where the combined forces of Liu Bei and Sun Quan successfully repel Cao Cao's massive army. This battle showcases the strategists' brilliance and the warriors' courage.

This literary masterpiece has had a profound impact on Chinese culture and society. It has inspired countless literature, theater, film, and video game adaptations. The novel has become a symbol of Chinese identity and has shaped how people perceive and understand the Three Kingdoms period of Chinese history.

78. The Decameron (Giovanni Boccaccio, ca. 1350)

"Kissed mouth doesn't lose its fortune,
on the contrary it renews itself just as the moon does."

— *Giovanni Boccaccio, The Decameron*

The Decameron is a collection of 100 stories told over ten days by seven young women and three young men who have fled the *Black Death* epidemic in Florence and taken refuge in a villa outside the city. On each day, one of the group members recites a story. The first day begins with Pampinea, who tells a tale about two lovers who trick their parents into allowing them to marry. This sets the tone for many of the following stories, which involve deception and clever ruses to achieve desired ends. On the second day, Filostrato narrates a tale that varies in subjects similar to the other stories in the collection. Neifile recounts a story on the third day about an old man whose daughter falls in love with a knight despite his disapproval. Each group member takes turns telling stories involving different themes such as betrayal, infidelity, unrequited love, loyalty, chivalry, and revenge. Many of these stories involve characters from different social classes interacting with one another or struggling against oppressive systems such as feudalism or patriarchy. Throughout all ten days of storytelling, there is much discussion among the characters about life's joys and sorrows, as well as philosophical musings on human nature and morality.

The Decameron is renowned for its description of characters and variety of style, ranging from romance to satire, and for its influence on subsequent works, including Geoffrey Chaucer's Canterbury Tales. By blending elements from antiquity with contemporary issues relevant during his period (such as social class differences), Boccaccio created a unique narrative style that is both entertaining and thought-provoking.

79. Water Margin (Shi Naian, ca. 1370)

> *"Any food when you're hungry,*
> *When you're cold rags save life;*
> *Any road when you're frightened,*
> *When you're poor any wife."*

> — *Shi Naian, Water Margin*

This highly acclaimed 14th-century Chinese novel, offers a vivid account of the adventures and exploits of 108 outlaws led by the charismatic Song Jiang. Situated at the intersection of historical fact and folklore, the narrative is set against political instability and social unrest. The epic tale unwraps as these disaffected individuals, driven to society's margins by corruption and injustice, converge at the remote outpost of Mount Liang. Here, they form a sizable army determined to fight against the systemic corruption of the ruling class and the stark societal inequalities that plague their land. The central figure Song Jiang emerges as a figure of defiance and courage. Together with his loyal associates, they traverse the length and breadth of China, rallying their cause and expanding their ranks with the oppressed and disenfranchised. The outlaws, each with a unique backstory and distinct personality traits, eventually become known as the *108 Stars of Destiny*, a direct reference to the Taoist tradition where the deity Shangdi banishes 108 rebellious overlords. Despite their status as outlaws, these figures are portrayed not as mere bandits but as individuals driven to rebellion by the insurmountable pressures of an unjust system. The climactic battles lead to their eventual triumph over hostile forces, reinstating peace and justice in a land once marred by turmoil.

Water Margin holds a seminal place in the canon of Chinese fiction for its masterful characters development and the dynamic interplay of socio-political subjects.

Water Margin

80. The Tale of the Heike (Anonymous, 1371)

> *"The proud do not endure; they are like a dream on a spring night;*
> *the mighty fall at last; they are as dust before the wind."*

— *Anonymous, The Tale of the Heike*

The Tale of the Heike, also known as *Heike Monogatari*, is a monumental epic that artfully captures the historical realities and philosophical nuances of late 12th-century Japan. Predominantly focusing on the *Genpei War*, a brutal civil strife between the Taira and Minamoto clans that lasted from 1180 to 1185, the epic paints a rich and immersive picture of the era's tumultuous political landscape. The story commences in the immediate aftermath of the Taira clan's disastrous defeat at the *Battle of Dan-no-ura*, where the tides of fortune shifted in favor of the Minamoto. The narrative swiftly retreats into the past; plunging into the heart of the complex court intrigues; the capricious shifts in power; and the relentless march toward the clan's inevitable downfall. The aftermath of the battle is marked by tragedy. Emperor Antoku, the young figurehead of the Taira clan, is drowned in the turbulent sea, symbolizing the sinking fortunes of his clan. The Taira clan's leader Kiyomori had previously passed away, but his ambition and actions had led his clan to this fate. The story concludes on a somber note, demonstrating the cyclical and ephemeral nature of power dynamics, deeply ingrained in the Buddhist concept of impermanence. The Minamoto clan's victory, while a cause for celebration, is also a reminder of the transient nature of glory and the inexorable cycle of rise and fall.

The tale's enduring cultural impact can be seen in its profound influence on various Japanese art and literature forms. It has inspired countless poems, plays, and visual art forms. Its tense characterization, evocative descriptions, and blend of historical fact and fiction have solidified its reputation as an exemplary work of Japanese epic literature.

81. Sir Gawain and the Green Knight (Unknown, ca. 1375)

> *"And now, Gawain: think. Danger is yours to overcome*
> *And this game brings you danger. Can this game be won?"*

> —— *Unknown*, Sir Gawain and the Green Knight

Sir Gawain and the Green Knight is a Middle English poem that portrays Sir Gawain, one of the Knights of the Round Table from King Arthur's court. On New Year's Day, a mysterious Green Knight arrives at Arthur's court and issues a challenge: he will allow any knight to strike him with his axe on the condition that he can return the blow one year and one day later. King Arthur initially offers to take up the challenge, but Sir Gawain bravely insists on accepting it in his stead. Gawain beheads the Green Knight, but to everyone's astonishment, the Green Knight picks up his head and reminds Gawain of their agreement. Gawain sets off on a perilous journey to find the Green Knight and fulfill his part of the challenge. Along the way, he stays at a lord's castle, where he becomes involved in a series of tests of his chivalry and honesty. Eventually, Gawain arrives at the Green Chapel to meet the Green Knight for their fateful encounter. The Green Knight swings his axe at Gawain but stops short as a test. On the third swing, he nicks Gawain's neck. The Green Knight then reveals that he is actually the lord of the castle where Gawain stayed, and the challenge was a test of the chivalry and honor of Arthur's knights. Gawain returns to Camelot, wearing a green sash as a symbol of his failure to fully uphold his knightly virtues and learning experience. The court, however, celebrates his honesty and bravery.

Sir Gawain and the Green Knight is one of the earliest and most revered works written in Middle English and is known for its intricate structure, rich language, and exploration of themes such as chivalry, honor, and human nature. It has influenced subsequent literature and continues to be studied as a significant piece of early English literature.

82. Piers Plowman (William Langland, 1377)

> *"But all the wickedness in the world which man may do or think*
> *is no more to the mercy of God than a live coal dropped in the sea."*

— *William Langland, Piers Plowman*

Piers Plowman is an intricate *Middle English* allegorical poem that evolves through a series of dream-visions experienced by the protagonist, known as *Will*, who embarks on a profound spiritual quest. The opening vision introduces a sprawling field of people representing the breadth of societal hierarchies, from peasants to church officials. A key figure in the tale is *Piers Plowman*, a hardworking peasant, symbolic of humble Christian virtue and the personification of patient toil. Will is told to seek Truth, which becomes his journey's motivating force. Throughout the poem, Will engages with various allegorical characters such as the *Seven Deadly Sins*, *Lady Meed* (representing materialistic desire), and personifications of theological virtues. One notable sequence is Will's encounter with Lady Meed, where he is brought into a critique of political and ecclesiastical corruption when Lady Meed is proposed to be wed to False, an act vehemently opposed by Conscience. This episode, set in the House of Commons, exposes the greed and corruption prevalent in society's upper echelons. As the narrative progresses, Will is introduced to allegorical characters who represent *Do-Well*, *Do-Better*, and *Do-Best*, embodying escalating moral and spiritual perfection levels. Through these interactions, the poem explores complex issues of faith, ethics, and societal responsibilities. The poem urges love for God above everything to maintain social harmony and reflects Christian morality and the quest for truth.

With its unique narrative structure, alliterative verse, and compelling allegory, Piers Plowman is a landmark of Middle English literature, greatly influencing future works, including Chaucer's "Canterbury Tales" and the morality plays of the late Middle Ages.

83. Troilus and Criseyde (Geoffrey Chaucer, ca. 1385-1388)

> *"Time, force and death, do to this body what extremity you can;*
> *But the strong base and building of my love*
> *is as the very centre of the earth, drawing all things to it."*

> — *Geoffrey Chaucer, Troilus and Criseyde*

Troilus and Criseyde is a poem that vividly portrays the doomed love story between Troilus, the valiant young prince of Troy, and Criseyde, a noble Trojan widow. The tale begins as Troilus, the son of King Priam of Troy, attends a temple in the city, where he first lays eyes upon the beautiful and virtuous Criseyde. He is instantly consumed by love as profound as it is unrequited. He suffers in silence until his dear friend Pandarus, Criseyde's uncle, discerns his affliction. Sympathetic to Troilus's plight, Pandarus facilitates their love by arranging secret meetings and becoming their confidant. They exchange vows of love, but their joy is ephemeral, for fate soon conspires against them. Criseyde's father Calchas, who defected to the Greeks, bargains with his new allies to exchange a Trojan prisoner for his daughter. This agreement forces Criseyde to abandon Troilus and Troy. Despite her initial resistance to leaving Troilus, Criseyde makes a promise that she will find a way to return to him within ten days. However, as she stays longer among the Greeks, she is pursued by Diomedes, a Greek warrior. Overwhelmed by her circumstances and swayed by Diomedes, she eventually breaks her vow to Troilus, who is heartbroken. Troilus never recovers from his loss, and his life is cut tragically short when he is killed in combat without ever seeing his beloved again.

Chaucer's masterpiece is a landmark of English literature that successfully weaves love, destiny, and deceit motives. It influenced other works, including Shakespeare's "Troilus and Cressida," and drew from earlier sources, such as Boccaccio's "Il Filostrato." The poem is considered a vital precursor to the Renaissance's humanist writings.

84. The Canterbury Tales (Geoffrey Chaucer, 1387-1400)

"You're doing nothing else but wasting time.
Sir, in a word, you shall no longer rhyme."

— *Geoffrey Chaucer, The Canterbury Tales*

The tales present a richly detailed, often humorous, and sometimes profoundly critical portrait of 14th-century English society. The narrative spreads as a collection of stories told by a diverse group of pilgrims journeying from a London inn to visit the shrine of Saint Thomas Becket in Canterbury. They agree on a storytelling contest to entertain each other during their long travels. The inn's host will judge the stories, and the best storyteller will be awarded a free meal at the inn upon their return. The collection comprises 24 tales, though it appears that Chaucer initially intended to include more. These stories vary widely in genre by encompassing courtly romance, beast fable, moral allegory, saintly life, chivalric fantasy, and sermon. They are narrated by characters as varied as their tales: a knight, miller, reeve, wife of Bath, pardoner, and nun's priest. Among the memorable adventures, the *Knight's Tale* presents a romantic saga of two knights competing for a lady's love. In contrast, *Miller's Tale* is a farcical story involving a carpenter, his young wife, and her two admirers. The *Wife of Bath's Tale* recounts a knight who must discover what women desire most as punishment for his crime. The *Pardoner's Tale* focuses on three young men who let their greed lead them to a tragic end, and the *Nun's Priest's Tale* narrates the story of a rooster named Chauntecleer who outwits a sly fox.

Chaucer's narrative style brilliantly integrates the vernacular of his contemporary world with sophisticated literary forms, marking a significant moment in the evolution of English literature. The collection is a fascinating historical document providing insights into medieval life, including its social classes, gender roles, beliefs, and practices. Above all, it exhibits Chaucer's incisive wit, understanding of human nature, and skill in characterization.

The Canterbury Tales

85. Revelations of Divine Love (Julian of Norwich, 1395)

> *"All shall be well and all shall be well*
> *and all manner of things shall be well."*

— *Julian of Norwich, Revelations of Divine Love*

Revelations of Divine Love is recognized as the first English-language book written by a woman. It chronicles Julian's series of sixteen mystical visions or showings of divine love, which she received during a severe illness when she believed she was near death. These visions inspire a profound theological meditation on the nature of God, Christ's passion, divine providence, and the problem of evil. Julian devotes her life to solitude and contemplation as an anchoress living in a small cell attached to a church. The visions range from witnessing the suffering of Christ to beholding the entirety of creation contained within a hazelnut. These divine encounters, punctuated with the assuring phrase "all shall be well," inspire her to explore and question the deep mysteries of Christianity, such as the concept of sin, salvation, and divine compassion. Challenging conventional religious doctrine, her ideas are initially met with skepticism from the Church authorities, even accusations of heresy, especially for her audacious ideas about God's *motherly* nature and the nonexistence of eternal damnation. However, her profound teachings resonate with many Christians, gradually gaining popularity. Her unique interpretation of divine love and optimism in the face of adversity inspires many believers, transforming Julian into a celebrated spiritual guide.

Revelations of Divine Love is a testament to Julian's deep faith, capacity for theological reflection, and courage to question established norms. Julian's reflections on divine love, sin, and redemption provide a compassionate alternative to the stern theology of her time. She emphasizes God's love and understanding as the path to spiritual growth and redemption, a powerful and relevant message today.

86. The Book of the City of Ladies (Christine de Pizan, 1405)

"To me, the City of Ladies seems like a dream,
for I have never seen or heard anything about such a city before."

— *Christine de Pizan, The Book of the City of Ladies*

The Book of the City of Ladies is an allegorical text widely considered one of the first works of *feminist* literature. The narrative is propelled by a dream of Christine herself, who is disheartened by her readings of women's inferiority and vilification in literature. Three personifications of virtues visit her – *Lady Reason, Lady Rectitude,* and *Lady Justice* – who commission her to construct an emblematic *City of Ladies.* The edification of this city is not a physical task but an intellectual one, where each *brick* is a tale of a remarkable woman from history, myth, and the bible. Christine dismantles misogynistic assumptions pervasive in her society by amassing stories of valiant and virtuous women like Queen Esther, the Amazons, and Saint Catherine. She challenges the contemporary discourse that unfairly slanders women, arguing that women's perceived inferiority is not due to their nature but their lack of access to education and opportunities. The women whose stories form the city's foundation highlight female strength, wisdom, virtue, and potential, proving that women can significantly contribute to society, religion, and culture. With the city's completion, Christine offers an alternative model for understanding women's roles, advocating recognition of women's worth beyond their traditional confines.

The Book of the City of Ladies is a notable defense of women's potential and an attack against misogynistic prejudice. Its emphasis on female empowerment and its groundbreaking critique of patriarchal norms marks it as an essential work in the canon of feminist literature. Pizan's achievement underscores women's historical contributions and offers a space of validation and affirmation for women's value in society by collecting the stories of numerous virtuous women in one place.

87. The Book of Abramelin (Abraham of Worms, 1458)

> *"Attempt no other thing but to excite thee*
> *unto the research of this Sacred Magic."*
>
> — *Abraham of Worms, The Book of Abramelin*

The Book of Abramelin, also known as *The Sacred Magic of Abramelin the Mage,* is an occult grimoire believed to have been written by Abraham von Worms, a German Jewish scholar. The book presents a system of ceremonial magic and spiritual development. It follows the story of Abraham, who embarks on a quest to obtain the knowledge and conversation of his *Holy Guardian Angel.* He travels to Egypt, where he encounters an Egyptian *mage* named Abramelin, from whom he learns the sacred rites and practices. These include prayer, fasting and the evocation of divine names and forces. Through these actions, the magician seeks to establish a personal relationship with their Guardian Angel and gain access to magical powers and divine wisdom. The book provides detailed instructions on the rituals, purification methods, and angelic invocations required to achieve the desired spiritual goals. It emphasizes the importance of moral and ethical conduct and the dedication and discipline needed for success in the magical arts.

The Book of Abramelin, known for its comprehensive approach to spiritual transcendence and magical practice, has left an indelible mark on the Western occult tradition. Notable for its emphasis on achieving spiritual enlightenment through the knowledge and conversation of the Holy Guardian Angel, it has offered a unique and profound methodology that has resonated with various occultists and spiritual seekers. Its influence has extended to prominent figures within the occult world, including Samuel Liddel MacGregor Mathers, a co-founder of the Hermetic Order of the Golden Dawn, who translated the work into English in the late 19th century. It has also significantly influenced Aleister Crowley, a prominent British occultist, who adopted and expanded upon Abramelin's teaching methods.

The Book of Abramelin

88. Le Morte d'Arthur (Thomas Malory, 1485)

> *"And ever Sir Launcelot cried unto his lord King Arthur for help;*
> *and so did many other knights that were with him;*
> *but all was lost for Sir Launcelot had no might to help himself."*

— *Thomas Malory, Le Morte d'Arthur*

Le Morte d'Arthur chronicles the legend of King Arthur, from the tale of his conception and birth to his eventual demise. Uther Pendragon, King Arthur's father, dies early in the narrative. Amidst a tumultuous power struggle for the throne, the enigmatic wizard Merlin intervenes, enchanting a sword and embedding it firmly within an anvil. Only Arthur, destined to be the rightful heir, possesses the strength and purity of heart to extract the legendary sword, solidifying his claim to the throne. Arthur later receives another sword, *Excalibur*, with mystical powers. Guided by a vision of unity and justice, Arthur gathers noble knights across Britain, establishing the illustrious *Round Table*. Bound by oaths of loyalty and camaraderie, these valiant warriors become the embodiment of chivalry and honor. With Excalibur in his hand and his trusted knights by his side, Arthur strives to create a realm of harmony and virtue. Within the heart of Camelot, a forbidden love takes root. Queen Guinevere, ensnared by the alluring presence of Sir Lancelot du Lac, succumbs to a love that defies the boundaries of loyalty and duty. The revelation of their clandestine affair disgraces Lancelot, leading to his banishment from Camelot by the betrayed and heartbroken Arthur. As whispers of discontent echo through the kingdom, the foundations of Arthur's noble realm begin to crumble. The conflict among the knights intensifies and culminates with Arthur being mortally wounded.

Le Morte d'Arthur shapes the essence of English literature as one of the earliest works composed in prose. By bringing these enchanting tales to the common people, Malory opened the gates to a world of knights, quests, and grandeur, forever etching the Arthurian legend into the collective imagination.

89. Malleus Maleficarum (H. Kramer, J. Sprenger, 1486-1487)

"But devils are subservient to certain influences of the stars,
because magicians observe the course of certain stars
in order to evoke the devils."

—— *H. Kramer, J. Sprenger, Malleus Maleficarum*

Considered one of the primary driving forces behind the witch hunt fervor that swept through Europe from the 15th to 17th centuries, the book's fame was bolstered by its claim of receiving an official endorsement from the highest echelons of the Catholic Church. This claim was false, but it contributed significantly to the book's widespread use. The work is divided into three distinct sections, each serving a different purpose of establishing, identifying, and prosecuting witchcraft. The first section primarily concerns establishing the reality and gravity of witchcraft and sorcery, arguing vigorously against those who did not believe in or downplayed their existence. They discuss the Devil's role in these practices, contending that witches entered pacts with the Devil and renounced their faith. The second section provides a catalog of the alleged activities of witches and their supposedly harmful consequences. The authors drew heavily from folklore, superstitions, and their interpretations of religious texts to detail the damages they attributed to witches. Furthermore, they wrote about witches' abilities to shape-shift, fly, and become invisible. The third section is a procedural manual for the detection, prosecution, and execution of witches. It provides an intricate, detailed guide to conducting witch trials: starting from the accusation process; gathering evidence; conducting interrogations (including torture); and finally, the methods of execution.

The Malleus Maleficarum was widely distributed with the help of the then-recently invented printing press. Many of the stereotypes and images we associate with witches, such as their ability to fly on broomsticks or their supposed gatherings known as "sabbaths," were popularized in this book.

THE RENAISSANCE

The Library of Humanity

THE RENAISSANCE

The seeds of the Renaissance were indeed sown in 14th-century Florence through the contributions of literary figures like Dante and Petrarch. However, it was the discovery of America in 1492 that truly brought about a cultural revolution on a broader European scale. The exploration of this new continent expanded horizons, ignited curiosity, and sparked a thirst for knowledge and exploration. The Renaissance, which had previously been an abstract ideal or an emerging movement within enlightened cities or wealthy courts, became a tangible reality that transformed history.

At the core of the Renaissance was *humanism*, an ideal that emphasized the potential of the individual rather than religious or spiritual matters. It celebrated human values such as reason, creativity, self-expression, and personal fulfillment, paving the way for the belief in human freedom and the ability to shape one's own destiny.

The discovery of the Americas impacted geographical perspectives and challenged established beliefs. It prompted a re-evaluation of traditional dogmas, particularly those of the Church, while simultaneously reigniting interest in rediscovering classical culture from ancient Greece and Rome. Writers drew inspiration from Greek mythology, incorporating its characters and plots into their stories. They also utilized Latin words in their writings, giving them a touch of sophistication and erudition.

Alongside these classical influences, Renaissance literature began to embrace contemporary elements. Some authors explored topics such as wars, poverty, and inequality, often using satire or allegory to indirectly convey political or moral messages. Notable works in this regard include Erasmus' *In Praise of Folly* and Rabelais' *Gargantua and Pantagruel*.

Narrative prose gained popularity during the Renaissance, replacing epic and chivalric adventures. The drama also took center stage with comedies filled with humor, satire, and tragedies, delving into deep emotions and philosophical reflections. Playwrights like Christopher Marlowe and William Shakespeare emerged and established a new pinnacle in literary and theatrical performance by creating works that blended fascinating stories, intricate plotlines, love, betrayal, and complex subjects.

While the Renaissance witnessed advancements in science, politics, and literature, the invention of printing by Gutenberg in 1453 played a crucial role in rapidly disseminating knowledge. The printing press facilitated the widespread distribution of books across different segments of society, gradually transforming a modern concept of readership, mainly comprised of scholars, to a broader audience.

Overall, the Renaissance marked a period of immense intellectual and artistic growth and democratization of knowledge. It remains a pivotal era that continues influencing and inspiring contemporary society.

90. Columbus's Letter on the First Voyage (Christopher Columbus, 1493)

> *"On the thirty-third day after leaving Cadiz I came into the Indian Sea,*
> *where I discovered many islands inhabited by numerous people.*
> *I took possession of all of them for our most fortunate King*
> *by making public proclamation and unfurling his standard,*
> *no one making any resistance."*

> — *Christopher Columbus, Letter on the First Voyage*

Columbus set sail from Spain on August 3, 1492, with three ships and a crew of over 90 men. His goal was to find a new trade route to the *East Indies*. After a stop in the Canary Islands, he resumed sailing, and after over a month at sea the crew spotted land on October 12. Columbus believed he had arrived in the *Indies (in Asia)* but had reached the Caribbean. He named the land *San Salvador*, though it was known as *Guanahani* by its indigenous inhabitants, the *Lucayan Tainos*. During the expedition, Columbus wrote a letter informing King Ferdinand and Queen Isabella of his discoveries. The letter detailed the beauty of the lands he had encountered and praised God for guiding him safely across the ocean. He also noted that he had found gold in some places. In a controversial move, Columbus enslaved several native people and took them back to Spain. As proof of his discoveries, Columbus brought back tobacco plants, cocoa beans, and exotic animals such as parrots. Upon arriving in Palos de la Frontera on March 15, 1493, Columbus presented his findings to King Ferdinand and Queen Isabella, who were pleased with what they heard and saw. They immediately ordered more ships to be built to further explore and conquer the newly discovered lands across the Atlantic.

Columbus's letter marks the beginning of European exploration in America and has had lasting effects on our world today – including new trade routes, food sources, and cultures. However, it is important to acknowledge the devastating impact of European colonization on the native populations, such as disease, enslavement, displacement, and eradication of local culture.

91. Amadís de Gaula (Rodríguez de Montalvo, 1508)

> *"If I were to fear the dreadful things,*
> *I would do so with more reason in the present things*
> *that happen to me every day*
> *than in the hidden ones that are yet to come."*

— *Rodríguez de Montalvo, Amadís de Gaula*

Amadís de Gaula follows the adventures of the knight-errant Amadís, who is born to a royal family but is abandoned at birth and raised by the knight Gandales. Amadís falls in love with Princess Oriana, and his quest for her love takes him through numerous trials and battles. Throughout the story, Amadís demonstrates his exceptional bravery, chivalry, and honor, which won him the admiration and respect of his peers. He defeats various foes, from giants and dragons to sorcerers and rival knights. However, Amadís also faces challenges to his honor, including false accusations of adultery and treachery. The central love story of Amadís de Gaula is between Amadís and Oriana, a strong and independent character who resists the advances of Amadís until she is convinced of his worthiness. The two lovers face many obstacles, including Oriana's imprisonment by her father and Amadís's self-imposed exile after he is accused of wrongdoing. But at last they are reunited, and their love triumphs over all. The story is also notable for its political themes, as Amadís is eventually revealed to be the rightful heir to the throne of Gaula, and he fights to reclaim his rightful place. The story is full of intrigue, deception, and machinations, as various factions jostle for power.

Garci Rodríguez de Montalvo compiled, edited, and added to the Amadís de Gaula, publishing his version around 1508. However, the tales of Amadís de Gaula existed in earlier versions, which are believed to date back to the 14th century. Amadís de Gaula is considered a precursor to the modern novel due its complex plotlines and dynamic characters. This work inspired many authors, including Miguel de Cervantes.

92. In Praise of Folly (Desiderius Erasmus, 1511)

> *"I am the one and indeed the only one whose divine powers*
> *can gladden the hearts of gods and men."*
>
> —— *Desiderius Erasmus, In Praise of Folly*

The essay is a satirical speech by *Folly*, the goddess of foolishness, addressed to an audience of philosophers and theologians. Folly asserts herself to be the offspring of *Plutus*, the deity associated with wealth, and the nymph *Youth*. She claims to have been raised by *Ignorance* and *Drunkenness*. Folly begins by ironically praising herself for bringing joy and pleasure into the lives of humans. She criticizes, using an ironic and satirical tone, those who are too serious about their studies and religious beliefs, arguing that they have no sense of humor or understanding of human nature. Folly then discusses various topics such as marriage, education, politics, religion, philosophy, literature, and art. For each case, she presents an argument favoring foolishness over wisdom, but in a *satirical* manner meant to highlight the follies and vices of society. For example, she argues that marriage should be based on love rather than social status or wealth; that education should focus more on developing the mind than memorizing facts; that war should not be glorified; that politicians should act with honesty rather than self-interest; that religion should be based on faith rather than dogma; that philosophy should be *open-minded* rather than dogmatic; that literature should provide entertainment rather than instruction; and finally that art should bring beauty into people's lives rather than serve as a tool for propaganda. The final section examines the misuse and corrupt practices within the Church; the perspective, however, never extends to God, the only perfect being, who, even in His perfection, possesses a *trace of madness*.

The book's satire provided readers with an alternative viewpoint on how we should approach life and society − one rooted more deeply in humor and critical thinking than piety or strict adherence to tradition alone.

93. Orlando Furioso (Ludovico Ariosto, 1516)

"I sing of knights and ladies,
of love and arms, of courtly chivalry, of courageous deeds
all from the time when the Moors crossed the sea from Africa
and wrought havoc in France."

— *Ludovico Ariosto, Orlando Furioso*

Orlando Furioso is an epic poem that spans a dazzling array of chivalric adventures, heroic exploits, and romantic quests. It boasts a diverse cast, primarily focusing on knights, set against the backdrop of the wars between *Christian* and *Saracen* forces. The narrative begins with Charlemagne's court and swiftly introduces many individuals. Orlando, one of the central figures in the poem, is a valiant Christian knight who falls head over heels for the enchanting pagan princess Angelica. His unrequited love eventually drives him to the brink of madness. Another significant figure is Rinaldo, another Christian knight, while Agramante, the Saracen king who invades Europe, also plays a prominent role. Orlando's bouts of rage and the herculean feats he performs during his frenzies are some of the most memorable aspects of the poem. Central to many subplots, Angelica becomes an object of desire for numerous other characters. She is eventually kidnapped by the wizard Atlante, leading both Orlando and Rinaldo on a quest to rescue her. The ongoing conflicts between the Christian and Saracen armies are parallel to these adventures, and individuals often find themselves caught between their duties and the passions that tug at their hearts.

Orlando Furioso exemplifies Renaissance literature by marrying classical elements from mythology with the chivalric traditions of the Middle Ages. Ariosto's masterful use of the 'ottava rima' (an Italian verse form) adds a lyrical quality to the depth and complexity of the characters. While the knights pursue honor and glory, they are also depicted as deeply human, with all the frailties and emotions of the human condition.

94. Utopia (Thomas More, 1516)

> *"This your island,*
> *which seemed as to this particular*
> *the happiest in the world,*
> *will suffer much by the cursed avarice*
> *of a few persons."*
>
> — *Thomas More, Utopia*

Utopia is a work of fiction and political philosophy that describes the imaginary island of Utopia and its religious, social, and political customs. The book's main character is Raphael Hythloday, an explorer who has returned from his travels to Europe with tales of a perfect society he encountered on an island in the *New World*. He recounts his experiences to More and other friends. Raphael's description of Utopia paints a picture of a society based on reason, justice, equality, and communal property ownership. The people are content with their lives and live in harmony with one another. There is no private property or money, and goods are shared equally among all citizens. All labor is voluntary, and there are no classes or hierarchies; everyone works together for the common good. The government comprises elected officials who serve for life terms but can be removed from office if they fail to fulfill their duties. Education is compulsory for all citizens and includes academic studies and practical skills such as farming or carpentry. Religion is tolerated but not enforced, and citizens are encouraged to pursue spiritual enlightenment through contemplation and study rather than dogma or ritualism. At the end of the book, More concludes that while it may not be possible to create such an ideal society, it serves as an example of how people should strive to live together in harmony regardless of class or status differences.

Utopia is historically significant as it was one of the earliest works to propose a theory for an idealized society. It sets the foundation for many later utopian literary works from authors such as Huxley and Wells.

95. The Prince (Niccolò Machiavelli, 1532)

> *"It is better to be feared than loved,*
> *if you cannot be both."*
>
> — *Niccolò Machiavelli, The Prince*

Machiavelli's doctrine is about how a prince should acquire and maintain power. It is considered a groundbreaking work in political philosophy because it rejects the belief that abstract ideals or religious principles should guide rulers. Instead, Machiavelli emphasizes the importance of practical considerations, such as military strength, the support of the people, and the need to maintain order and stability. Some scholars argue that The Prince marks the beginning of modern political philosophy because it prioritizes empirical observation and practical wisdom over abstract theory or metaphysical speculation. It was also in direct conflict with the time's dominant Catholic and *scholastic* doctrines concerning politics. In his princedom, Machiavelli divides principality into two types: hereditary and new. In addition, Machiavelli addresses several issues: *free will* versus *fate* or fortune; whether princes should rely on their judgment or depend on advisors; how much cruelty is necessary for a prince; what kind of military forces are best; and whether they should engage in foreign wars or concentrate on internal administration. Throughout his work, Machiavelli warns against relying too heavily on traditional ideas about governing and cautions against following conventional morality when it could prove disastrous for the state or ruler. He advocates for realism when dealing with difficult situations – a concept now known as "the ends justify the means."

The Prince is regarded as one of the most influential works ever written about politics. Niccolò Machiavelli offers pragmatic advice on how a ruler should act while governing effectively at the same time. The book's insights continue to shape our understanding of leadership and power dynamics.

96. Gargantua and Pantagruel (François Rabelais, 1532-1534)

> *"By this each king may learn, rook, pawn, and knight,*
> *That sleight is much more prevalent than might."*

— *François Rabelais, Gargantua and Pantagruel*

Gargantua and Pantagruel is a satirical and absurd novel comprised of five books that follows the exploits of two giants, father and son, as they discover a world filled with eccentric characters and outlandish situations. The story begins with the birth of Gargantua, who is born fully grown and with an insatiable appetite. Gargantua rises to become a fearsome warrior, but he eventually becomes disillusioned with the world and sets off on a journey of self-discovery. In the second book, the focus shifts to Gargantua's son Pantagruel, who is even larger and more powerful than his father. Pantagruel sets off on a series of adventures with his friend Panurge, a cowardly but clever rogue. Along the way, they encounter various characters, including scholars, lawyers, priests, and clowns. Through their travels, Rabelais satirizes his time's multiple institutions and professions, exposing their greed, corruption, and foolishness. During one of their voyages, Pantagruel and his companion seek the oracle of the Divine Bottle in search of answers to life's most profound questions. They also encounter the enigmatic and seductive Queen Whims, who leads them on a merry chase through bizarre and absurd scenarios. The series' final book finds Pantagruel and his companion embarking on new adventures, including a visit to the utopian land of Lanterns, where the inhabitants are perpetually drunk and happy. The novel's ending celebrates life through the joys and pleasures of human existence.

This seminal work of Renaissance humanism is filled with bawdy humor, puns, and wordplay, as well as erudite references to classical literature and philosophy. Rabelais masterfully uses his characters and their absurd situations to comment on the human condition and the follies of society.

97. De revolutionibus orbium coelestium (Nicolaus Copernicus, 1543)

"For it is the duty of an astronomer
to compose the history of the celestial motions
through careful and expert study."

— *Nicolaus Copernicus, De revolutionibus orbium coelestium*

De revolutionibus orbium coelestium (*On the Revolutions of the Celestial Spheres*) is one of the most influential books in history, as it proposed a *heliocentric model* of the universe, which displaced Earth from its central position in cosmology (the ancient Greek Aristarchus of Samos had already presented a heliocentric model in the third century BCE, but Copernicus was most likely unaware of it). Copernicus' model of the universe argues that the Sun is at rest near the center of the universe and that all other planets revolve around it in circular orbits. This theory was revolutionary for its time, as it contradicted traditional Ptolemaic models, which placed Earth at the center of all motion. Copernicus describes how his model explains astronomical phenomena, such as retrograde motion and precession, more accurately than Ptolemy's geocentric system. He also discusses his calculations for determining planetary positions using trigonometry and epicycles. He concludes by discussing how his model can be used to predict future astronomical events. De revolutionibus orbium coelestium laid out a new vision for understanding our place in the cosmos and set into motion a scientific revolution that eventually led to modern astronomy and cosmology.

This book advanced scientific thinking. It changed our understanding of our view of the universe by proposing that Earth was not at the center but instead revolved around the Sun — something that had not been suggested before in such a detailed way. It contributed significantly to many future discoveries in astronomy and other fields like philosophy and mathematics, making it an essential milestone for humanity's development over time.

98. Popol Vuh (Unknown, 1550-1554)

> *"They were endowed with intelligence,*
> *they succeeded in knowing all that there is in the world.*
> *[Then the Creator said]:*
> *They know all ... what shall we do with them now?*
> *Let their sight reach only to that which is near;*
> *let them see only a little of the face of the earth!"*

— *Unknown, Popol Vuh*

Popol Vuh is an ancient Mayan book of creation stories and mythological tales. It gives an account of the gods and goddesses who created the world and the adventures of their descendants, the *Hero Twins*. The first part of Popol Vuh begins with the creation of Earth by the *Heart of Heaven*, a divine being. The gods start with animals but find that they cannot speak and praise them. They then attempt to generate humans from mud, but these mud beings could not speak or multiply and are dissolved by rain. The gods make another attempt, this time fashioning humans from wood, but these wooden beings lacked souls, emotions, and intellect. Finally, humans are successfully created from maize. The second part of Popol Vuh tells the story of the *Hero Twins Hunahpu* and *Xbalanque*. They are sent to Xibalba, a place ruled by evil lords, where they must face many tests to prove their worthiness. The twins ultimately succeed in defeating their enemies and restoring peace to Xibalba. The third part of Popol Vuh focuses on how humans were instructed in various aspects of life: agriculture, hunting, fishing, weaving, pottery-making, music-making, and writing. It also tells how humans were given laws by which to live and how they should honor their gods with offerings and sacrifices. Finally, Popol Vuh ends with a prophecy about a future time when humans will be destroyed by floodwaters but will eventually be reborn into a new world better than the previous.

The Popol Vuh gives a unique perspective on ancient Mayan civilization's beliefs, mythology, and culture.

99. Les Prophéties (Nostradamus, 1555)

> *"Indeed, the hereditary gift of prophecy
> will go to the grave with me."*
>
> —— *Nostradamus, Les Prophéties*

Les Prophéties consists of a series of poetic four-line verses known as *quatrains*, which are said to predict future events. Nostradamus wrote his quatrains in a blend of French, Latin, Greek, and Occitan, employing symbolic and metaphorical language. This resulted in the text being shrouded in ambiguity, which has led to numerous interpretations throughout the years. In terms of structure, Les Prophéties is organized into *centuries*. Although the term *century* suggests 100 years, it is merely a label used by Nostradamus to describe a group of 100 quatrains. The range of topics Nostradamus covers is broad and includes wars, natural disasters, conflicts, political upheavals, religious shifts, and other significant events. The open-ended nature of Nostradamus's language has allowed for many interpretations, with some claiming that his quatrains have predicted major historical events such as the rise of Napoleon, the *French Revolution*, and *World War II*. Various languages, mixed metaphors, and cryptic symbolism reflect the Renaissance's fascination with classical learning, mysticism, and the unknown. This *obscurity* in the language is often regarded as a deliberate attempt by Nostradamus to protect himself from accusations of heresy and to allow the quatrains to be adapted to various contexts over the centuries.

Les Prophéties can be seen as an example of prophetic and apocalyptic writings. The mystique surrounding Nostradamus and his quatrains has influenced various forms of popular culture, including literature, films, and other media. Its blend of poetry, prophecy, and enigmatic language continues to leave readers both fascinated and perplexed, and its influence on popular culture is indelible.

Les Prophéties

100. Lives of the Most Excellent Painters, Sculptors, and Architects (Giorgio Vasari, 1568)

> *"I think that anyone who will take the trouble*
> *to consider the matter carefully*
> *will arrive at the same conclusion as I have,*
> *that art owes its origin to Nature herself,*
> *that this beautiful creation the world supplied the first model,*
> *while the original teacher was that divine intelligence*
> *which has not only made us superior to the other animals,*
> *but like God Himself, if I may venture to say it."*

— *Giorgio Vasari, Lives of the Most Excellent Painters, ...*

Commonly known as *The Lives*, the book comprises biographies of notable artists from the late 13th century to Vasari's own time. The Lives is organized chiefly by artists, beginning with Cimabue and Giotto, whom Vasari saw as the instigators of the *Renaissance* rebirth of the arts, and it moves on to encompass artists such as Leonardo da Vinci, Michelangelo Buonarroti, and Raphael. Vasari provides details about the artists' lives and the *techniques employed* in their works and offers insights into their personalities and their relationships with patrons and other artists. Vasari's book is significant because it established the genre of the artist's biography with historical context and emphasized the artist's role as a creator. He also considered art history to progress and improve over time, a concept that influenced subsequent historical evaluations. Furthermore, the text analyzes *aesthetic principles* and commentary on composition, color theory, and materials. His admiration for the great masters of the Renaissance is evident in his enthusiastic and sometimes embellished accounts.

The Lives marked a critical moment in history when knowledge about art became codified into one definitive source, providing insight into how people historically viewed great works of art and allowing readers to better understand cultural attitudes at the time.

101. Os Lusíadas (Luís Vaz de Camões, 1572)

> *"Let the world tremble as it senses*
> *all you are about to accomplish."*

> — *Luís Vaz de Camões, Os Lusíadas*

Os Lusíadas is regarded as one of the most significant literary works in the Portuguese language. This epic poem narrates the voyage of Vasco da Gama to India in 1497-1499 and celebrates the *Age of Discovery*, during which Portugal established itself as a global maritime and colonial power. However, Os Lusíadas transcends a mere historical account, serving as an homage to the Portuguese people, their history, and their achievements. The poem commences with an invocation to the Muses and an address to King Sebastian of Portugal, who is portrayed as a symbol of national hope. The narrative encompasses a series of episodes, including the discovery of the Cape of Good Hope, the arrival in India, and the diplomatic encounters with Indian rulers. Camões highlights the virtues of the Portuguese, such as bravery, perseverance, and piety, and underscores the significance of exploration and discovery. The character of Vasco da Gama is depicted as a heroic figure who surmounts immense challenges to achieve his objectives. Additionally, Os Lusíadas is replete with digressions and musings on diverse topics, encompassing history, philosophy, and theology. Camões draws on classical and biblical references to explore subjects like love, fate, and the divine. The poem is also deeply allegorical, incorporating Greek and Roman mythology and portraying Portugal's endeavors as divinely ordained.

Os Lusíadas has become an emblem of Portuguese national identity and pride, epitomizing the country's Golden Age. A notable aspect of Os Lusíadas is its linguistic and poetic richness. Camões employs a vast and varied lexicon by innovating new words and expressions and incorporating terms from other languages. He utilizes literary devices such as alliteration, rhyme, and metaphor to craft a vibrant and captivating narrative.

102.   An Apology for Poetry (Philip Sidney, ca. 1580)

"The poet, he nothing affirmeth,
and therefore never lieth."

— *Philip Sidney, An Apology for Poetry*

An Apology for Poetry, also known as *The Defence of Poesy*, is an essay written as a defense of poetry, which was criticized for its perceived lack of moral or practical utility. Sidney wrote this essay in response to *Stephen Gosson's The School of Abuse*, which expressed antipathy towards imaginative literature. In his eloquent defense, Sidney extols the nobility of poetry and contends that it holds an important place in society. He posits that poetry's power emanates from its capacity to simultaneously instruct and delight its audience, a notion that aligns with the views of the ancient Roman poet Horace. Significantly, Sidney recasts *Plato's critique of poets*, who had reproached them for potentially deceiving audiences through untruths. Sidney counter-argues a poet is, in fact, *the least liar* among writers since he does not claim absolute truth but rather engage in imaginative creation that explores alternative perspectives and possibilities. Thus, poets are not beholden to established authority or conventional wisdom and are not constrained by these bounds. Instead of propagating falsehoods, poets open up alternate interpretations of reality through the lens of imagination. To bolster his argument, Sidney employs classical rhetorical tools, including evocative descriptions and references to illustrious figures from antiquity. He further argues that poetry can serve educational purposes and furnish solace in times of grief or hardship.

An Apology for Poetry is heralded as one of the most seminal treatises on aesthetics within English literature. Sidney's groundbreaking notions about art as a wellspring of inspiration and an instrument for elevating human thought and emotion have been profoundly influential.

103.   The Spanish Tragedy (Thomas Kyd, 1587-1592)

> *"Then haste we down to meet thy friends and foes;*
> *To place thy friends in ease, the rest in woes.*
> *For here though death doth end their misery,*
> *I'll there begin their endless tragedy."*

— *Thomas Kyd, The Spanish Tragedy*

Hieronimo, the *Knight Marshal of Spain*, searches for vengeance for the brutal murder of his son Horatio. The story is introduced with the ghost of Don Andrea and the embodiment of revenge, crafting a foreboding atmosphere that foreshadows the tragic events. Hieronimo's son Horatio falls victim to a violent plot orchestrated by Lorenzo and Balthazar due to convoluted romantic interests and political intrigues. Lorenzo, the nephew of the King of Spain, is enamored with Bel-Imperia, who, in turn, is in love with Horatio. Bel-Imperia is also Lorenzo's sister. On the other hand, Balthazar, the son of the King of Portugal, is also smitten by Bel-Imperia. This complex web of relationships leads to the cold-blooded murder of Horatio, setting the stage for the subsequent cycle of vengeance. As Hieronimo discovers the shocking truth behind his son's death, he allies with Bel-Imperia, Horatio's bereaved lover. Together, they devise an intricate plan to meet out justice to the culprits. The grand stage for their revenge opens during a court play. In an ingenious turn of events, Hieronimo manipulates the theatrical performance into a horrifying spectacle of violence, leading to the real-time murders of Lorenzo and Balthazar, thereby shocking the unsuspecting audience. Their quest for justice climaxes in a sequence of suicides that engulfs the main characters.

The Spanish Tragedy presents an insightful examination of 'metatheatre' (a play within a play), blurring the line between reality and fiction, which enhances its theatrical impact. This exploration of 'metadrama' became a significant stylistic feature in subsequent dramatic literature, especially in Shakespearean works.

104. Friar Bacon and Friar Bungay (Robert Greene, 1588-
1592)

> *"Why looks my lord*
> *like to a troubled sky*
> *When heaven's bright shine*
> *is shadow'd with a fog?"*

— Robert Greene, Friar Bacon and Friar Bungay

Friar Bacon and Friar Bungay is a play that follows the titular
characters, both adept in magic and science. Their relationship
is tainted with rivalry as they continuously vie to demonstrate
their intellectual superiority. One of the play's most intriguing
storylines features Friar Bacon's audacious project to create a
brazen head, a magical object imbued with the power to prophesy
and protect England against threats, potentially elevating
Bacon to unparalleled fame and fortune. However, Bacon's
ambition ultimately proves to be his downfall. Meanwhile,
another narrative thread follows the romantic entanglement of
Prince Edward and Margaret, a fair maid of Fressingfield. As
the story progresses, the characters are embroiled in schemes
involving love, magic, and ambition. Friar Bacon and Friar
Bungay is notable for exploring issues such as the perils of over-
ambition and the duality between science and magic. Through
engaging dialogue and wit, it raises questions about human
nature and the ethical implications of meddling with forces
beyond understanding. It reflects the curiosities and anxieties of
the *Elizabethan era*, where science and magic often connected,
and ambitious pursuits were both admired and cautioned
against.

With its blend of comedy, romance, and moral introspection, Friar Bacon
and Friar Bungay captures the essence of English Renaissance drama in its
complexity. The portrayal of multifaceted characters and the use of magical
elements contribute to its enduring appeal.

105.   Tamburlaine (Christopher Marlowe, 1588)

> *"That perfect bliss and sole felicity,*
> *the sweet fruition of an earthly crown."*

— *Christopher Marlowe, Tamburlaine*

Tamburlaine is a compelling dramatic work in two parts describing the rise and reign of a *Scythian shepherd*, Tamburlaine, based on the historical Central Asian Emperor, *Timur the Lame*. He ascends to power by triumphing over nations, transforming into a formidable conqueror. The narrative begins with Tamburlaine defeating the Persian King Mycetes in battle and subsequently assuming the Persian throne. Emboldened by his victory, he embarks on a sweeping campaign to conquer all of Asia. His ruthless exploits earn him immense wealth and power but also incite the wrath of other rulers who perceive his ambition as a looming threat. Tamburlaine then targets the Sultan of Damascus and takes him captive in battle. He further forays into Egypt to face off against the influential ruler Bajazeth. After overpowering Bajazeth, Tamburlaine arrogantly declares himself the *Emperor of the World*. He extends his conquest to Africa and Europe. During his relentless win, Tamburlaine encounters Zenocrate, the daughter of an African king. He succumbs to his affection for her, and they become husband and wife. Despite his numerous victories, Tamburlaine's lust for power remains insatiable. He employs strategic ingenuity in his battles to extend his rule over Europe and Asia Minor. However, an illness claims his life before he can realize his ultimate ambition of ruling over all of humanity.

Tamburlaine is a milestone in English Elizabethan drama, paving the way for later works through its expressive language, rich imagery, and intricately structured plot. The play delves into profound topics, such as the tension between free will and fate, and the role of morality in politics, offering insights into human nature that remain pertinent today.

106.   The Jew of Malta (Christopher Marlowe, 1590)

"For whilst I live,
here lives my soul's sole hope,
And when I die,
here shall my spirit walk."

— *Christopher Marlowe, The Jew of Malta*

The Jew of Malta is centered around Barabas, a wealthy Jewish merchant living on the island of Malta. The governor of Malta, Ferneze, confiscates Barabas's wealth to pay off the tribute demanded by the Turks. Enraged by the loss of his wealth, Barabas is driven to seek revenge. He resorts to treacherous means, including manipulation, deceit, and murder. Barabas's daughter Abigail discovers his treachery and, wracked by guilt, converts to Christianity and enters a convent. Barabas, undeterred, uses betrayal and poison to cause further deaths; he poisons his own daughter to prevent her from revealing his crimes. As the play progresses, Barabas forms an alliance with the Turkish invaders and assists them in laying siege to Malta. However, when the Turks appoint him as governor of Malta, he switches allegiance again, betraying them and helping the Maltese. His relentless pursuit of revenge and power ultimately leads to his own downfall. Barabas is ensnared in a trap set by Ferneze and perishes.

The Jew of Malta is a seminal work of Elizabethan drama, notable for its complex, Machiavellian protagonist and darkly comic tone. It deals with religious hypocrisy, the corrupting influence of wealth, and the perils of unchecked ambition. The character of Barabas is seen as an early example of the anti-hero, and his cunning and ruthlessness have often been compared to Shakespeare's Richard III. The play has also been discussed for portraying anti-Semitic stereotypes prevalent during the Elizabethan era. Its exploration of moral relativism and the ambiguity of human motives offers valuable insights into the complexities of human nature, setting a precedent for character development in subsequent literature.

The Jew of Malta

107.   Doctor Faustus (Christopher Marlowe, 1592-3)

> *"O soul, be chang'd into little water-drops*
> *And fall into the ocean, ne'er be found.*
> *My God, my God, look not so fierce on me."*

> — *Christopher Marlowe, Doctor Faustus*

Doctor Faustus, a scholarly man frustrated with the confines of traditional disciplines, studies the forbidden world of necromancy in his thirst for more profound knowledge and power. In a daring act, Faustus conjures Mephistopheles, a servant of Lucifer, and strikes a perilous pact: Faustus will be granted omnipotent power and the service of Mephistopheles for twenty-four years. In return, Faustus must forfeit his soul to Lucifer at the term's end. The contract signed in Faustus's blood seals his doom but empowers him to transcend human limitations. Faustus begins a life of indulgence and excess. He leverages his supernatural abilities to perform feats that astound the common folk and aristocrats alike, ranging from summoning spirits from Hell to creating illusions of historical figures. He travels extensively with Mephistopheles while showcasing his capabilities to various European dignitaries. Notably, he plays tricks on the Pope and revives the long-deceased Alexander the Great to entertain the Holy Roman Emperor. As his life of earthly pleasures and unchecked power progresses, the inevitable end of his contract looms ominously. He grapples with his impending doom, fruitlessly attempting to annul his pact with Lucifer and seek divine intervention. Yet, Mephistopheles is always present to remind him of the irrevocability of his bargain. In its climactic conclusion, Faustus faces his tragic destiny. Despite his pleas for mercy and attempts at repentance, he is condemned to his agreed fate.

Through various literary devices such as allegory, irony, and symbolism, Marlowe weaves a narrative masterpiece that grapples with philosophical and metaphysical questions of faith, destiny, free will, and the human condition.

108.   Edward II (Christopher Marlowe, 1592)

"All live to die, and rise to fall."

—— *Christopher Marlowe, Edward II*

Edward II begins with King Edward II's fervent devotion to his beloved friend and possible lover, Piers Gaveston. Gaveston had been in exile, but upon Edward's ascension to the throne, he recalls Gaveston to England and bestows him with titles and privileges. The English nobles, led by the earls of Lancaster, Warwick, and Mortimer Junior, deeply resent Gaveston's influence over the king. They perceive Gaveston as threatening the nobility and the kingdom's stability. King Edward's relentless favoritism towards Gaveston infuriates the nobles, who demand Gaveston's exile. The king reluctantly agrees but soon arranges for Gaveston's return. The nobles, in turn, capture Gaveston and execute him. Grief-stricken, Edward vows revenge. As the conflict escalates, Queen Isabella, the wife of Edward, feels neglected and allies herself with Mortimer Junior. Together, they gather support from France and lead an army against Edward. Edward is eventually captured and imprisoned. While Edward is in prison, his son is crowned King Edward III, with Queen Isabella and Mortimer Junior effectively ruling on his behalf. Mortimer Junior arranges for the murder of King Edward II in prison. However, as Edward III matures, he learns of Mortimer Junior's treachery and the role he played in his father's downfall and death. Young King Edward III takes control, has Mortimer Junior executed for treason, and seizes his mother Queen Isabella. The play concludes with Edward III establishing his rule while reflecting on the tragic events that brought him to power.

Marlowe explores the abuse of power and the human cost of political ambitions. Edward II is groundbreaking for its time as it portrays the intimate relationship between two men. Bertolt Brecht adapted Marlowe's Edward II with his own language premiering in Germany in 1924.

109.   Richard III (William Shakespeare, 1592-1593)

> *"True hope is swift, and flies with swallow's wings;*
> *Kings it makes gods, and meaner creatures kings."*

— *William Shakespeare, Richard III*

Richard III is a *historical play* that dramatizes the *Machiavellian* rise to power and the short reign of King Richard III of England. The play begins with Richard, Duke of Gloucester, expressing bitterness over his brother Edward IV's ascent to the English throne. Richard is portrayed as physically deformed and morally corrupt (in Shakespeare's depiction) and resolves to take the throne for himself. Through manipulation, deceit, and murder, Richard begins eliminating those in line for the throne. He orchestrates the murder of his brother George, Duke of Clarence. When King Edward IV dies, Richard becomes *Lord Protector of England*, overseeing Edward's young sons, the *Princes in the Tower*. Richard has the young princes declared illegitimate and subsequently has them killed, securing his claim to the throne. Richard becomes King Richard III but finds his position unstable due to the bloody and treacherous means he obtains. He grows increasingly paranoid and continues his murderous spree. Richard's wife Anne Neville dies under mysterious circumstances, and Richard attempts to marry his niece Elizabeth of York to further solidify his claim. However, opposition grows as the Earl of Richmond (*Henry Tudor*) gains support to overthrow Richard. His promised marriage to Elizabeth of York strengthens Richmond's claim to the throne. The play culminates in the *Battle of Bosworth Field*, where Richard is ultimately killed by Richmond's forces. Richmond is then crowned as *King Henry VII*. His marriage to Elizabeth of York ends the *Wars of the Roses* by uniting the rival houses of *Lancaster* and *York*, the *red* and *white* roses.

Shakespeare's complex and fascinating Richard III is a dark portrayal of ungovernable ambition, betrayal, and the pursuit of power at any cost.

110.   Dido, Queen of Carthage (Christopher Marlowe, 1594)

"If he forsake me not,
I never die,
For in his looks I see eternity,
And he'll make me immortal with a kiss."

— *Christopher Marlowe, Dido, Queen of Carthage*

Dido, Queen of Carthage, is a character based on the classical myth of Dido and Aeneas. Dido is the founder and first queen of Carthage. Her husband Sychaeus was killed by her brother Pygmalion, which led to Dido's flight from Tyre and the subsequent establishment of Carthage. Dido's life takes a dramatic turn when Aeneas, a Trojan warrior, arrives in Carthage with his fleet of ships. He had been shipwrecked during his journey to Italy and is searching for refuge. Dido and Aeneas fall in love, but their relationship is ill-fated. In an attempt to prevent Aeneas from fulfilling his destiny of founding Rome, the goddess Juno encourages Dido's love for Aeneas. However, Jupiter sends Mercury to remind Aeneas of his duty to proceed to Italy. Aeneas reluctantly decides to leave Dido to accomplish his mission. He does not initially tell Dido about his departure. When Dido learns of Aeneas' intentions to leave, she is heartbroken. Despite her pleas for him to stay, Aeneas remains committed to his destiny. Devastated by his departure, Dido decides to end her own life. Before her death, she curses Aeneas and his descendants.

Dido, Queen of Carthage, is one of Marlowe's earliest plays and is considered a significant example of Elizabethan tragedy. It explores the tragic consequences of love, duty, and fate and reflects on the classical text of the Aeneid by Virgil, where the story of Dido and Aeneas is prominently featured. Through its exploration of personal sacrifice for public duty, it poses timeless questions about the tension between personal desire and societal expectations.

111. A Midsummer Night's Dream (William Shakespeare, 1595)

> *"Love looks not with the eyes,*
> *but with the mind."*

— *William Shakespeare, A Midsummer Night's Dream*

Theseus, the Duke of Athens, is preparing to marry Hippolyta, the Queen of the Amazons. Meanwhile, Hermia is in love with Lysander, but her father wants her to marry Demetrius. Unwilling to follow her father's wishes, Hermia and Lysander plan to elope and agree to meet in the woods outside Athens. Helena, a friend of Hermia, is in love with Demetrius, who once loved her but now desires Hermia. In the same forest, Oberon and Titania, King and Queen of the Fairies, are in a quarrel. Oberon seeks to play a trick on Titania and sends his mischievous servant Puck to obtain a magical flower. When applied to someone's eyes while they sleep, the juice of this flower causes them to fall in love with the first creature they see upon waking. Oberon overhears Helena and Demetrius arguing and orders Puck to use the flower on Demetrius so that he will love Helena. However, Puck mistakenly applies the juice to Lysander's eyes, causing him to fall in love with Helena. To correct this, Puck later applies the fluid to Demetrius's eyes, but this leads to both men pursuing Helena, to Hermia's dismay. Oberon also uses the flower on Titania, causing her to comically fall in love with Bottom, whose head Puck has transformed into a donkey. Eventually, Puck reverses the spell on Lysander, and Oberon does the same for Titania. By morning, Hermia, Lysander, Helena, and Demetrius are happily paired and married alongside Theseus and Hippolyta.

A Midsummer Night's Dream has been adapted into numerous versions due to its timeless exploration of themes such as love and fate. With its wit, lighthearted tone, and Shakespeare's masterful use of language in colorful descriptions of the mythical world, the play creates a dream-like atmosphere that captivates audiences.

112.   The Faerie Queene (Edmund Spenser, 1590-1596)

"Fierce wars and faithful loves shall moralize my song."

—— *Edmund Spenser, The Faerie Queene*

The Faerie Queene is an allegorical epic celebrated for its intricate blend of romantic narrative and moral allegory. Written in *Spenserian stanzas*, the work comprises six books and an unfinished seventh, each focusing on a knight who embodies a particular virtue. In Book I, the protagonist is the *Redcrosse Knight*, symbolizing *Holiness*. He is accompanied by *Una*, representing *Truth*, on a quest to defeat a dragon and rescue Una's parents. Along the way, they face deceptive characters such as *Archimago*, symbolizing *religious hypocrisy*, and *Duessa*, embodying *falsehood*. Book II follows *Sir Guyon*, who embodies *Temperance*. He is portrayed as a disciplined and restrained knight who quests to destroy a bower of bliss, representing excess and earthly pleasure. In Book III, the story introduces *Britomart*, a female warrior who represents *Chastity*. She is searching for her destined love Artegall, and her journey is marked by female empowerment and the importance of steadfast love. Book IV focuses on several knights, chiefly Cambell and Triamond, and symbolizes *Friendship*. This book emphasizes the bonds of friendship and loyalty as the knights face various challenges and adversities. Book V follows the knight *Artegall* on his adventures, representing *Justice*. Artegall, also Britomart's betrothed, is on a mission to combat injustice and tyranny throughout the land. In Book VI, the narrative follows Sir *Calidore*, whose adventures revolve around *Courtesy*. Sir Calidore's quest is to capture the *Blatant Beast*, representing *slander* and *malicious gossip*, and to highlight the importance of courtesy and civil behavior. An unfinished fragment of a seventh book also features Sir Calidore's character.

Spenser's Faerie Queene is praised for its poetic form and has been lauded by later Romantic poets such as John Keats and William Wordsworth.

113.   Romeo and Juliet (William Shakespeare, 1595)

> *"My bounty is as boundless as the sea,*
> *My love as deep; the more I give to thee,*
> *The more I have, for both are infinite."*

— *William Shakespeare, Romeo and Juliet*

Romeo and Juliet is one of Shakespeare's most famous plays. It tells the tragic love story of two young star-crossed lovers from feuding families in Verona. Romeo Montague and Juliet Capulet fall deeply in love at first sight. Despite the animosity between their families, they decide to marry secretly with the help of Friar Laurence, who hopes their union might reconcile the Montagues and Capulets. However, fate takes a grim turn when Romeo gets involved in a duel and ends up killing Tybalt, Juliet's cousin. Romeo is banished from Verona. Desperate to avoid a marriage to Paris, which her parents arranged, Juliet seeks Friar Laurence's help. The Friar provides her with a potion that will simulate death. She plans to take the potion, be declared dead, and reunite with Romeo when she awakens. Unfortunately, Romeo does not receive the message explaining the plan and buys poison, believing that Juliet is truly dead. He goes to Juliet's tomb, where he encounters and kills Paris. Thinking Juliet is gone, he drinks the poison. When Juliet awakens to find Romeo dead beside her, she takes her life with his dagger. The play concludes with the grieving families agreeing to end their feud in honor of their deceased children.

Romeo and Juliet is a timeless tragedy that illustrates the consequences of hatred and the transcendental nature of love. Its poignant narrative and poetic language has made it an enduring classic in literature. The play's themes of love, tragedy, and social conflicts continue to resonate with audiences today, making Romeo and Juliet an immortal masterpiece of literature.

Romeo and Juliet

114.   Jin Ping Mei (Lanling Xiaoxiao Sheng, 1596-1610)

> *"When a beautiful woman takes an idea firmly into her head,*
> *even if the walls are ten thousand feet high,*
> *she cannot be prevented from carrying it out."*

— *Lanling Xiaoxiao Sheng, Jin Ping Mei*

Jin Ping Mei, or *The Plum in the Golden Vase*, is a Chinese novel that centers on Ximen Qing, a wealthy and corrupt merchant in a *Northern Song Dynasty* setting. Ximen Qing's insatiable desire for power and sensual pleasure leads him into a web of complex and dangerous relationships with his multiple wives and concubines. He amasses wealth and status through manipulation and treacherous means. The novel opens with Ximen Qing's seduction and subsequent marriage to Pan Jinlian, the young and beautiful widow of his friend Wu Dalang. This sets the stage for a series of decadent exploits as Ximen Qing indulges in extramarital affairs. One of his notable liaisons is with Li Ping'er, who becomes one of his favored concubines. Meanwhile, Pan Jinlian, resentful of Ximen's infidelities, schemes against him with her maidservant Wu Yueniang. They orchestrate Ximen Qing's downfall and eventual death through cunning plots, including poison. While set in the Northern Song Dynasty, the novel's detailed portrayal of characters and society reflects the cultural and social milieu of the *late Ming Dynasty*, during which the author lived. Through its rich narrative, Jin Ping Mei explores various subplots and many characters connected to Ximen Qing, focusing on the consequences of lust, greed, and deceit.

Written in vernacular Chinese, Jin Ping Mei is renowned for its realistic characterization and intricate depiction of Chinese society. Although it gained notoriety for its explicit content, leading to bans in certain periods, the novel transcends the erotic genre by providing a multifaceted and critical examination of human nature and society.

115.   Essays (Francis Bacon, 1597)

> *"The best part of beauty is*
> *that which no picture can express."*
>
> — *Francis Bacon, Essays*

Essays are a collection of philosophical reflections on a variety of topics, including death, truth, friendship, love, marriage, and more. At the heart of each essay is Bacon's exploration of how best to use one's reason. He argues that knowledge should be used to improve life rather than simply accumulate it. Bacon emphasizes the importance of moderation in all aspects of life and encourages readers to strive for a balance between physical pleasures and intellectual pursuits. He also calls for an honest approach to living by warning against self-deception and hypocrisy. The essays also reflect Bacon's views on religion and morality. He stresses the need for humility before God and condemns excessive pride or ambition as foolishness. In addition, he believes that true morality comes from within, not from external sources such as laws or customs. In his essays, Bacon also discusses various political, economic, and scientific topics. He speaks out against tyranny, poverty, and disease; advocates for economic justice by encouraging honest trade practices; and suggests methods for alleviating poverty. His views on science are progressive for his time, promoting experimentation over superstition and indicating that natural phenomena should be studied to understand their causes rather than relying solely on religious explanations. Overall, Bacon's Essays provide thoughtful insight into many different aspects of human life while emphasizing the importance of reason in achieving a meaningful existence.

This book was one of the first significant works to explore self-reflection and personal development by stressing the importance of truth-seeking and independent thought.

116. The Merchant of Venice (William Shakespeare, 1597)

"You speak an infinite deal of nothing."

— *William Shakespeare, The Merchant of Venice*

The Merchant of Venice follows the story of Antonio, a wealthy Venetian merchant who borrows money from Shylock, a Jewish moneylender, to help his dear friend Bassanio woo the wealthy heiress Portia. Shylock despises Antonio, partly because Antonio has insulted and mistreated him for being a Jew. Shylock agrees to lend the money but demands gruesome collateral: if the loan is not repaid on time, Antonio must forfeit a pound of his own flesh. Confident that his ships will return to port in time, Antonio agrees. Bassanio wins Portia's heart, and they marry. However, Antonio's ships are reported lost at sea, and Shylock, bitter because his daughter Jessica has eloped with a Christian, insists on exacting the pound of flesh from Antonio. The case goes to court. In court, disguised as a lawyer, Portia makes a famous argument based on the *literal interpretation* of the contract − Shylock can take a pound of Antonio's flesh but not a drop of his blood. Since it is impossible to do this without shedding blood, Shylock is prevented from claiming what he is owed. Furthermore, Portia reveals that according to Venetian law, because Shylock sought to take the life of a citizen, he must forfeit his property, and his life is at the mercy of the Duke. The Duke spares Shylock's life but orders him to surrender half of his wealth to Antonio and half to the state. Antonio renounces his claim to Shylock's wealth on the condition that Shylock converts to Christianity and leaves his estate to his daughter Jessica and her husband Lorenzo upon his death. Shylock, defeated, accepts the conditions.

Shakespeare explores the depths of human nature, exposing the intricacies of greed, justice, and prejudice. One of the most remarkable aspects of the play is Shakespeare's ability to create characters with multifaceted personalities and emotions.

117.   Every Man in His Humour (Ben Jonson, 1598)

> *"He that is so respectless in his courses,*
> *Oft sells his reputation at cheap market."*

— *Ben Jonson, Every Man in His Humour*

Every Man in His Humour is comedy satirizing the behaviors and *humours* (dominant personality traits) of various characters woven into the complex web of *Elizabethan society*. The central character Knowell is an old man who is obsessed with the actions of his son Edward Knowell. Concerned that his son is leading a licentious life, Knowell sends his servant Brainworm to spy on him. In contrast, Kitely, a wealthy merchant, constantly fears his wife is unfaithful. His obsessive jealousy manifests itself in amusing yet poignant ways, reflecting Jonson's genius in portraying character traits or *humours* that dominate an individual's behavior. Simultaneously, Captain Bobadil, a braggart soldier, and Matthew, an affected poet, provide ample humor through their inflated self-importance and affectation. The play's multiple storylines intersect when a letter intended for Edward falls into his father's hands, resulting in a series of misunderstandings and comic mishaps. The narrative unfolds in the bustling commercial district of London, presenting a colorful slice of life from the Elizabethan era. The characters, each driven by their dominant humor or obsessive inclinations, present a humorous yet insightful critique of human follies and pretensions.

Every Man in His Humour is a comedy of errors and a study of human qualities and society's pretensions. Through its clever plot and intricate characterizations, Jonson's play urges audiences to examine their own humor and provides a timeless commentary on the human condition. It also marks Jonson's commitment to a more realistic portrayal of life and character, setting the stage for his later works.

118.   Hamlet (William Shakespeare, 1601)

> *"To be, or not to be*
> *– that is the question."*
>
> —— *William Shakespeare, Hamlet*

Hamlet, the Prince of Denmark, is plunged into mourning after his father's sudden death. His grief turns to a burning desire for revenge when his father's ghost reveals that he was murdered by Hamlet's uncle King Claudius. To confirm the ghost's story, Hamlet devises a plan to stage a play that re-enacts the circumstances of his father's murder, and Claudius's reaction convinces Hamlet of his guilt. However, Hamlet struggles with internal conflicts and is indecisive about revenge. Meanwhile, Polonius, the father of Ophelia, believes that Hamlet's erratic behavior is due to his love for Ophelia and shares his thoughts with Claudius. In a fit of rage, Hamlet kills Polonius, mistaking him for Claudius, which leads to his banishment. Claudius sends Hamlet to England with orders for his execution, but Hamlet escapes and returns to Denmark. He discovers that Ophelia has drowned, which some interpret as suicide due to her madness. In the climax, Hamlet engages in a duel with Laertes, Polonius's son. During the duel, Gertrude accidentally drinks poisoned wine intended for Hamlet and dies. Hamlet is wounded by an envenomed sword but manages to stab Claudius with the same blade, forcing him to drink the poisoned wine before dying.

Hamlet is one of the most renowned plays of all time. The play has been studied extensively due to its themes such as mortality, betrayal, and revenge. Shakespeare uses various literary techniques to convey these complicated emotions, such as soliloquies, and metaphors which create a tragic and intense atmosphere. Hamlet's existential reflections have profoundly influenced Western thought, giving rise to numerous philosophical and psychological interpretations. The character's notorious indecision has been analyzed from Freudian, existentialist, and absurdist perspectives.

119.   The City of the Sun (Tommaso Campanella, 1602)

"On the interior wall of the first circuit
all the mathematical figures are conspicuously painted,
figures more in number
than Archimedes or Euclid discovered."

— *Tommaso Campanella, The City of the Sun*

The City of the Sun envisioned an ideal society where harmony reigns supreme, thanks to wise laws and regulations set forth by its spiritual and philosophical ruler. The City is built on high mountains near the equator, giving it an eternal spring climate, and its inhabitants live simple but comfortable lives in harmony with nature sharing all resources. The main temple is dedicated to the Sun god and contains schools, gardens, and laboratories where people can learn and study philosophy, science, mathematics, and astronomy. Instead of commerce, people pursue leisure activities such as music, poetry, theatre, and artistry to express their creativity. Some rules prohibit religious intolerance or superstition, and all citizens are taught to respect each other's beliefs without judgment or prejudice. The government focuses on education rather than war; instead of creating weapons, they develop tools for building houses and machinery for farming crops so that everyone can benefit from them equally without difference or discordance between classes or social standings.

Campanella, a Dominican friar, imagined an ideal society under spiritual and philosophical guidance, emphasizing understanding the world through empirical observations and scientific exploration, which aligns with the rise of scientific thought during the Renaissance period. The City of the Sun parallels Thomas More's Utopia. However, there are also some significant differences: The City of the Sun ideates a mystical, scientifically-oriented society, while Utopia focuses more on social and political aspects. Campanella's work signifies a notable shift in utopian thought, highlighting the growing prominence of scientific rationalism as a path towards societal perfection during a period of intense intellectual upheaval.

120.   Othello (William Shakespeare, 1604)

"I will wear my heart upon my sleeve, for daws to peck at."

—— *William Shakespeare, Othello*

Iago, an ensign of Othello's army, is plotting revenge against Othello for passing him over for a promotion, which was given instead to Cassio. To accomplish his revenge, Iago – one of the most sinister villains in literature – finds an unlikely ally in Roderigo, a wealthy Venetian desperately in love with Desdemona, the beautiful daughter of the Venetian senator Brabantio. Desdemona, however, is already secretly married to Othello, a character navigating his identity as a black man in white society while also representing a high-ranking military officer. The marriage becomes public knowledge and creates tension since Desdemona's father had expected her to marry a white Venetian nobleman. Iago fabricates stories and manipulates a handkerchief, a gift from Othello to Desdemona, as a piece of evidence to convince Othello that Desdemona has been unfaithful to him with Cassio. This sends Othello on a destructive path of jealousy and rage. Desdemona, innocent and confused by Othello's sudden change in behavior, attempts to reason with him but to no avail. Othello, consumed by misguided passion, strangles his beloved Desdemona. The climax is followed by the arrival of Iago's wife Emilia. Unaware of her husband's devious plot, Emilia learns of the unjust accusations against Desdemona and bravely exposes Iago's scheming. Coming face-to-face with the brutal realization of his fatal error, Othello tragically ends his life. Iago is arrested, facing justice and leaving a reminder of the damage that deceit and jealousy can cause.

The play explores the vulnerability of human emotions and the deep-seated societal and racial prejudices, attesting to the timeless appeal of Shakespeare's genius. This masterful depiction of human nature underscores his keen insight into psychological complexities and individual motivations.

Othello

121.   King Lear (William Shakespeare, 1605-6)

"Nothing will come of nothing."

—— *William Shakespeare,* King Lear

The aging King Lear decides to divide his kingdom among his three daughters – Goneril, Regan, and Cordelia. Lear plans to measure their love by their proclamations, and in response to Cordelia's refusal to flatter him, Lear disinherits her and divides her share of the kingdom between her two sisters Goneril and Regan. Once they secure their inheritance, Goneril and Regan quickly reveal their true, greedy, and power-hungry natures. They ruthlessly usurp their father's remaining authority, reducing him to a shell of his former self. The now helpless Lear descends into madness: left to wander the wilderness during a violent storm, accompanied only by his Fool and the loyal, but banished, Earl of Kent. In the intervening time, Cordelia, who has married the King of France, returns with a French army to save her father and reclaim his kingdom. Parallel to this, a subplot involving the Earl of Gloucester and his two sons Edgar and Edmund echoes the motifs of power, betrayal, and filial ingratitude. As the conflict arises, treachery is revealed and justice is served in the most tragic ways. Due to their destructive ambitions, Goneril, Regan, and Edmund meet their ends. However, victory comes at a steep price. Cordelia is unjustly executed, and Lear dies from a broken heart, holding her lifeless body. The only solace is that the virtuous Edgar defeats his villainous brother Edmund, though he and Kent are left to mend a shattered kingdom.

King Lear is a masterwork of Shakespeare, blending themes of power, love, loyalty, and the devastating consequences of betrayal. It offers an unsparing examination of human nature and the catastrophic effects of pride and misplaced trust. This play is a testament to Shakespeare's enduring legacy as one of the greatest playwrights in history for its exploration of universal subjects, unparalleled characterization, and profoundly tragic narrative.

122.   Macbeth (William Shakespeare, 1606)

> *"Out, out, brief candle! Life's but a walking shadow,*
> *a poor player that struts and frets his hour upon the stage*
> *and then is heard no more; it is a tale told by an idiot,*
> *full of sound and fury signifying nothing."*

— *William Shakespeare, Macbeth*

On his victorious return from a battle, Macbeth – a celebrated general serving King Duncan of Scotland – encounters three witches who prophesy that he will ascend to the throne of Scotland. The prophecy sparks a burning desire within Macbeth and his ambitious wife Lady Macbeth to hasten their path to the throne. They conspire and successfully murder King Duncan during his visit to their castle, leading to Macbeth's ascension to the throne. However, the path to power is soaked in blood, guilt, and obsession. Consumed by guilt and the fear of being discovered, Macbeth descends into paranoia and hallucinations, leading him to commit more murders. He orders the death of his friend Banquo, fearing that his offspring might threaten his reign as per the witches' prophecy. Meanwhile, the slain king's sons Malcolm and Donalbain, fearing for their safety, flee to England and Ireland, respectively. Macduff, a nobleman, suspects Macbeth's treachery and allies with Malcolm. They gather an army to reclaim the throne from Macbeth. In the final act, overcome by guilt and madness, Lady Macbeth commits suicide, and Macbeth, armed with a misguided confidence instilled by the prophecy, faces Macduff in a battle. Macduff reveals that he was born through a *Caesarian section*, making him technically *not born of a woman*, as per the witches' prophecy. Macduff slays Macbeth and hails Malcolm as Scotland's rightful king.

Shakespeare's Macbeth is a tale of ruthless ambition and its tragic consequences. Its profound exploration of the psychology of guilt, haunting narrative, poetic richness, and deep thematic depth make it one of the most impactful works in English literature.

123.   L'Orfeo (Claudio Monteverdi, 1607)

"I am Music, who in sweet accents,
Can make peaceful every troubled heart,
And so with noble anger, and so with love,
Can I inflame the coldest minds."

— *Claudio Monteverdi, L'Orfeo*

The opera recounts the tragic Greek myth of Orfeo, who descends into the Underworld to rescue his beloved wife Eurydice from the clutches of death. When Eurydice dies, Orfeo is stricken with grief. He embarks on a perilous journey to the Underworld to retrieve her. He manages to persuade Charon, the ferryman of the river Styx, to allow him passage through a soulful and plaintive song that underscores his deep love for Eurydice. Once in the Underworld, Orfeo meets Pluto, the King of Hades, and his wife Proserpina. They are touched by Orfeo's courage and his soul-stirring music. Consequently, they agree to let Eurydice return to the living world with Orfeo, but under the condition that he must not look back at her until they have reached the world of the living. Unable to resist his temptation to turn around and look at his beloved before their arrival, Orfeo does not do what was asked of him, and Eurydice dies for the second time. Stricken with grief and despair at having lost Eurydice again, Orfeo is visited by Apollo, the god of music, who persuades him to ascend to heaven, where he will attain immortality and be free of his earthly desires.

L'Orfeo is a landmark work in the history of opera, as it is one of the earliest operas still regularly performed. Its fusion of music, drama, and dance set the foundation for the future development of the genre. The opera is particularly noted for its effective use of recitatives and monodies, which helped establish a new standard for musical composition. The universal themes of love, loss, and devotion resonate with audiences today — a testament to their enduring relevance and power.

124.   Vespro della Beata Vergine (Claudio Monteverdi, 1610)

> *"Be exalted for His might: for He has done marvelous things."*
>
> —— *Claudio Monteverdi, Vespro della Beata Vergine*

Also known as *Monteverdi Vespers*, it is one of the most ambitious musical compositions of the early 17th century and is recognized for its grandeur, spiritual depth, and innovative use of vocal and instrumental music. The composition comprises 13 parts, including five *psalms*, four *hymns*, and several *motets*, each displaying a unique aspect of Monteverdi's compositional range. The work opens with *Domine ad adjuvandum me festina*, a lively and dramatic call for God's assistance. This is followed by the first Psalm setting *Dixit Dominus*, a work of vocal virtuosity where multiple choirs interact in an impressive demonstration of polychoral technique. The sequence of Psalms interspersed with motets continues to showcase Monteverdi's innovative approach to each piece. For instance, the motet *Nigra sum*, known for its expressive text from the *Song of Solomon*, offers a lush and sensual solo vocal line against a simple instrumental accompaniment. The heart of the Vespers is *Ave Maris Stella*, a hymn to the Virgin Mary. Monteverdi constructs this movement as a series of variations over the chant and creatively employing a wide range of textures, from a simple two-part setting to a complex six-part counterpoint. This grand structure of the Vespers concludes with an intricate and expansive set of the *Magnificat*. Monteverdi proves his mastery of diverse musical forms by alternating between dramatic choral sections, elaborate solos, and intricate duets.

Throughout Vespro della Beata Vergine, Monteverdi blends the traditional with the innovative. He uses traditional plainsong as a structural basis, adding dramatic text settings, expressive dissonances, and virtuosic vocal writing, a hallmark of the new "seconda pratica" style he helped pioneer. The groundbreaking composition is a true landmark in the transition from the Renaissance to the Baroque period.

THE 17th CENTURY

The Library of Humanity

THE 17ᵗʰ CENTURY

The 17th century was a time of tremendous change and transformation in ideas and society. It was a period characterized by a whirlwind of intellectual and social movements as new scientific concepts, philosophical doubt, and political and religious conflicts swept across the Western world. Amid this dynamic era, brilliant minds like Descartes, Hobbes, and Locke emerged, leaving an indelible mark on the annals of Western history.

The influence of these eminent thinkers reverberated not only in the realms of philosophy and politics but also in the realm of literature. Writers of the 17th century found themselves attracted by the shifting currents of their time, and their literary works became a reflection of their evolving understanding of the world. Engaging in contemporary debates about religion, politics, and science, these authors set off on a quest to explore new literary forms that would encapsulate their changing reality.

The *English Civil War* (1642-1651) profoundly influenced literary output. This conflict split English literature into two distinct periods: before 1660, characterized by the closure of theaters due to civil unrest, and after 1660, marked by the restoration of the monarchy under Charles II. Amidst this backdrop, writers such as John Milton ventured into the world of epic poetry, employing their creative prowess to address pressing issues like freedom from tyranny and censorship. Concurrently, Andrew Marvell explored *metaphysical poetry*, aiming to reconcile traditional Christian beliefs with the discoveries of modern science.

The audience for literature in the 17th century experienced a significant transformation. The proliferation of printing technology led to an increase in literacy rates and the rise of a more educated and discerning readership. Expanding intellectual horizons paved the way for a broader intellectual class, actively engaging with literary works. Moreover, the popularity of narrative prose played a vital role in shaping this cultural shift, as writers began to embrace innovative forms that mirrored their evolving worldview and participated in the ongoing dialogues about religion, politics, and science.

The 17th century witnessed a departure from the established canons of the Renaissance. The spirit of the *Baroque* era, characterized by dramatic expression, elaborate ornamentation, and contrast, influenced writers to break free from traditional conventions. There was a growing appetite for linguistic experimentation and even extravagance. An emblematic example of this literary transformation is Miguel de Cervantes' *Don Quixote*, which stands as a pinnacle of Spanish literature and heralds the advent of the *modern novel* era.

In summary, the 17th century was an era defined by daring experimentation, boundless innovation, and unparalleled creativity. Its literary legacy continues to endure, as the echoes of this transformative period can still be heard in contemporary literature.

125.   Don Quixote (Miguel de Cervantes, 1605-1615)

> *"The truth may be stretched thin, but it never breaks,*
> *and it always surfaces above lies, as oil floats on water."*

— *Miguel de Cervantes,* Don Quixote

Don Quixote, fully titled *The Ingenious Gentleman Don Quixote of La Mancha* (*El ingenioso hidalgo don Quijote de la Mancha* in Spanish), is an epoch-defining masterpiece that tells the story of an ordinary *hidalgo* – a member of the Spanish lower nobility – named Alonso Quixano. Consumed by tales of knights and chivalry, Quixano's reality morphs into a romantic dream world, leading him to adopt the persona of *Don Quixote de la Mancha*. Mounted on his horse Rocinante and accompanied by his loyal squire Sancho Panza, Don Quixote embarks on a quest for noble adventures across Spain. As Don Quixote journeys through the countryside, he encounters everyday occurrences that he interprets as epic challenges befitting a knight-errant. From tilting at windmills, believing them to be evil giants, to viewing a peasant girl as the ladylove he must honor and protect, Don Quixote's delusions make for moments of comedy, tragedy, and profound reflection. The narrative takes a cruel turn when the Duke and Duchess manipulate Don Quixote and Sancho for their amusement, playing into and exacerbating Quixote's delusions. The novel ends with a heartbroken Don Quixote who renounces his delusions and the chivalric ideals he held so dear.

The genius of Don Quixote lies in its multi-faceted exploration of reality and imagination, sanity and madness, idealism and pragmatism. Cervantes utilizes satire, irony, and metafiction to critique the romantic literature of his time while also portraying his characters' profound humanity and enduring spirit. Don Quixote is not merely a tale of a delusional knight-errant and his commonsensical squire but a deep and enduring exploration of the human desire for meaning, the power of imagination, and the boundaries of reality. Its universal themes and innovative narrative structure have firmly placed it as a timeless classic in world literature.

126.   The Duchess of Malfi (John Webster, 1612-1614)

"Ambition, madam, is a great man's madness."

— *John Webster, The Duchess of Malfi*

The Duchess of Malfi is a widowed noblewoman who defies societal expectations by falling in love with and secretly marrying her steward Antonio. This personal act of defiance ignites the fury of her brothers Ferdinand and the Cardinal, who are keen to preserve their inheritance and family status. They hire Bosola, a former convict, to spy on the Duchess. Unknown to them, the Duchess had three children with Antonio. Eventually, Bosola discovers the Duchess's secret. Ferdinand, portrayed as unhinged, threatens his sister and severs ties. To escape their oppressive control, the Duchess and Antonio plot to feign financial deceit necessitating Antonio's exile. The Duchess, trusting Bosola, involves him in the scheme. However, Bosola is loyal to Ferdinand and the Cardinal, who intercept the plan. Antonio flees with their eldest son, but the Duchess and her two younger children are captured. Following Ferdinand's orders, Bosola's henchmen kill them. This event deeply affects Bosola, who then resolves to avenge the Duchess. Meanwhile, the Cardinal's malevolence escalates as he confesses his involvement in the Duchess's death to his mistress Julia, and murders her to keep her from speaking. The climax sees Bosola overhearing the Cardinal plotting against him. Seeking revenge, Bosola attacks him in a dark chapel but mistakenly kills Antonio, who had returned to reconcile. Bosola then slays the Cardinal. A subsequent struggle leads to Bosola and Ferdinand mortally wounding each other.

This intricate play is a powerful commentary on the destructive nature of power and societal constraints, particularly regarding women's autonomy. It grapples with themes of forbidden love, patriarchal control, betrayal, revenge, and the ultimate quest for redemption.

127.   Novum Organum (Francis Bacon, 1620)

"Nature, to be commanded, must be obeyed."

—— *Francis Bacon, Novum Organum*

Novum Organum presents a new method for generating and validating knowledge. With its title meaning *New Instrument*, Novum Organum alludes to Aristotle's Organon and signifies Bacon's intent to replace the syllogistic logic and deductive reasoning that Aristotle espoused with a new inductive method based on empirical observation and experimentation. Bacon asserts that the foundation of true knowledge lies in direct practical experience and empirical observation rather than solely relying on the accepted wisdom of classical texts or a priori reasoning. He proposes a method of investigation called *induction*, which involves the meticulous collection of observations, their classification, and the subsequent derivation of general laws from specific instances. This revolutionary approach by Bacon forms the basis of today's scientific method. Central to Bacon's theory is the logical fallacies that hinder the pursuit of proper knowledge. He introduces a classification system for these errors, which he terms *Idols*. The *Idols of the Tribe* are common to humanity and arise from human nature. The *Idols of the Cave* pertain to individual prejudices and preferences. The *Idols of the Marketplace* are engendered by language and societal communication. The *Idols of the Theatre* are born out of dogmatic philosophical systems. Bacon believed these *Idols* prevented individuals from perceiving the world accurately. He therefore advocates for an objective and open investigation of the natural world, free from preconceptions and prejudices and apt to discover the true will of God manifested in nature.

By emphasizing the critical role of empirical observation and by laying the foundations of the inductive method, Bacon established the modern-era scientific paradigm for generating and validating knowledge. His work is regarded as a crucial turning point in the history of science and philosophy.

128.   The Anatomy of Melancholy (Robert Burton, 1621)

> *"Be not solitary, be not idle...*
> *Exercise thyself rather with men than alone;*
> *for which of us can enough avoid*
> *or enough endure his own thoughts?"*

— *Robert Burton, The Anatomy of Melancholy*

The Anatomy of Melancholy is a comprehensive exploration into the labyrinth of melancholia and depression. Divided into three core sections – the *Introduction, Digest,* and *Epistle* – Burton presents a detailed description in decoding the phenomenon of *melancholy.* In the Introduction, he outlines numerous theories attributing melancholy to physical, moral, or spiritual influences and guides readers on recognizing and treating varying forms of melancholy with medical and philosophical remedies. The Digest examines diverse melancholic cases, from love, friendship, death, time, money, and fame. Burton explores different theories of melancholy's causes and remedies. It even includes Burton's own hypothesis on melancholy, founded on the *humors theory,* which postulates that our emotions are guided by four *bodily fluids* that must stay balanced for good health. The concluding Epistle is a letter from Burton to a pseudonymous *Democritus Junior* (pen name used by Robert Burton himself to engage in a dialogue with the reader) giving advice on living without succumbing to depression or melancholy-associated maladies. He champions engaging in activities like reading quality books, having meaningful dialogues with friends, traveling, and appreciating nature as a way to enrich life and combat feelings of despair and emptiness.

This fundamental work explores the complexities of depression and melancholia, and Burton provides an insightful analysis of the causes and cures for this affliction. The use of anecdotes from classical authors helps illustrate his points while giving historical context for his ideas.

129. The Changeling (Thomas Middleton and William Rowley, 1622)

"Why should my hope of fate be timorous?"

—— *Thomas Middleton and William Rowley, The Changeling*

The play is a tragic tale set in Alicante, Spain. Its plot revolves around Beatrice, whose father pledges her in marriage to Alonzo, but Beatrice's heart is won by Alsemero, a nobleman from Valencia. In her desperation to be with Alsemero, Beatrice plots Alonzo's murder, employing De Flores, her father's servant, as the executioner. De Flores demands Beatrice's virginity as payment, to which she yields begrudgingly. A parallel comic subplot transpires in a mental asylum, where two men disguise themselves as madmen to court Isabella, the young wife of an old doctor named Alibius. The interplay of Antonio, the asylum's fool, and a madman named Franciscus, who is also smitten by Isabella, adds a further layer of humor. As the asylum prepares for a performance at Beatrice's wedding, it offers a moment of respite from the tense main plot. When Beatrice and Alsemero marry, she fears he will discover she is not a virgin. To deceive him, she conspires with her maid Diaphanta, to switch places with her on the wedding night. However, as Diaphanta's absence prolongs, Beatrice becomes suspicious and fears betrayal. The plot thickens as secrets unravel. The slain Alonzo's brother Tomazo seeks revenge, while Vermandero demands justice for the murder. Finally, Beatrice's secrets are laid bare, forcing her to confess her crimes. The distraught Alsemero locks her and De Flores in a closet. When all the characters gather, Alsemero reveals the truth, and Beatrice and De Flores confess their crimes before dying.

This tragicomedy is an exploration of the destructive power of jealousy. Middleton and Rowley frequently use puns, which help bring out the humor within certain situations while maintaining an overall sense of tension.

130.   Dialogue Concerning the Two Chief World Systems
(Galileo Galilei, 1632)

> *"The Sun, with all those planets revolving around it and dependent on it,*
> *can still ripen a bunch of grapes*
> *as though it had nothing else in the Universe to do."*

> — *Galileo Galilei, Dialogue Concerning the Two Chief World Systems*

Galileo invites readers to eavesdrop on a riveting conversation between three characters: Salviati, Sagredo, and Simplicio. The stakes are high as they wrestle with a controversial concept: the Copernican *heliocentric* model posits that the Earth revolves around the Sun, a stark departure from the dominant Aristotelian view of Earth as the universe's center. Galileo establishes the context in the preface, referencing the ban on the belief in a moving Earth and his endorsement of Copernicus's revolutionary theory. As the first day passes, the trio scrutinizes Aristotle's assertions about the world's completeness and perfection based on its three dimensions. Salviati, armed with evidence of celestial changes like new stars and sunspots, questions the idea of an immutable heavenly realm. On the second day, the characters engage in a spirited debate about celestial motion, specifically Earth's rotation. Salviati proposes that this rotation could account for the stars' daily movement. As the third day dawns, objections to Earth's annual motion are brought to the fore. Salviati argues that Earth's position is not central to the universe, citing the fluctuating distances of the planets from Earth as evidence. Theology enters the conversation, alongside the consideration of the immense distances to fixed stars. During the last day of the discussion, Salviati elucidates the influence of Earth's motion on tides, tackling their daily, monthly, and annual variations.

Galileo's seminal work articulates the compelling case for the Copernican model, boldly challenging the Aristotelian worldview and underscoring the vital role of empirical evidence in unraveling the universe's secrets.

131.   Le Cid (Pierre Corneille, 1636)

> *"Love is a tyrant which spares no one."*
>
> — *Pierre Corneille, Le Cid*

In 11th-century Seville, Don Sancho and Don Rodrigue, both enamored with Chimène, find themselves entangled in a power play. The situation escalates when Count de Gormas, Chimène's father, challenges Rodrigue's father to a duel out of jealousy, hurling an insult that ignites Rodrigue's sense of honor. Despite knowing his decision could jeopardize his relationship with Chimène, Rodrigue fights. The King disapproves of the Count's rash actions, and his anxiety mounts as the Moorish navy advances. When Rodrigue triumphs over the Count in the duel, the King is deprived of a valuable warrior just when he needs one the most. Racked with guilt, Rodrigue sends a message to Chimène through her nursemaid, expressing his readiness to face death as retribution for her father's demise. Returning from the war as a celebrated hero, the Moors bestow Rodrigue with the title *The Cid*. Spotting an opportunity, Don Sancho offers to fight Rodrigue for Chimène's hand in marriage. Caught in a dilemma, Rodrigue decides to face death rather than live with Chimène's scorn. But Chimène compels him to fight, desperate to avoid a future with Sancho. When Sancho appears bearing a bloodied sword, Chimène fears the worst and declares her love for Rodrigue, even suggesting to prefer the convent's solitude over marrying Sancho. When the King reveals Rodrigue's survival, he proposes that Chimène marry Rodrigue, but only after a year, giving her time to grieve her father's death. Until then, Rodrigue is tasked with continuing his battles against the Moors and earning his honor.

Le Cid is lauded for its intricate narrative and nuanced characters who, despite their conflicts, are portrayed as empathetic figures: their actions are not derived from malevolent intent but understandable motivations.

132.   Discourse on the Method (René Descartes, 1637)

> *"Divide each difficulty into as many parts*
> *as is feasible and necessary to resolve it."*

— *René Descartes, Discourse on the Method*

Descartes seeks to establish a new framework based on doubt, to discern a sound basis for understanding. He decides to question everything that can be confuted, including the testimony of his senses and the authority of established knowledge. Using radical skepticism, Descartes aims to eliminate uncertainties and achieve *indubitable truths*. He argues that even if all his beliefs are illusory, the very act of doubting requires a thinking entity, a self that exists. This *thinking self* becomes the foundation of certainty on which Descartes will build his philosophical system, famously captured in the phrase *Cogito, ergo sum* ("I think, therefore I am"). As a result of his philosophical investigations, Descartes advocates breaking down complex problems into simpler parts and analyzing them methodically. Descartes' methodological approach lays the foundation for his later works in philosophy and science, where he seeks to establish a complete understanding of the natural world. Descartes suggests that the physical world comprises matter and motion governed by *mathematical laws*. Accordingly, the human body operates as a *complex machine* that functions independently of conscious thought. This separation of mind and body, known as *Cartesian dualism*, constitutes an essential aspect of his philosophy. Finally, Descartes grapples with the notion of God's existence, presenting several arguments supporting his belief. He argues that the idea of God as a perfect being cannot have originated from himself as an imperfect being. Therefore, God must exist as the *source* of this idea.

Descartes' fundamental work provided a revolutionary basis for many later philosophical theories about scientific methodology.

133.   Meditations on First Philosophy (René Descartes, 1641)

"Man being of a finite nature,
his knowledge must likewise be of limited perfection."

—— *René Descartes, Meditations on First Philosophy*

Meditations expands the philosophical system of *Discourse on Method*. The First Meditation explores the doubt and skepticism that the Meditator experiences. He aims to rebuild his knowledge on certain foundations by doubting everything. He considers the possibility of being deceived by his senses, acknowledging that senses can sometimes be unreliable. In the Second Meditation, Descartes explores the nature of the human mind and argues that the mind is more known than the body. He develops a theory of *representationalism*, stating that we only have access to the *world of our ideas*, and these ideas represent things that are external to the mind. In the Third Meditation, Descartes presents arguments for the existence of God. He categorizes ideas into *innate*, *fictitious*, and *adventitious*, asserting that *the idea of God is innate* and placed in us by God. He argues that the cause of an idea must have at least as much formal reality as the idea itself, and since he has a concept of God with infinite objective reality, the cause of this must be an eternal and perfect being. In the Fourth Meditation, Descartes addresses the problem of error. He argues that error is not a positive reality but rather a *lack of what is correct*. In the Fifth Meditation, Descartes explores the existence and nature of external material objects. He examines the perception of these objects as they exist in his thoughts and distinguishes between clear and distinct ideas and confused and obscure ones. In the Sixth Meditation, Descartes delves into the distinction between mind and body, arguing that they are different substances.

By addressing solipsism and skepticism, Descartes establishes a framework of reality consisting of God, finite minds (including his own), and external things.

134.   Dokkōdō (Miyamoto Musashi, 1645)

"Perception is strong and sight weak.
In strategy it is important to see distant things as if they were close
and to take a distanced view of close things."

— *Miyamoto Musashi, Dokkōdō*

Dokkōdō (*The Way of Walking Alone*) is a set of 21 precepts written by a legendary samurai, philosopher, and writer, shortly before his death. The precepts cover various aspects of life: acceptance of the world's ways, self-discipline, detachment from desires, non-attachment to the past, avoidance of jealousy and regret, letting go of grudges, steering clear of attachments, and avoiding preferences and luxuries. Musashi's teachings emphasize humility, self-reliance, clarity of mind, and the pursuit of personal development. The writer outlines his philosophy on life, including the principles that form its foundation: living with courage and conviction; being aware of one's environment; cultivating an appropriate mental attitude; understanding the importance of continual learning; preserving harmony with nature; developing martial skills for self-defense purposes only; embracing death as part of life's cycle rather than fearing it; and seeking power through knowledge. Musashi cautions against complacency or overconfidence when fighting opponents, emphasizing adaptability as a critical element for success in any conflict situation. By continuously aiming for perfection while embracing errors as chances for growth rather than setbacks, this principle becomes achievable through the two fundamental qualities of patience and resilience.

Dokkōdō offers advice on how to live life with integrity and courage while developing strength and wisdom through physical and mental training; it speaks to anyone seeking self-improvement.

135.   Leviathan (Thomas Hobbes, 1651)

> *"In such condition, there is no place for industry,*
> *because the fruit thereof is uncertain:*
> *[...] and which is worst of all,*
> *continual fear and danger of violent death;*
> *and the life of man solitary, poor, nasty brutish and short."*

>   — *Thomas Hobbes, Leviathan*

The central argument in Leviathan is that civil peace and social unity are best achieved by establishing a commonwealth through a *social contract*. Hobbes begins by arguing that all people naturally seek peace, safety, and security: they desire to be free from the violence of others. He then argues that any state of nature without some kind of political authority will inevitably dissolve into a "warre of every man against every man" due to competition for resources, which he characterized as a "perpetuall condition of meer Warre." In order to escape this state, people must enter into a social contract in which they agree to surrender their natural rights to an absolute sovereign power that will guarantee their security from external threats. Hobbes also argues that there can be only one sovereign power over a given territory at any given time; otherwise, there would be no ultimate source of law or justice. The sovereign must possess both military and legislative powers; otherwise, it cannot enforce its laws or protect its citizens from foreign invasion. Furthermore, Hobbes believes that the sovereign should have absolute control over all aspects of life within its borders – including religion – to prevent internal conflict among its citizens. Finally, he discusses monarchy, aristocracy, and democracy as forms of government, preferring monarchy but not categorically rejecting the others.

Leviathan provides a framework for understanding rights and obligations as individuals within the society. It also provides a theory on how governments should be structured.

136.   Of Plymouth Plantation (William Bradford, 1651)

> *"Being thus passed the vast ocean,*
> *and a sea of troubles before in their preparation*
> *(as may be remembered by that which went before),*
> *they had now no friends to wellcome them*
> *nor inns to entertain or refresh their weatherbeaten bodies;*
> *no houses or much less towns to repair too; to seek for succor."*

— *William Bradford, Of Plymouth Plantation*

William Bradford, one of the leaders of the Plymouth Colony, chronicles the Pilgrims' voyage on the Mayflower and their subsequent settlement at Plymouth, in what is now Massachusetts. The Pilgrims arrived at Cape Cod in November 1620. The first winter was extremely difficult, with half of the colonists dying due to inadequate shelter and lack of food. In March 1621, the colonists established a treaty with the *Wampanoag tribe*, which allowed them access to land for farming and fishing rights. The following year was successful, with an abundant harvest that provided sustenance. In August 1623, Governor Bradford declared *a day of Thanksgiving* to celebrate the good fortune they had experienced since arriving in America. This event is widely considered to be America's first *Thanksgiving* celebration. As time passed, more settlers arrived, and new towns were founded throughout New England. By 1630 there were 11 towns established in Massachusetts alone. In October 1636, a group of settlers led by Roger Williams was banished from Massachusetts for refusing to accept state-sanctioned religion, establishing *Providence Plantation* (Rhode Island) as a safe haven for those seeking religious freedom. By 1645 there were nearly twenty towns established across New England; this growth was not without conflict as Indian tribes resisted the encroachment on their lands leading up to *King Philip's War* (1675-1676).

Of Plymouth Plantation provides insight into how settlers were able to survive such harsh conditions and how their values shaped early America.

Of Plymouth Plantation

137.   To His Coy Mistress (Andrew Marvell, 1649-1660)

> *"Had we but world enough, and time,*
> *This coyness, Lady, were no crime."*

— *Andrew Marvell, To His Coy Mistress*

To His Coy Mistress is a classic carpe diem poem by a prominent *Metaphysical poet*. The term *carpe diem* means *seize the day*. Marvell's poem vividly reflects this concept because the speaker employs persuasive and eloquent arguments to convince his beloved to embrace and act upon their love without delay. The poem is structured in three distinct sections. In the first part, the speaker indulges in whimsical and hyperbolic expressions to describe how, if they were not bound by the constraints of time, he would spend centuries adoring her and lavishing praise upon her beauty and grace. He portrays a grandiose image where her resistance to his courtship would be admissible if they had eternity. In the second part, there is a drastic shift in tone. The speaker switches from using dreamy hypotheticals to confronting the stark reality of human mortality. He paints a rather bleak and macabre picture, reminding his beloved that their time on earth is limited; if she continues to be coy, she will take with her to the grave her virtues, unappreciated and untasted. Finally, in the last section, the speaker proposes that they should seize the moment and engage in passionate love. He urges his beloved to be amorous while her beauty still flourishes, as this is the only way to triumph over the inexorable march of time.

To His Coy Mistress is a masterful poetic expression of urgency and desire in the face of life's transience. Its elaborate metaphors and eloquent language embody the tension between the yearning for eternal love and the reality of human temporality. It serves not only as a romantic persuasion but also as a philosophical reflection on life's ephemerality. Moreover, the poem exemplifies the Metaphysical poet's penchant for intellectual playfulness, ingenuity, and wit.

138.   Tartuffe (Molière, 1664)

> *"Brightness of wit and ready speech*
> *will get a man respect;*
> *But if his sense is shallow like a brook,*
> *All his fine words are mere pretense and talk."*

— *Molière, Tartuffe*

Tartuffe is a comedic play first performed in 1664. The story centers on the deceit and hypocrisy of the titular character *Tartuffe*, who feigns religious piety to manipulate and exploit a gullible man named Orgon and his family. Orgon, blinded by Tartuffe's pretended holiness, offers him unwavering trust and a place in his household, despite the clear skepticism of his family and servants. Orgon even promises his daughter Marianne's hand in marriage to Tartuffe, although she is in love with another man named Valère. Elmire, Orgon's astute wife, is not fooled by Tartuffe's facade and concocts a plan to expose him. She convinces Orgon to hide under a table while conversing with Tartuffe, wherein she pretends to be receptive to his advances. Tartuffe, believing they are alone, reveals his lecherous intentions and lack of true piety. Having heard everything from his hiding place, Orgon realizes the depth of Tartuffe's deceit. However, before Orgon can act against Tartuffe, he learns that Tartuffe has already gone to the authorities with incriminating documents that Orgon had entrusted him, placing Orgon's estate and family at risk. In a final twist, Tartuffe is arrested by an officer of the King for his crimes, and Orgon's family is saved.

Tartuffe is a sharp satire of religious hypocrisy and gullibility. Through wit and humor, Molière criticizes how people can be deceived by appearances and blind faith and how hypocrites can exploit religion for personal gain. The play also portrays strong female characters, such as Elmire and Dorine (the sharp-witted maid), who stand up to deceit and manipulation. Molière cleverly depicts the conflicts and interactions between characters from different social classes, highlighting societal issues of his time.

139.   The Misanthrope (Molière, 1666)

> *"If you don't appreciate me for who I am,*
> *why should I pretend to be someone else?"*

—*Molière, The Misanthrope*

The play centers on the character Alceste, who abhors the deceit and flattery prevalent in the French aristocratic society of his time. Alceste prides himself on his honesty and straightforwardness but is at odds with societal norms. His closest friend Philinte is more pragmatic and tries to temper Alceste's bluntness with diplomacy, but to no avail. Alceste is in love with Célimène, a coquette known for her wit and charm, but her flirtatious and insincere nature is at odds with his ideals. As the story progresses, Alceste's frankness creates conflicts, especially when he candidly criticizes the mediocre poetry of Oronte, a fellow courtier. Meanwhile, Célimène continues to entertain multiple suitors, much to Alceste's chagrin. Célimène's character is further complicated by her dealings with Arsinoe, a seemingly virtuous lady who, under the pretense of moral guidance, attempts to undermine Célimène. However, Arsinoe's own hypocrisy is laid bare in the process. The play reaches its climax when letters written by Célimène, in which she mocks her various suitors, are revealed. Each suitor, upon reading the disparaging comments about himself, leaves Célimène. With the dishonesty and artifice surrounding him, Alceste decides to withdraw from society to avoid its deceit and hypocrisy. Before he leaves, he asks Célimène to join him, but she refuses, reluctant to abandon her social life.

One of the play's most notable achievements is its complex and nuanced portrayal of its main character Alceste. Molière's skillful use of dialogue contributes to the play's greatness, and his use of satire is particularly effective, as he skewers the social conventions and hypocrisies of the French court with a deft touch that is both scathing and entertaining.

140.   Paradise Lost (John Milton, 1667)

> *"The mind is its own place,*
> *and in itself can make a Heaven of Hell,*
> *a Hell of Heaven."*
>
> — *John Milton, Paradise Lost*

The poem begins with Satan and his fellow rebel angels being cast into Hell after their failed rebellion against God. In Hell, Satan and his demons construct *Pandemonium*, their capital, and debate whether or not to continue the war against Heaven through more direct means. In Heaven, God foresees the fall of man and decides to offer *grace* and a chance for *redemption*. He also foretells the eventual sacrifice of his Son to save humanity. Motivated by envy and a desire for revenge, Satan travels through chaos and night to reach Earth. He discovers the beauty of Eden, where God has placed the first humans, Adam and Eve. They live in harmony and innocence but are warned not to eat from the *Tree of Knowledge of Good and Evil*. Satan, taking on the form of a serpent, successfully tempts Eve to eat the forbidden fruit. Eve, in turn, offers the fruit to Adam, who knowingly chooses to eat it out of love for her. Their innocence is lost, and they become ashamed of their nakedness. God sends the archangel Michael to pass judgment. Adam and Eve are expelled from the *Garden of Eden*, but not before Michael shows Adam a vision of humanity's future, including the eventual *redemption* through the sacrifice of Jesus. Satan returns to Hell and is briefly celebrated as a hero, but he and the fallen angels are ultimately turned into serpents as a punishment for their deeds.

Paradise Lost is celebrated for its rich language and verse and its complex characters, particularly Satan, who is depicted with tragic grandeur. Milton's portrayal of the fall and its universal ramifications combines a rich classical tradition with deep religious subjects, making it one of the greatest epic poems in English literature.

141.   Ethics (Baruch Spinoza, 1677)

> *"God, or a substance consisting of infinite attributes,*
> *each of which expresses eternal and infinite essence."*
>
> — *Baruch Spinoza, Ethics*

Ethics is a philosophical treatise by Baruch Spinoza that examines the nature of reality, the relation between mind and body, and the path to spiritual enlightenment. The work is *geometrically structured*, modeled after *Euclid's Elements*, and is divided into five parts. In Part One, Spinoza argues that there is only *one substance*, which he identifies with God or Nature, and that this substance has *infinite attributes*. He holds that everything, including human beings, is part of this one substance. He asserts that humans can perceive only two attributes: *thought* and *extension*. His conception of God is often described as *pantheistic*. Part Two examines the nature of the human mind and its relation to the body. Spinoza asserts that the mind and body are two aspects of a single reality. He introduces the concept of *conatus*, the inherent inclination of a thing to continue to exist and enhance itself. Part Three focuses on human emotions and desires, where Spinoza argues that emotions are natural and understanding them is key to controlling them. He posits that freedom arises from understanding the causal chains that bind us. Part Four is devoted to human servitude and the power of emotions, and he highlights the detrimental effects of negative emotions. In Part Five, titled Of Human Freedom, Spinoza discusses how reason and knowledge of the true nature of reality can liberate humans from emotional bondage. He explains that through reason and understanding, one can achieve an *intellectual love of God*, which is the highest form of knowledge and leads to true happiness.

Ethics is a profound philosophical work that combines metaphysics, epistemology, psychology, ethics, and the philosophy of mind to provide a path to human freedom and happiness.

142.   Phèdre (Jean Racine, 1677)

"Innocence has nothing to dread."

— *Jean Racine, Phèdre*

The tragic play revolves around Queen Phaedra, the wife of King Theseus, who falls in love with her stepson Hippolytus. This passionate but forbidden love sets the stage for a tragic outcome. Phaedra confides her feelings to her nurse Oenone, who advises her to reveal her desires to Hippolytus. Hippolytus is horrified by the confession, and in his dismay, he admits his love for Aricia, a rival to the throne who had been banned from marrying by Theseus. The news of Theseus's return complicates matters, leading to a plan to protect Phaedra's secrets. Theseus, unaware of Phaedra's passion, is puzzled by her cold reception. Oenone falsely accuses Hippolytus of attempting to seduce Phaedra, infuriating Theseus, who banishes his son and uses one of the three wishes granted by Neptune to curse him. In the meantime, Phaedra struggles with her guilt over Hippolytus's punishment and her jealousy of Aricia. Eventually, the truth begins to surface. Oenone's lies become evident when she commits suicide out of shame. Through his father's curse, Hippolytus is killed by a sea monster sent by Neptune. Before dying, Hippolytus maintains his innocence and asserts his eternal love for Aricia. Full of remorse, Phaedra confesses her role in the tragedy to Theseus before taking her own life. Devastated and left alone, Theseus makes a final act of redemption by adopting Aricia as his daughter and allowing her to succeed him on the throne.

Phèdre is a gripping tale of forbidden love, betrayal, and tragic fate. Set in a court filled with secrets and suppressed desires, the characters grapple with their emotions, conclusively leading to their downfall. Racine's tragedy is a masterful exploration of human passion and its destructive potential, providing insights into the moral tensions of 17th-century French society.

143.   Discourse on Metaphysics (Gottfried W. Leibniz, 1686)

"The monad is the real atom of nature; there are no others."

— *Gottfried W. Leibniz, Discourse on Metaphysics*

Leibniz explores the nature of God, the fundamental substances of reality, and the interplay between matter, form, and soul. He asserts that God, *being supremely perfect*, chose to create this world among infinite possibilities, as it allows for the *maximal diversity of phenomena* while maintaining the *simplest laws*. A significant portion of the Discourse is dedicated to exploring the nature of substances. Leibniz introduces the concept of *monads – indivisible, immaterial entities that constitute the fabric of reality*. In a groundbreaking departure from traditional substance theories, he posits that *each monad reflects the entire universe* in a unique way, and they do not interact with each other directly. Instead, Leibniz suggests that God synchronizes the internal states of all monads in a *pre-established harmony* such that their changes reflect a coherent and coordinated world. Leibniz also delves into the nature of physical objects, which he regards as aggregates of monads. In his view, what seems to be physical causation in the world results from the *harmonious coordination* among monads established by God. This leads him to discuss the intricate relationship between the immaterial soul and the material body, suggesting that *souls are a special monad with perceptions*. Another essential aspect is Leibniz's take on human freedom and the problem of evil. He contends that, although God predetermined everything, human beings possess freedom through their capacity for rational reflection and choice by reason. As for the existence of evil, Leibniz maintains that it is a necessary consequence of the limitations of created beings.

Leibniz's bold philosophical system has provided foundational insights into science, mathematics, and rationalist philosophy. His innovative concepts, such as monads and pre-established harmony, have had a lasting impact, making Discourse a crucial text in the history of philosophy.

144. Philosophiæ Naturalis Principia Mathematica (Isaac Newton, 1687)

"I frame no hypotheses."

—— *Isaac Newton, Philosophiæ Naturalis Principia Mathematica*

Philosophiæ Naturalis Principia Mathematica (also known as the *Principia*) is a landmark work in physics and astronomy, consisting of three books within a single volume. Written by Isaac Newton and first published in 1687, the Principia formulates the laws of motion and universal gravitation. In Book I, *The Motion of Bodies*, Newton lays out his three laws of motion, which describe the relationship between the motion of an object and the forces acting upon it. He uses rigorous mathematical reasoning to analyze the consequences of these laws and considers various cases of motion under a central force. Book II is concerned with the motion of bodies through resisting mediums, such as air or water. Here, Newton investigates the properties of fluids and the effects of resistance on motion, laying the groundwork for the development of fluid mechanics. In Book III, *The System of the World*, Newton presents his law of universal gravitation, establishing that every mass attracts every other mass in the universe with force proportional to the product of their masses and inversely proportional to the square of the distance between them. He applies this law to explain a wide range of astronomical phenomena, including the elliptical orbits of planets, which had previously been described by Kepler's laws.

The Principia is a scientific excursion that leverages mathematics to account for natural phenomena previously shrouded in mystery. By forming the basis of classical mechanics, it shaped the course of physics and had far-reaching implications for fields as diverse as engineering and astronomy. Its legacy permeates modern scientific thought and testifies to its enduring importance.

THE 18th CENTURY

THE 18ᵗʰ CENTURY

The 18th century was a period of significant change and intellectual ferment, characterized by a desire for knowledge and progress. This period, particularly in Europe, was marked by the *Enlightenment*, a movement that sought to enlighten society's intellectual and cultural life through reason, science, and the promotion of individual rights. Literature played a crucial role in this movement, as it aimed to be useful and practical, offering guidance on how to live a good life and be a productive member of society. As Voltaire, one of the prominent figures of the Enlightenment, wrote in his Philosophical Dictionary, it was a time when "men began to think for themselves, to trust their reason, to respect the rights of others, and to value the blessings of freedom."

The 18th century witnessed the rise of journalism, facilitating the spread of culture and ideas. This development led to the formation of discussion groups, the founding of academies, the publication of journals, and the gathering of intellectuals in cafes. These spaces promoted free thought outside the confines of traditional cultural hierarchies and contributed to the democratization of knowledge.

During this period, nature was often seen as a model for human behavior, and many writers and thinkers stressed the importance of living according to its laws. Jean-Jacques Rousseau was a key figure in this respect. In his book *Emile, or On Education*, he emphasized the importance of individualism and self-expression, advocating for education that catered to each student's unique needs and interests.

In addition to the Enlightenment, the late 18th century in Germany saw the emergence of the *Sturm und Drang* movement. Spearheaded by figures like Johann Wolfgang Goethe, Sturm und Drang celebrated individualism and emotional intensity, often critiquing established society. It laid the groundwork for *Romanticism*, which would further explore these topics in the 19th century.

The 18th century also heralded significant social, political, and economic changes. The *Industrial Revolution*, which began during this period, had a profound impact on society. Furthermore, the concept of the social contract and the notion of individual freedoms and rights started to take hold, encouraging active political participation.

This era also saw the beginnings of revolutionary changes, such as the *French Revolution*, which was partly a product of the intellectual shifts of the time. These revolutions contributed to laying the foundation for the development of modern democratic societies.

While focusing on Europe, it is important to note that the 18th century was also a period of change and development globally. Different parts of the world experienced their own cultural, social, and intellectual movements.

In summary, the 18th century was a pivotal time in history characterized by intellectual awakenings; cultural shifts; and the beginnings of modern social, political, and economic systems. Its legacies continue to shape the contemporary world.

145.   The Fable of the Bees: Or Private Vices, Public Benefits
(Bernard Mandeville, 1714)

> *"Do we not owe the growth of wine to the dry shabby crooked vine?*
> *which, whilst its shutes neglected stood, choak'd other plants, and ran to wood."*

— *Bernard Mandeville, The Fable of the Bees*

At the heart of Mandeville's work is a paradoxical proposition that *private vices*, often considered detrimental to societal harmony, can inadvertently result in *public benefits*. Mandeville utilizes the beehive metaphor to symbolize a dynamic, complex society. This hive teems with bees that, guided by their selfish instincts, tirelessly compete for resources and goods. On the surface, these behaviors appear inimical to the communal spirit, but Mandeville astutely observes that they drive the prosperity and growth of the hive. However, Mandeville does not romanticize these private vices. He notes that if unchecked, they can fuel social unrest and destabilize societal structures, primarily due to escalating inequality and dissatisfaction. A wise bee proposes a governance strategy that channels these private vices within defined societal rules. This idea posits that if the individual's pursuit of personal desires were controlled and moderated, they could potentially be harnessed for collective benefit. For instance, personal ambition could drive economic growth, while a desire for personal health could inspire enhanced healthcare accessibility. Mandeville underscores that this approach is not a panacea that completely resolves the tension between individual desires and the collective good. Instead, it establishes a sustainable equilibrium where personal ambitions contribute to societal welfare.

Mandeville's insightful fable has significantly influenced subsequent thinkers. Adam Smith, often dubbed the father of modern economics, has borrowed from Mandeville's paradoxical view of vice and virtue. Smith's concept of the 'invisible hand,' where individual self-interest inadvertently contributes to societal welfare, parallels Mandeville's views.

146.   Robinson Crusoe (Daniel Defoe, 1719)

> *"I learned to look more upon the bright side of my condition,*
> *and less upon the dark side,*
> *and to consider what I enjoyed,*
> *rather than what I wanted."*

— *Daniel Defoe, Robinson Crusoe*

The eponymous hero Robinson Crusoe is a young man with a restless spirit and a thirst for seafaring adventure. His spirit remains unbroken despite numerous disastrous voyages, including a shipwreck and a stint of enslavement by Salé pirates. Defying the well-meaning advice of his family, he leaves port on yet another journey. Fate, however, strikes again, and a violent storm leaves Crusoe as the sole survivor on a desolate island. Over the years, Crusoe builds a self-sufficient life: growing crops, raising animals, and creating tools. He turns to religion for comfort. Eventually, he encounters cannibals visiting the island. Rather than attacking them, Crusoe rescues a captive, whom he names *Friday*. He teaches Friday English and converts him to Christianity. They rescue two more prisoners, including Friday's father and a Spaniard. Before they can execute a plan to escape the island with other Spaniards, an English ship arrives with mutineers planning to maroon their captain. Crusoe helps retake the ship, and they set sail for England, leaving the mutineers on the island with guidance on survival. Crusoe reaches England in 1687 after almost three decades of being away. He finds his family presumed him dead. He then travels to Lisbon to claim his Brazilian plantation profits. With newfound wealth, he travels overland to England with Friday. During this journey, they have a final adventure fighting wolves in the Pyrenees.

Robinson Crusoe is a classic adventure tale exploring survival, self-reliance, and human perseverance in extreme hardship. Widely regarded as one of the first novels in the English language, it notably fuses fiction and non-fiction elements, giving readers an engrossing narrative rich in detail and realism.

147.   Gulliver's Travels (Jonathan Swift, 1726)

"Undoubtedly, philosophers are in the right when they tell us that nothing is great or little otherwise than by comparison."

— *Jonathan Swift, Gulliver's Travels*

The narrative follows the adventures of Lemuel Gulliver, an English ship surgeon, as he ventures to four fantastical and distinct lands, each offering a unique perspective on humanity. In the land of Lilliput, Gulliver finds himself a giant amongst diminutive inhabitants embroiled in petty disputes, reflecting the absurdities of political conflicts in Swift's contemporary society. Conversely, in Brobdingnag, Gulliver becomes a dwarf in a land of giants, highlighting the vulnerability and insignificance of humans. On the flying island of Laputa, Swift satirizes the impracticality of theoretical knowledge devoid of common sense, symbolized by its inhabitants engrossed in abstract speculations while ignoring practical affairs. Finally, in the land of Houyhnhnms, Gulliver encounters a race of rational, virtuous horses and the barbaric, brutish Yahoos, embodying the best and worst of humanity. These varied experiences lead Gulliver to question the norms and values of his own society, leading to his disillusionment with humanity. Upon his return to England, he isolates himself from society, preferring the company of horses over humans. Yet, in the end, Gulliver realizes he cannot entirely reject society, denoting his understanding that social flaws require reform rather than absolute rejection.

Swift uses satire to critique the follies of humanity throughout the novel. He examines various aspects of society. By exaggerating some features of these topics, he reveals how absurd some behaviors can be when taken to extremes. Gulliver's Travels provides an entertaining yet thought-provoking look into human nature and clever use of satire.

148.   A Modest Proposal (Jonathan Swift, 1729)

"I have been assured
by a very knowing American of my acquaintance in London,
that a young healthy child well nursed is at a year old
a most delicious nourishing and wholesome food,
whether stewed, roasted, baked, or boiled."

— *Jonathan Swift, A Modest Proposal*

A Modest Proposal is a remarkable example of satirical literature that provides a scathing social commentary on the desperate condition of 18th-century Ireland. Swift astoundingly proposes a solution to the severe poverty and overpopulation problem: selling poor Irish children as culinary delicacies for the wealthy classes. He argues that this would alleviate poverty, reduce crime, increase employment, and provide more money for public works projects. Swift begins by outlining how dire the situation in Ireland has become due to extreme poverty and excessive population growth, which leads him to propose his radical solution. He then goes on to argue why selling children as food is an acceptable option; he claims that it would benefit both the poor parents who have too many mouths to feed and those with large fortunes looking for new sources of nutrition. Furthermore, he states there will be no shortage of customers since people are always ready "to gratify their palates" with exotic dishes such as these. Throughout his proposal, Swift employs various rhetorical strategies, including irony and sarcasm, to make his points more effective while, at the same time, mocking what he perceives as illogical or careless thinking among members of society when considering social issues like poverty or overpopulation.

A Modest Proposal is considered one of the greatest works of satire due to its biting social commentary on poverty and inequality and its influence on modern satirical writing.

149.   Pamela, or Virtue Rewarded (Samuel Richardson, 1740)

> *"Why should the guiltless tremble so,*
> *when the guilty can possess their minds in peace?"*

> — *Samuel Richardson, Pamela, or Virtue Rewarded*

Pamela Andrews is a virtuous and attractive young servant working for Lady B, a wealthy widow. After Lady B's death, her son Mr. B becomes infatuated with Pamela. He tries to seduce her multiple times, leveraging his social status and wealth to coerce her into becoming his mistress. These unwelcome advances put Pamela in a precarious position, struggling to protect her virtue against the relentless pursuits of her employer's son. The novel is composed mainly of Pamela's letters to her impoverished parents, in which she animatedly recounts her ordeal. Her accounts present her strong personality, moral steadfastness, and religious piety; these are virtues that she refuses to compromise, regardless of Mr. B's persistent attempts or the potential for an improved social standing. Her integrity and strength of character, manifested in her resistance, earn her the respect of other characters within the narrative. This includes Mrs. Jewkes, the initially stern housekeeper in Mr. B's estate, who admires Pamela's unwavering fidelity to her principles. As the story progresses, Mr. B's desire morphs from physical attraction to genuine admiration for her character. Struck by her uncompromising virtue, he proposes marriage, offering Pamela a legitimate route to rise above her low social standing. Initially suspicious of his intentions due to his past actions, Pamela eventually accepts the marriage proposal, and she finally becomes a respected lady.

Richardson's narrative provides an insightful commentary on the stark class distinctions and power dynamics of 18th-century England, illustrating how virtue can triumph over the corrupting influence of power and wealth. The novel stands as a pioneering work of psychological realism and preserves a nuanced exploration of characters and their motivations.

150. An Enquiry Concerning Human Understanding (David Hume, 1748)

> *"Reason is, and ought only to be the slave of the passions."*

—— *David Hume, An Enquiry Concerning Human Understanding*

Throughout this work, Hume challenges traditional conceptions of knowledge, arguing that human understanding is based on experience rather than on innate ideas or principles. He argues that our beliefs are determined by habit and custom rather than reason or evidence. Hume argues that we cannot perceive causal relationships directly but instead must infer them from patterns observed in past experiences. This leads him to reject the notion of necessary connections between events as an illusion created by our own minds; instead, he claims that all cause-effect relationships can be explained through inductive reasoning. He then discusses different types of knowledge, such as mathematics and morality, and analyzes their foundations. He further questions whether there can be any certainties in life given how unreliable our perceptions may be. Finally, Hume turns his attention to religion and suggests that religious belief should not depend upon arguments or evidence but simply upon personal faith alone; without this faith, it would be impossible for us to have meaningful lives at all. In conclusion, Hume proposes a skeptical view of human understanding, which holds that we cannot achieve certainty in any area due to the limitations imposed upon us by our minds and senses.

Hume's seminal work is foundational to modern epistemology. He considers various skeptical arguments that challenge our ability to know anything with certainty. Hume's work has had a lasting impact on philosophical thought, inspiring later generations of empiricists such as John Stuart Mill and Bertrand Russell.

151.   Tom Jones (Henry Fielding, 1749)

"It is not enough that your designs, nay that your actions,
are intrinsically good,
you must take care they shall appear so."

— *Henry Fielding, Tom Jones*

The novel's protagonist Tom Jones is an orphan discovered as an infant by the honorable Squire Allworthy at his estate Paradise Hall in Somerset. Squire Allworthy, a noble and compassionate man, raises Tom as his own. Despite the benevolent influence of his adoptive father, Tom grows into a spirited and impetuous young man known for his good looks and charm. His vivacious nature often lands him in trouble, particularly with the opposite sex. Tom's heart, however, belongs to the virtuous and beautiful Sophia Western, who lives nearby. Sophia's grace and goodness serve as a stark contrast to Tom's sometimes reckless behavior. The affection between Tom and Sophia is reciprocated, but their differing social statuses and the manipulations of those around them, including scheming relatives and jealous suitors, create hurdles in their path to union. Adding depth to the narrative are the adventures and misadventures that Tom experiences. He is falsely accused of theft, gets into brawls, has chance encounters with highwaymen, makes daring rescues, and becomes entangled with several women. Through these escapades, Fielding paints a vivid picture of 18th-century English society, complete with its virtues, vices, hypocrisies, and follies. Sophia, resolute in her love and integrity, remains a guiding light for Tom, whose character evolves throughout the story. After many twists and turns, including a revelation regarding Tom's lineage, the young couple's resilience and love are rewarded.

Tom's journey explores the redeeming quality of love and the importance of personal growth. The novel is praised for its vibrant and diverse cast of characters and Fielding's deft blending of comedy and drama.

152.   Candide (Voltaire, 1759)

> *"I have wanted to kill myself a hundred times,*
> *but somehow I am still in love with life.*
> *This ridiculous weakness is perhaps*
> *one of our more stupid melancholy propensities,*
> *for is there anything more stupid than to be eager to go on*
> *carrying a burden which one would gladly throw away?"*

> — *Voltaire, Candide*

Candide is a *satirical novel* that follows the adventures of a young man named Candide. Raised in a baronial castle, Candide is nurtured on the *philosophy of optimism* by the ever-optimistic tutor Dr. Pangloss, who asserts that they live in the *best of all possible worlds* based on *Leibnizian philosophy*. Candide's naive belief in Pangloss's teachings is tested when he is expelled from the castle for being romantically involved with the Baron's daughter Cunégonde. Embarking on a series of travels and misadventures, Candide witnesses the horrors of war, natural disasters, and human cruelty. Along the way, he meets a diverse group of characters, including the disillusioned Martin. Candide's experiences provoke him to question the validity of Pangloss's optimistic philosophy. Despite the calamities he endures, he persists in his search for Cunégonde, whom he hopes to marry. Candide eventually reunites with Cunégonde, whose beauty has faded, and also with Pangloss, who, despite the miseries endured, has not abandoned his optimistic beliefs. By the novel's end, Candide's experiences have moderated his outlook on life. Instead of subscribing to philosophical optimism, he concludes that practical work and a simple life may be the keys to contentment. He famously ends with: "we must cultivate our garden," implying that people should focus on their primary duties.

Candide is celebrated as a hallmark of Enlightenment literature due to its scathing satire on dogma and philosophical optimism. Voltaire critiques the intellectual constructs and advocates for the use of reason instead.

153.   The Life and Opinions of Tristram Shandy, Gentleman
(Laurence Sterne, 1759)

> *"I have a strong propensity in me*
> *to begin this chapter very nonsensically,*
> *and I will not balk my fancy.*
> *Accordingly I set off thus."*

—— *Laurence Sterne, The Life and Opinions of Tristram Shandy, Gentleman*

The Life and Opinions of Tristram Shandy, Gentleman, is a groundbreaking novel that defies conventional narrative structure. Told through the eyes of the eponymous protagonist Tristram Shandy, the story is a collection of digressions, anecdotes, and character sketches, which combine to portray Tristram's eccentric family and his observations on life. One prominent example of the novel's humor and unconventionality is the incident regarding Tristram's name. His father Walter Shandy had planned to give him a distinguished name, but through a series of comic mishaps and much to his father's chagrin, he becomes christened Tristam. The novel includes an array of quirky characters. Tristram's father Walter is a pedantic gentleman obsessed with theories and systems, which seldom work in practice. Uncle Toby, Tristram's good-hearted uncle, is preoccupied with military history and spends his time reenacting battles. Throughout the book, Tristram attempts to narrate his life story, but his countless digressions lead him to cover many topics ranging from his conception and birth to philosophical musings on life, time, and causality.

Sterne's novel is famous for its inventive narrative techniques, including blank pages, visual aids, and non-linear storytelling. This avant-garde approach to narrative was ahead of its time and has influenced modernist and postmodernist writers. The Life and Opinions of Tristram Shandy, Gentleman, is celebrated for its wit, humor, and narrative innovation and remains a landmark in the history of the novel.

154.   Emile, or On Education (Jean-Jacques Rousseau, 1762)

"To live is not to breathe but to act.
It is to make use of our organs, our senses, our faculties,
of all the parts of ourselves
which give us the sentiment of our existence.
The man who has lived the most
is not he who has counted the most years
but he who has most felt life."

— *Jean-Jacques Rousseau,* Emile, or On Education

In Emile, or *On Education,* Rousseau presents his philosophy on the importance of natural education and individual experience. The book is divided into several sections, each corresponding to different stages of a person's life: infancy, childhood, adolescence, and adulthood. In each section, Rousseau provides detailed advice and principles on how to nurture a child's development naturally at every age. In infancy, Rousseau believes children should be allowed plenty of freedom to explore within safe boundaries. Physical activities such as walking or riding are recommended for fostering health and curiosity. He suggests stimulating their intellectual growth during childhood through practical engagement with the world rather than through books. Rousseau asserts that adolescence is the time for introducing abstract thinking and moral values. Upon reaching adulthood, Rousseau promotes independent thought by exposing individuals gradually to diverse ideas, allowing them to make informed decisions in life. Love, respect for others, and avoiding harsh punishments form the basis of his moral education. According to Rousseau, the ultimate goal is to produce a virtuous citizen who can think independently and live in harmony with nature.

Emile is not merely a book about child-rearing methods and guidance; it is a comprehensive philosophical work that profoundly reflects human nature and societal norms. It laid the foundation for modern educational theory and continues to significantly influence parenting and teaching practices today.

155.   The Social Contract (Jean-Jacques Rousseau, 1762)

> *"Let us then admit that force does not create right,*
> *and that we are obliged to obey*
> *only legitimate powers."*

— *Jean-Jacques Rousseau, The Social Contract*

In The Social Contract, Jean-Jacques Rousseau explores the concept of political authority and the nature of society. Rousseau posits that genuine political authority originates not from divine right or conquest but from a voluntary contract among free individuals. This social contract, he contends, seeks to balance the sometimes conflicting demands of individual liberty and societal order. Rousseau advocates for a political community where all citizens are equal, and laws are established based on the *general will* – a concept central to his theory, representing the common good or public interest. He argues that this *general will* should be the guiding principle for creating and enforcing laws. He also discusses the concept of sovereignty, arguing that it resides entirely in the hands of the people, who can choose to delegate it but never surrender it. This social contract's purpose is to preserve each individual's natural rights, ensuring equal access to justice and freedom of speech while maintaining public order. Rousseau believed that any legitimate government must strive to protect its citizens, allowing room for societal evolution and change, which can only be achieved through collective deliberation and respect for human dignity.

Jean-Jacques Rousseau's work is a foundational text of modern political philosophy. In it, Rousseau argues that the best form of government is based on an agreement between the people and their rulers, where all citizens are equal under the law and have a say in how they are governed. Rousseau's work was highly influential during the Age of Enlightenment and has been widely studied for its insights into human nature and its implications for democratic governance.

156.   The Castle of Otranto (Horace Walpole, 1764)

"The Castle and Lordship of Otranto should pass from the present family whenever the real owner should be grown too large to inhabit it."

— *Horace Walpole, The Castle of Otranto*

The novel is set in the medieval era, and its plot weaves together elements of romance, tragedy, and supernatural mystery. The narrative begins with a tragic event: Manfred, the Prince of Otranto, is gripped by desperation as his son Conrad is crushed to death by a colossal helmet that mysteriously materializes in the castle's courtyard. Manfred panics, aware of an ancient prophecy declaring that Otranto "should pass from the present family, whenever the real owner should be grown too large to inhabit it." He resolves to secure his lineage by divorcing his wife Hippolita and marrying Isabella, Conrad's betrothed. However, Isabella, terrified and unwilling, flees Manfred's advances. In the castle's underground crypt, Isabella encounters Theodore, a young, noble peasant who assists her. Theodore plays an increasingly central role. When Manfred attempts to enact his tyrannical desires, supernatural elements intercede. More enormous armor pieces appear, and apparitions haunt the castle. Blinded by his ambition, Manfred fails to recognize the unraveling of the prophecy that threatens his rule. Theodore is revealed to be the *true heir* of Otranto, being a descendant of Alfonso, the original and rightful ruler. The revelation culminates in the spectral appearance of Alfonso, the castle being partially swallowed by the earth, and Manfred's downfall. Theodore's noble virtues contrast starkly against Manfred's hubris and tyranny. Theodore and Isabella's union symbolizes the restoration of rightful and virtuous governance to Otranto.

Thanks to its blend of medieval romance with supernatural elements, The Castle of Otranto is widely recognized as the pioneering work of the "Gothic fiction" genre.

The Castle of Otranto

157. Philosophical Dictionary (Voltaire, 1764)

> *"Superstition is to religion what astrology is to astronomy,*
> *the mad daughter of a wise mother."*

— *Voltaire, Philosophical Dictionary*

In the dictionary, Voltaire expounds his views on various topics ranging from science to religion, politics to ethics, and morality. He examines these topics through both historical analyses as well as personal commentary. Throughout his writings in this dictionary, Voltaire addresses controversial issues such as atheism and freedom of speech, advocating for religious tolerance while criticizing superstition or dogmatism within the organized religion. He also criticizes government censorship laws that stifle free expression or creativity; he argued instead for an environment where people could express their thoughts openly without fear of retribution or persecution from authority figures or institutions. Fundamentally what unites all these disparate ideas together throughout this philosophical dictionary is its central premise: reason should be used above all else when seeking knowledge and understanding about oneself and others to lead a life based upon just principles rather than illusory ones dictated by force or fraudulence alone (as so much had been done historically). Through his work, he encourages readers to use reasoned thinking rather than force or false doctrines when seeking knowledge.

Voltaire's Philosophical Dictionary is a masterpiece of the Enlightenment era that continues to shape contemporary thought and discourse. One of the most striking features of the Philosophical Dictionary is its ability to transcend time and remain relevant today. It delves into issues that remain critical to modern society, such as the tension between progressivism and traditionalism and the impact of social norms on individual freedom. Furthermore, Voltaire's work is intellectually stimulating and masterfully written. His prose is engaging, and his wit make the work a delight to read.

158.   Encyclopédie (Denis Diderot, 1751-72)

> *"As long as the centuries continue to unfold,*
> *the number of books will grow continually,*
> *and one can predict that a time will come*
> *when it will be almost as difficult*
> *to learn anything from books*
> *as from the direct study of the whole universe."*
>
> — *Denis Diderot, Encyclopédie*

Denis Diderot, a philosopher, writer, and art critic residing in Paris, conceived an idea for an encyclopedia that would encompass world knowledge like never before. Motivated by this grand vision, Diderot began recruiting contributors and editors. He was soon joined by mathematicians, scientists, and scholars from across Europe, who brought their expertise and insights to the project. As the work progressed, additional volumes were added to the collection, totaling 35 volumes. The Encyclopédie garnered attention for its comprehensive content and the controversial views on religion and politics expressed in some of its entries. This led to resistance from authorities who sought control over information dissemination, banning parts of the Encyclopédie. However, many still accessed it due to its wide distribution throughout Europe. After over two decades of dedication, Diderot's monumental work was published in volumes between 1751 and 1772.

The Encyclopédie amassed a plethora of information on science, technology, philosophy, and more, contributed by European experts. This groundbreaking work revolutionized education during its time and democratized Enlightenment thinking for all, regardless of class or wealth. Moreover, the Encyclopédie played a pivotal role in fueling political revolutions, including the French Revolution, through its significant effect on public opinion and introducing radical ideas into mainstream discourse.

159. The Sorrows of Young Werther (Johann Wolfgang Goethe, 1774)

"Sometimes I don't understand
how another can love her, is allowed to love her,
since I love her so completely myself, so intensely, so fully,
grasp nothing, know nothing, have nothing but her!"

— *Johann Wolfgang Goethe, The Sorrows of Young Werther*

In Goethe's seminal work, the protagonist Werther is tormented by a deep, unrequited affection for a young woman named Charlotte, who is already betrothed to Albert. Werther's soul becomes inexorably attached to Charlotte's enchanting presence, and in secrecy, he cannot let go of the dream of winning her heart despite the impossibility of his longing. As Charlotte's marriage approaches, Werther's mental state plunges into abysmal depths. His life becomes an emotional tempest; the winds of despair and depression buffet him as he grapples with his unattainable love. He bids farewell with a final letter addressed solely to Charlotte before taking off into the woods one last time; unlike all prior occasions, this time he was armed with a pistol and not only his thoughts and emotions. As expected, tragedy ensues when Werther takes his own life soon after, leaving behind immense sorrow among those who knew him well, including friends and family.

This novel, representative of the "Sturm und Drang" literary movement, is a heart-wrenching exploration of human emotions. Its innovative and evocative prose dived into the depths of despair and romantic longing with an intensity rarely seen before. The novel is a poignant beacon in literary history, paving the way for generations to explore complex emotions and the human psyche through the written word. It remains a testament to the power and peril of unbridled passion.

The Sorrows of Young Werther

160.   Ugetsu Monogatari (Ueda Akinari, 1776)

> *"Shape I may take, converse I may, but neither god nor Buddha am I,
> rather an insensate being whose heart thus differs from that of man."*

— *Ueda Akinari, Ugetsu Monogatari*

Ugetsu Monogatari is an enchanting collection of nine supernatural tales steeped in the ambiance of *medieval Japan*. The collection epitomizes the rich tradition of Japanese *ghost stories*, interlacing delicate human emotions with the ethereal presences. Akinari's deft narrative style creates an otherworldly atmosphere, where spectral figures and humans often cross paths, leading to interactions that underscore the impermanence and frailty of human life. For instance, one of the stories, *The Reed-Choked House*, explores the haunting sorrow of unfulfilled love, while another, *The Blue Hood*, delves into the eerie repercussions of one's past actions. What distinguishes Akinari's storytelling is his seamless fusion of *Buddhist* and *Shinto* beliefs with the supernatural elements characteristic of *traditional Japanese folklore*. His tales are not just ghost stories; they often carry deeper moral and philosophical undercurrents. The world is portrayed not merely as a source of horror but as reflecting human existence's yearnings and tragedies. Akinari's prose is replete with lush imagery and refined poetic sensibilities, and the psychological depth of his characters adds a dimension of realism to the fantastical elements, allowing the reader to empathize with the characters' dilemmas and emotions.

In the canon of Japanese literature, Ugetsu Monogatari holds a distinguished place as a pioneering work in the realm of supernatural fiction. Its blend of atmospheric horror with deep emotional and philosophical reflections has influenced countless writers and artists. Akinari's legacy lives on, and his masterful tales continue to captivate readers with their timeless resonance and poetic beauty.

Ugetsu Monogatari

161.   An Inquiry into the Nature and Causes of the Wealth of
Nations (Adam Smith, 1776)

> *"Little else is requisite to carry a state*
> *to the highest degree of opulence*
> *from the lowest barbarism*
> *but peace, easy taxes, and a tolerable administration of justice;*
> *all the rest being brought about by the natural course of things."*

> —— *Adam Smith, An Inquiry into the Nature and Causes ...*

An Inquiry into the Nature and Causes of the Wealth of Nations
is a seminal text in political economy, presenting foundational
principles that allow individuals and nations to understand and
pursue their economic interests. Smith outlines his theory on
why some nations are wealthier than others. He believes it
comes down to four main factors: division of labor, capital
accumulation, population growth, and foreign trade. Smith
explains how each element contributes positively or negatively
to a nation's wealth. Regarding the division of labor, he states
that it increases efficiency because workers specialize in specific
tasks rather than having an entire workforce focused on one job.
In terms of capital accumulation, Smith claims this leads to
increased productivity since money can be invested more
efficiently, such as in machinery or tools. Population growth
also has benefits; countries with large populations tend to have
higher revenues due to the larger number of consumers buying
goods produced by businesses within those economies. Foreign
trade is seen as beneficial since importing cheaper raw materials
from other countries while exporting more expensive finished
products helps increase profits. His work laid the foundations
for modern economics.

An Inquiry into the Nature and Causes of The Wealth of Nations by Adam
Smith is one of the most influential works on economics due to its
revolutionary theories regarding free market capitalism and government
intervention in markets.

162.   Critique of Pure Reason (Immanuel Kant, 1781)

> *"Space is nothing else than the form of all phenomena of the external sense, that is, the subjective condition of the sensibility, under which alone external intuition is possible."*

> — *Immanuel Kant, Critique of Pure Reason*

This influential work in philosophy attempts to bridge the gap between *rationalism* and *empiricism*, two dominant schools of thought at the time. Rationalism is the philosophical view that regards reason as the chief source of knowledge rather than sensory experience, with some rationalists even believing in *innate ideas* (present in mind from birth). On the other hand, empiricists believe all knowledge comes from sensory experience and that the mind at birth is a blank slate or *tabula rasa*. Kant argues that knowledge can be gained from both pure reason and experience, but it must be appropriately understood through careful analysis. He begins by exploring human understanding and its limitations when attempting to gain knowledge about reality. Then, he discusses his concept of synthetic a priori judgments – propositions that are true independently from experience but whose contents cannot be derived solely from reason. This leads him to his famous discussion on space and time as forms imposed by our minds on certain objects to make sense of them, as well as other topics such as causality and freedom versus determinism. Kant ultimately asserts that all concepts, whether derived from logical reasoning or sensory input, must undergo processing by our subjective faculties before they crystallize into meaningful knowledge. Essentially, each individual imposes their own mental categories on experiences to make sense of them.

Critique of Pure Reason is one of the most influential writings ever produced on epistemology (the study of how we acquire knowledge) and metaphysics and emphasizes the limits of human understanding. The Critique has had a lasting influence on subsequent philosophical thought, with its ideas continuing to shape debates in contemporary philosophy.

163. Les Liaisons Dangereuses (Choderlos de Laclos, 1782)

"You may conquer her love of God:
You will never overcome her fear of the devil."

— *Choderlos de Laclos, Les Liaisons Dangereuses*

Les Liaisons Dangereuses is a fascinating *epistolary novel* that exposes the French aristocracy's dark intrigues and moral decadence on the eve of the *French Revolution*. The narrative revolves around the cunning and manipulative former lovers Vicomte de Valmont and Marquise de Merteuil. They craftily use seduction for amusement, revenge, and social dominance. Valmont, a notorious libertine, is challenged by Merteuil to seduce the virtuous Madame de Tourvel. Merteuil, on her part, desires revenge against a former lover and aims to use Valmont's talents in her vendetta. Initially, Valmont views the conquest of Madame de Tourvel as a game to prove his seductive powers. Still, as he gets to know her, he unexpectedly falls genuinely in love with her. This development complicates his intentions and the very essence of the game he is playing. Simultaneously, Merteuil is orchestrating her own schemes. She manipulates the affections of a young Chevalier and directs a series of betrayals, all while maintaining a facade of respectability. Her lack of remorse and her delight in the pain she inflicts reveal the chilling extent of her malevolence. Madame de Tourvel, who is deeply torn between her love for Valmont and her moral convictions, makes the painful decision to leave him. Valmont, seeking revenge against Merteuil for her role in this emotional maelstrom, ensures that her treachery is exposed. He meets his end in a duel, fatally wounded, but not before he sets in motion the downfall of Merteuil. Merteuil's reputation is annihilated, ultimately forcing her to flee Paris.

De Laclos's novel is a portrayal of the cynical and debauched world of the French aristocracy and a deep exploration of the complexities of human emotions, manipulation, and the consequences of unrestrained ambition.

Les Liaisons Dangereuses

164. A Vindication of the Rights of Woman (Mary Wollstonecraft, 1792)

"I do not wish them [women]
to have power over men; but over themselves."

— *Mary Wollstonecraft, A Vindication of the Rights of Woman*

The book argues that women should be given citizenship rights and not be confined to traditional societal roles. Wollstonecraft begins by criticizing current notions about women's education and nature; she believes these harm both genders. Women, for example, lack fundamental civil liberties such as freedom of speech or religious choice because they are seen as incapable of making rational decisions due to external influences like social expectations or male domination. She highlights how denying women equal education keeps them from becoming independent thinkers who can make informed choices regarding essential matters such as marriage or religion – something which has been denied to them historically. In order for progress towards equality between men and women to occur, Wollstonecraft insists that men must recognize the potential capabilities within each gender rather than using a person's sex to determine one's worthiness for specific roles in life (such as politics). Additionally, she argues that women's limitations result from societal expectations and religious teachings that discourage women's intellectual development. Wollstonecraft believes that if reason, which she sees as a *gift from God*, is considered the basis for human power and intelligence, then there should not be any gender-based differences.

One of the first books advocating for gender equality and women's rights, it was groundbreaking during a time when women were largely seen as inferior to men in society and had limited access to educational opportunities or economic independence. The book helped spark an important conversation about gender equality that has inspired many other works since its publication.

165.   Wilhelm Meister's Apprenticeship (Johann Wolfgang Goethe, 1795-96)

> *"We are shaped and fashioned by what we love."*
>
> —— *Johann Wolfgang Goethe, Wilhelm Meister's Apprenticeship*

Wilhelm Meister is a young man who sets out to become an actor and embarks on a journey of self-discovery. Along the way, he meets several people who help him grow as an individual and develop his skills as an actor. He also learns about philosophy and discovers what it means to be truly free. The novel follows Wilhelm's journey from being naive and immature to becoming more aware of himself and his place in the world. He encounters different characters, such as Mignon, Lothario, Philina, Felix, and Mariana, who all teach him something valuable about life that helps shape his growth into adulthood. Through their conversations, they explore love, friendship, freedom, and morality, which are essential for personal development. Throughout this process, Wilhelm learns how to make decisions based on reason rather than emotion while still maintaining sensitivity towards others' feelings; he also begins to understand why certain laws exist within society while developing the moral code that allows him independence without compromising social values or norms. In addition, he finds solace in nature, which serves as a refuge from the chaos of city life and provides insight into more profound truths about existence through its beauty and harmony with human emotions like joy or sorrow.

Wilhelm Meister's Apprenticeship is a landmark work notable for its "Bildungsroman" genre — it is one of the first instances of this genre that focuses on the protagonist's psychological and moral evolution from youth to adulthood, and it had a lasting influence on later culture, literature, and philosophy.

THE 19th CENTURY

THE 19th CENTURY

The early nineteenth century was a time of great change and upheaval in European history. This period was marked not just by the rise and fall of Napoleon Bonaparte, who contributed to spreading liberal reforms across Europe, but also by transformations in the social, economic, and cultural fabric.

The first half of this century saw a profound shift in literature and culture. The *Romantic movement*, with its roots by German intellectuals, rejected the *Enlightenment*'s focus on reason and embraced the power of emotion, imagination, and individual experience. Nature was revered as a source of inspiration, and the spiritual realm was idealized. Literary giants such as Goethe produced works that reflected these themes, with *Faust* and *Prometheus* among the most celebrated. This movement, which spread throughout Europe within two decades from Germany, profoundly influenced culture and arts. Topics such as individualization, return to nature, and idealization of the spirit were central during this time.

During the 19th century in England, a significant cultural shift occurred as literary studies became increasingly institutionalized. *Canons of English* studies were established, and academics began focusing on identifying and analyzing literary works that could be studied for future generations. This period also saw the rise of new principles of poetry from the Romanticism and Victorian periods. As writers sought to express their cultural identities through words, gender poetics gained popularity. These writers explored subjects of gender, sexuality, and social roles, often using their own experiences to inform their work.

Theatre in the 19th century enjoyed immense popularity. With the rise of theatre companies, there was a surge in the demand for plays and adaptations. Romantic and Victorian dramas mirrored the literature of the time and offered entertainment while reflecting Europe's evolving social fabric.

Mid-century Europe faced significant political upheavals, including the revolutions of 1848, which were fueled by desires for national sovereignty and liberal reforms. These events influenced literature, leading to the emergence of Realism as a reaction against *Romantic idealism*. *Realism* sought to depict life as it was, often focusing on ordinary details and people's everyday struggles.

Advancements in printing technology in the latter half of the 19th century ushered in a new era for literature. The novel became an especially popular form, with authors crafting stories to emotionally connect with a broader audience. This period also saw an unprecedented growth in print media, including newspapers and magazines, which became more accessible to the masses.

Notably, Russian literature experienced what is often considered a golden age in the 19th century. Authors like Leo Tolstoy and Fyodor Dostoevsky wrote seminal works such as *War and Peace* and *Crime and Punishment*. These authors navigated complex problems like morality, justice, and social conflict, achieving an extraordinary depth of human introspection.

Furthermore, the 19th century was a time of scientific discovery and technological innovation. The *Industrial Revolution* was in full swing, dramatically altering economies and societies. Charles Darwin's theory of evolution by natural selection became one of the most influential scientific theories.

166.   Phenomenology of Spirit (G. W. F. Hegel, 1807)

"The bud disappears when the blossom breaks through,
and we might say that the former is refuted by the latter;
in the same way when the fruit comes,
the blossom may be explained to be a false form of the plant's existence,
for the fruit appears as its true nature in place of the blossom."

— *G. W. F. Hegel, Phenomenology of Spirit*

Hegel explores how consciousness evolves from simple sensory awareness to complex *self-consciousness* of the *Spirit* through successive stages. The notion of *dialectic* is essential to Hegel's thought: he believes that knowledge and understanding progress through a process of *thesis, antithesis,* and *synthesis* (although his dialectic is more nuanced than this triadic formula suggests). This means that an idea or state (the thesis) naturally generates its opposite (the antithesis), and the conflict between them is eventually resolved in a *higher* form of truth (the synthesis). He then outlines specific shapes of this journey: sense-certainty, perception, understanding, force, and the understanding of life, reason, and Spirit. Each form contains positive aspects, such as knowledge acquired, and negative aspects, such as limitations encountered along the way due to errors in judgment or lack of comprehension about one's environment or oneself. Through these successive shapes, Hegel argues that proper understanding only emerges gradually from repeated experiences combined with reflection upon them, conclusively leading to self-awareness. He suggests that by recognizing this evolution, the Spirit rises above its limitations and becomes a fully conscious agent within history – a process he defines as *Absolute Knowing.*

Phenomenology of Spirit is a cornerstone of modern thought. Through his analysis, Hegel argues that we can achieve actual knowledge only through dialectical thinking – the process by which we move beyond binary oppositions.

167.   Faust (Johann Wolfgang Goethe, 1808)

"All theory is gray, my friend. But forever green is the tree of life."

— *Johann Wolfgang Goethe, Faust*

Faust is a scholar and philosopher who has devoted his life to pursuing knowledge. Still, despite his vast learning, he feels he has not lived and, in his desperate search for meaning, decides to make a pact with the devil, Mephistopheles, with whom he trades his soul for the chance to experience the full range of human emotions and pleasures. The parallel with *Doctor Faustus*, written by Christopher Marlowe in the late 16th century, cannot be overlooked. Although both works address the moral implications of Faust's pact with the devil, they do so in different ways. In Marlowe's work, Faustus is a proud and arrogant man who seeks knowledge and power beyond his mortal limits. On the other hand, Goethe's Faust is a man searching for meaning and purpose in life who makes a pact with the devil out of desperation rather than pride. The first part of the work is mainly about Faust's attempts to find happiness and fulfillment through the pleasures of the world. He becomes infatuated with a young woman named Gretchen, and his relationship with her eventually leads to his profound transformation. The play's second part is more abstract and philosophical, with Faust exploring metaphysical and existential questions. Throughout the play, Faust is inspired by music, poetry, and other forms of artistic expression. At last, Faust is redeemed through God's mercy, which acknowledges his continuous striving and capacity for growth and self-improvement.

Faust is a complex work that profoundly meditates the nature of human existence and the search for meaning and purpose. He is also notable for using symbolism and allegory, with many characters and events in the work representing broader philosophical and metaphysical concepts. Throughout the work, Goethe employs a wide range of experimental literary devices that incorporate drama, poetry, and prose elements.

168.   Pride and Prejudice (Jane Austen, 1813)

> *"Do anything rather than marry without affection."*
>
> — *Jane Austen, Pride and Prejudice*

The story, set in rural England during the Regency era, begins with the arrival in town of a wealthy bachelor, Mr. Bingley, and his friend Mr. Darcy. Elizabeth Bennet initially dislikes Mr. Darcy due to his haughty attitude. The process of her warming up to him is complex. She initially forms her negative opinion of him based on his dismissive treatment of her at a ball and his apparent arrogance. However, Elizabeth begins to see Mr. Darcy in a more nuanced light over time. Through a letter from Darcy, she learns about his positive interventions in matters concerning her family and the true character of Mr. Wickham, who had initially misled Elizabeth with his charm. This revelation leads Elizabeth to recognize her own prejudices and the errors in her initial judgments. She begins to see Mr. Darcy in a more positive light and eventually realizes that she has fallen in love with him despite their initial misunderstandings and differences in social class. At the same time, Elizabeth's younger sister Lydia Bennet runs off with the unscrupulous Mr. Wickham, causing distress for the whole family as they fear scandal and shame. Mr. Darcy eventually comes to the rescue by providing financial assistance so that Lydia can marry Wickham properly, thus salvaging the reputation of the Bennet family. Parallelly, Mr. Bingley, who is smitten with Elizabeth's elder sister Jane, overcomes his reservations and proposes to her. Elizabeth and Mr. Darcy admit their feelings for each other after overcoming various obstacles. In the end, they get married, much to the delight of Mrs. Bennet, who is pleased with the advantageous match due to Mr. Darcy's wealth.

The story is known for its commentary on the societal conventions faced by women during the Regency era. Through Elizabeth's character, Austen portrays a strong, independent woman who defies societal norms.

169.   Emma (Jane Austen, 1815)

> *"One half of the world*
> *cannot understand*
> *the pleasures of the other."*
>
> — *Jane Austen, Emma*

Emma is an attractive and wealthy young woman who lives with her widowed father in the village of Highbury. Emma, somewhat overconfident in her abilities, believes she has a knack for matchmaking and takes it upon herself to find a suitable husband for her friend Harriet Smith. However, her meddling leads to misunderstandings and unintended consequences, causing Emma to realize that she does not understand matters of the heart as well as she thought. Throughout the novel, Emma's misguided ventures in matchmaking, rooted in her naivety and high social standing, result in comedic and troublesome moments. Emma develops a deeper understanding of herself and those around her. She also learns the value of genuine affection and recognizes the importance of social considerations in her community. The novel deftly explores topics such as the social class structure in 19th-century Britain and its impact on relationships, gender roles, marriage expectations, and the power dynamics between men and women. Additionally, it reflects on personal growth through self-reflection and the pursuit of genuine happiness. Emma's journey through the narrative is one of maturation and self-discovery as she navigates her flaws and prejudices and, ultimately, finds a path that aligns with her heart.

Emma by Jane Austen is cherished for its incisive portrayal of its heroine's growth and keen observations of social constraints and character. It provides insight into the societal norms and expectations of the Regency era in England and remains a compelling exploration of young adulthood, social maneuvering, and human nature that resonates with readers today.

170.   Northanger Abbey (Jane Austen, 1817)

"Now I must give one smirk
and then we may be rational again."

— *Jane Austen, Northanger Abbey*

Northanger Abbey is a novel that chronicles the coming-of-age journey of Catherine Morland, an impressionable and imaginative young woman. Invited to the bustling city of Bath for the social season, she meets Henry Tilney and his sister Eleanor. Through her interactions with them, and other characters such as Isabella Thorpe, John Thorpe, and the imposing General Tilney, Catherine navigates the intricacies and deceptions of society, often learning through her own blunders. Her naivety leads her into a series of comical and awkward situations but, ultimately, plays a role in her growth as she learns essential lessons about love, friendship, and discernment. Her adventure extends to Northanger Abbey, the Tilney family's home; this is where her fertile imagination, fueled by gothic novels, makes her suspect a dark mystery surrounding General Tilney's deceased wife. This misadventure is particularly instructive for Catherine, teaching her the importance of discernment and not jumping to conclusions based on fancy or rumors. Throughout the novel, the reader witnesses Catherine's evolution from a guileless young lady, susceptible to the influence of romantic gothic novels, to a more discerning and judicious woman. Northanger Abbey is an amusing narrative, replete with Jane Austen's trademark wit and keen observations and an insightful commentary on growing up, the pitfalls of naiveness, and the balance between imagination and reason.

This novel marked a divergence from the conventional literature of the era, as it integrated a greater focus on the internal development of characters rather than solely concentrating on the plot. Its gentle satire illuminates the importance of moderation between imagination and practicality.

171.   Frankenstein (Mary Shelley, 1818)

> *"Beware; for I am fearless*
> *and therefore powerful."*
>
> — *Mary Shelley, Frankenstein*

Frankenstein is a horror novel that tells the tragic story of Victor Frankenstein, a young scientist obsessed with reanimating the dead. Through his experiments, Victor creates a sentient creature from various body parts. Initially, Victor has aspirations for the creature's beauty and benevolence, but when it comes to life, he is horrified by its grotesque appearance. Victor flees, abandoning the creature, who is confused and alone. As the creature navigates the world, it experiences rejection and cruelty from humans because of its monstrous appearance. Yearning for companionship, the creature attempts to befriend humans and learn their ways but is continuously rebuffed. In a desperate plea, the creature implores Victor to create a companion for him, but Victor, fearing the consequences, ultimately refuses. Feeling utterly forsaken, the creature seeks revenge against Victor by targeting his loved ones. This sets off a dark and consuming vendetta between creator and creation. Victor, wracked with guilt and desperation, endeavors to destroy the creature. His pursuit takes him to the icy expanses of the Arctic, where he is rescued by Captain Walton, an explorer. Through letters to his sister, Walton recounts Victor's tale and the profound reflections on ambition, responsibility, and humanity that their conversations invoke.

Frankenstein by Mary Shelley explores the perils of unchecked scientific ambition, the influences of society and loneliness on character, and the moral responsibilities accompanying creation. This Gothic novel, imbued with horror and science fiction elements, stands as an enduring and thought-provoking exploration of human nature and the consequences of our choices. Frankenstein is heralded as one of the pioneering works of science fiction.

Frankenstein

172.   Ivanhoe (Sir Walter Scott, 1819)

> *"Men talk of the blessings of freedom ... any wise man would teach me*
> *what use to make of it now that I have it."*

—— *Sir Walter Scott, Ivanhoe*

Ivanhoe is a historical novel set in 12th-century England during the reign of King Richard I (the *Lionheart*). The story follows the valiant Wilfred of Ivanhoe, a Saxon knight who has recently returned from the *Third Crusade*. Ivanhoe is estranged from his father Cedric the Saxon and due to his allegiance to the Norman King Richard and his love for Cedric's ward Lady Rowena. At the outset, Ivanhoe enters a tournament in disguise and proves himself a formidable knight. The novel intricately weaves the politics of the time, where Prince John, King Richard's brother, is plotting to claim the throne during Richard's absence. Ivanhoe finds allies in the legendary outlaw Robin Hood and his band of merry men. However, the narrative also introduces Rebecca, the daughter of a Jewish moneylender named Isaac of York. Rebecca plays a vital role in the story, nursing Ivanhoe to health after he is wounded in the tournament. Prince John's allies, including the ruthless knights Brian de Bois-Guilbert, Reginald Front-de-Boeuf, and Maurice de Bracy, scheme and engage in treachery. They kidnap Lady Rowena and Rebecca, leading to a valiant rescue attempt. Meanwhile, Rebecca is accused of witchcraft and faces a trial, during which Ivanhoe champions her cause. King Richard returns in disguise and ultimately reveals himself. In the ensuing events, there are confrontations, a trial by combat, and finally, the restoration of King Richard's authority.

The characters of Ivanhoe grapple with issues of chivalry, honor, and the cultural clash between the Saxons and Normans. The novel is rich with historical detail and exploration of the social dynamics of the era. Scott's portrayal of Rebecca and the anti-Semitic attitudes she encounters is especially noteworthy as a portrayal of the prejudices of the time.

173.   The Complete Poems (John Keats, 1814-1820)

> *"The air is all softness."*
>
> — *John Keats, The Complete Poems*

The collection The Complete Poems by John Keats encompasses various poems that explore transcendence, beauty, and the transience of life. In particular, the *Ode to the Nightingale* delves into the concept of seeking escape from mundane reality and yearning to merge with the enchanting melody of the nightingale. Keats employs symbolism and evocative language to convey the profound beauty of existence and its fleeting nature, which the speaker strives to transcend through the nightingale's song. Another notable poem, *Ode on a Greek Urn*, contemplates art and beauty's eternal and unchanging nature. *To Autumn* celebrates the splendor of the natural world and the fleetingness of life, depicting the season as an intimate companion. Keats skillfully utilizes personification to evoke a sense of both the captivating beauty and bitter transience of autumn and all aspects of life. Sensuous imagery is a significant device employed by Keats, as he appeals to the senses of sight, sound, taste, touch, and smell, creating a vivid sensory experience for the reader. For instance, in *The Eve of St. Agnes*, he describes the room filled with the gentle scent of incense and the resounding silver trumpets of the wind, establishing a lively and immersive atmosphere. Keats employs alliteration, assonance, and internal rhyme to infuse musicality into his language. He also embraces the concept of *negative capability*, which involves embracing uncertainty and ambiguity when confronted with complex emotions and experiences.

John Keats is recognized as one of the foremost Romantic poets of the early 19th century. His works eloquently reflect his profound admiration for the beauty and power of the natural world, his exploration of the intricate realm of human emotions, and his mastery of language and poetic craftsmanship.

174.   The Last of the Mohicans (James Fenimore Cooper, 1826)

> *"Tell them, that the Being we all worship, under different names,*
> *will be mindful of their charity;*
> *and that the time shall not be distant,*
> *when we may assemble around his throne,*
> *without distinction of sex, or rank, or color!"*

— *James Fenimore Cooper, The Last of the Mohicans*

Set in 1757 during the *French and Indian War*, the novel follows three central characters: Hawkeye, Uncas, and Chingachgook. Hawkeye, whose real name is Natty Bumppo, is a white man adopted by the Mohican tribe and living as a woodsman and scout. Uncas and Chingachgook are Mohicans, with Chingachgook being the father of Uncas. Their mission is to safeguard Cora Munro, her sister Alice Munro, Major Duncan Heyward, and a singing teacher named David Gamut as they traverse dangerous territory. Throughout their journey, they encounter various obstacles, including wild animals, treacherous terrain, and rival tribes. Despite these perils, they successfully reach Fort William Henry, where they are reunited with the British forces. The novel hints at a subtle romantic tension between Cora and Uncas, which is complicated by societal attitudes and taboos regarding interracial relationships during the period. Towards the novel's end, tragedy strikes as Uncas is killed by Magua, a vengeful Huron warrior seeking retribution against the British and his men. Cora, who is also killed by one of Magua's followers, had been captured along with Alice and Gamut earlier in the story.

The novel has garnered acclaim for its detailed descriptions of nature, action-packed plot, and exploration of matter such as racial tensions between Native Americans and white settlers. Cooper incorporates historical figures like General Montcalm to add authenticity to the narrative. The story offers a unique perspective on the clash of cultures between European settlers and Native Americans during this period.

The Last of the Mohicans

175.   The Betrothed (Alessandro Manzoni, 1827)

> *"Crime is a rigid, unbending master,*
> *against whom no one can be strong*
> *except by total rebellion."*

— *Alessandro Manzoni, The Betrothed*

The Betrothed (*I Promessi Sposi*) is an Italian historical novel set in Lombardy in the early 17th century. It is widely considered one of the greatest novels of Italian literature. The story is about two young lovers, Renzo and Lucia, who are engaged to be married. However, their plans are thwarted by a local baron named Don Rodrigo, who desires Lucia for himself and uses his power to prevent the marriage. After an attempt to marry in secret is thwarted by Don Rodrigo's henchmen, Renzo flees to Milan to escape Rodrigo's wrath, while Lucia seeks refuge in a nearby monastery. In Milan, Renzo gets involved in various misadventures and witnesses the *bread riots*. Don Rodrigo's henchmen eventually abduct Lucia and then unwittingly hand her over to a cruel nobleman known as *The Unnamed* (*L'Innominato*), who has a change of heart upon meeting Lucia. She is subsequently released and finds shelter in a safe house. Renzo is helped by a holy man named Father Cristoforo, and later, he survives the plague that struck Milan. Towards the novel's end, Renzo and Lucia are finally reunited after numerous hardships and separations. Don Rodrigo, who becomes a victim of the plague, eventually dies.

The novel explores love, power, justice, and faith, and gives a vivid portrayal of Italian society and culture during the 17th century. It is also notable for its depiction of the historical events and conditions of the time, including famine, disease, and the social unrest prevalent in Lombardy during that era. Alessandro Manzoni's richly detailed portrayal of characters, his use of regional dialects, and his reflection on the social conditions played a significant role in the Italian unification process during the 19th century.

176.   Notre-Dame de Paris (Victor Hugo, 1831)

> *"Large, heavy, ragged black clouds hung like crape hammocks*
> *beneath the starry cope of the night.*
> *You would have said that they were the cobwebs of the firmament."*

— *Victor Hugo, Notre-Dame de Paris*

Set in 15th-century Paris, the story primarily revolves around Quasimodo, an ugly hunchback living in the bell tower of Notre-Dame Cathedral; Esmeralda, a beautiful and kind-hearted Gypsy; and Claude Frollo, the archdeacon of Notre-Dame, who becomes obsessively infatuated with Esmeralda. The story begins with Frollo, who has raised Quasimodo as his ward, ordering the hunchback to kidnap Esmeralda. Quasimodo's attempt is foiled by Phoebus de Chateaupers, the captain of the King's Archers, and other nearby citizens. Quasimodo is subsequently put on trial and punished. During his punishment, Esmeralda shows him kindness, which leads Quasimodo to develop a deep affection for her. Esmeralda, meanwhile, becomes enamored with Phoebus. Frollo's jealousy peaks when he spies on them during a rendezvous. Unable to contain his envy, Frollo stabs Phoebus, who survives the attack, but Esmeralda is falsely accused of the crime and sentenced to death. As Esmeralda is about to be executed, Quasimodo rescues her by claiming sanctuary within the cathedral. Despite his efforts, Esmeralda is later captured and hanged. Following her death, Quasimodo is heartbroken and seeks refuge beside her body in the crypt. His skeletal remains are found years later, embracing Esmeralda's skeleton. Notre-Dame de Paris features extensive descriptions of the architecture and history of the cathedral and medieval Paris. Through these depictions, Hugo draws attention to the Gothic architecture, fallen into neglect.

Notre-Dame de Paris is renowned for its portrayal of medieval life and the complex, tormented characters. The cathedral itself plays an important role, serving as a symbol, throughout the novel.

177.   Canti (Giacomo Leopardi, 1835)

> *"This solitary hill has always been dear to me."*
>
> — *Giacomo Leopardi, Canti*

Leopardi's Canti (*Songs*) is a collection of poems that explores existential themes with a prevailing sense of disillusionment and melancholy. The collection delves into the inherent suffering of human life, the fleeting nature of existence, and the longing for an unattainable ideal. Leopardi exhibits a refined and meticulous approach, employing rich symbolism and intricate metaphors. His lyrical descriptions of nature, melancholic reflections, and introspective meditations showcase his mastery of language and evoke profound emotional responses. In the poem *The Infinite*, Leopardi examines the human yearning for the infinite and the limitations of human existence. The speaker, confined to a small hill, envisions the boundless expanse beyond, highlighting the contrast between the infinite and the finite and evoking a sense of wonder and melancholy. *To Silvia* pays homage to Silvia, a childhood infatuation of Leopardi's, capturing lines of unrequited love, the longing for lost innocence, and the transience of life. *To the Moon* addresses the moon as a symbol of transcendence and inspiration, reflecting Leopardi's fascination with the celestial realm and his yearning for a higher existence beyond earthly limitations. Leopardi drew significant inspiration from classical literature, including Greek and Roman poets, particularly Virgil and Horace, admiring their ability to convey deep emotions and philosophical ideas through elegant language and vivid imagery.

Giacomo Leopardi, a prominent figure in Italian literature, enchants readers with his profound and introspective poetry. His collection of poems, characterized by deep melancholy, philosophical contemplation, and keen observations on human existence, stands as a testament to his poetic genius.

178.   Oliver Twist (Charles Dickens, 1838)

"Please, sir, I want some more."

— *Charles Dickens, Oliver Twist*

The quote is from one of the most famous scenes in the novel, where young Oliver Twist gathers the courage to ask for more gruel at the workhouse where he's been living. Placed under the care of the workhouse authorities, Oliver endures a difficult existence, surviving on meager rations and enduring arduous labor. After being placed with an undertaker and suffering further mistreatment, he runs away to seek his fortune in London, hoping for a brighter future. However, his path takes a fateful turn when he becomes entangled with a group of pickpockets led by the cunning Fagin, who exploits vulnerable street children for his criminal activities. Amidst this perilous environment, Oliver encounters Nancy, a member of Fagin's gang who occasionally shows moments of kindness despite her affiliation with the criminal underworld. Simultaneously, Oliver encounters Mr. Brownlow, a benevolent individual who recognizes his potential and offers a glimmer of hope amidst the darkness. As events unfold, one of Fagin's associates orchestrates a scheme to frame Oliver for theft from Mr. Brownlow's residence. This development sets off a series of dangerous encounters as both Fagin and the brutish thug Bill Sikes seek revenge against the innocent Oliver. Through acts of bravery and the intervention of unlikely allies, Oliver manages to escape the clutches of Fagin and Sikes, emerging unharmed and taking his rightful place in society. Coincidence and inheritance play a role in Oliver's eventual rise in society. His heritage and true lineage are revealed, and he demonstrates that even in the face of immense hardship, justice can prevail.

The novel explores themes like poverty, crime, and injustice prevalent during the Victorian era in England. Through its characters, Dickens captures the struggles of those oppressed by poverty.

179. Democracy in America (Alexis de Tocqueville, 1835-40)

> *"The greatness of America lies not so much in being more enlightened than any other nation as in her ability to repair her faults."*

> —— *Alexis de Tocqueville, Democracy in America*

The French political thinker and historian, embarked on an extensive tour of America starting in 1831. During his journey, he carefully observed various aspects of American society, politics, and the economy. The work is divided into two volumes, each exploring distinct yet interconnected subjects. In the first volume, de Tocqueville focuses on the exceptional nature of American democratic institutions. He examines the functioning of these institutions within the executive, legislative, and judicial branches of government and the role of political parties in American democracy. De Tocqueville expresses admiration for the decentralization of American politics, where power is dispersed among different state and local institutions. He is particularly intrigued by Americans' propensity to form political, civil, and private associations, which he sees as a vital safeguard against the potential tyranny of the majority. In the second volume, de Tocqueville digs deeper into the broader social effects of American democracy. He explores topics such as social equality, majority rule, individualism, and materialism. Additionally, he discusses the role of religion in America, perceiving it as a crucial counterbalance to some of the potential excesses of democracy, such as unchecked individualism and materialism. De Tocqueville contends that the American democratic experiment exemplifies a successful balance between liberty and equality, highlighting principles like the *rule of law, freedom of the press,* and the presence of *civil society.*

Democracy in America stands as an unparalleled inquiry into the mechanics of American democracy, offering a lasting reflection on its virtues, vulnerabilities, and distinctive features relevant to the present day.

180.   Dead Souls (Nikolai Gogol, 1842)

"However stupid a fool's words may be,
they are sometimes enough to confound an intelligent man."

— *Nikolai Gogol, Dead Souls*

In the bleak landscapes of *Tsarist Russia*, Dead Souls emerges as a compelling satirical commentary on Russian society. The narrative, tinged with the absurd, centers around the scheming social climber Pavel Ivanovich Chichikov. His goal is to acquire *dead souls* – a term for deceased serfs still listed as property on the census, causing their owners to pay taxes on them. Chichikov seeks to purchase these *souls* at a reduced price, intending to exploit this seemingly substantial property to secure a loan and elevate his social status. He convinces landowners to sell these dead souls through cunning persuasion and deceit, presenting the transaction as a win-win situation where they can eliminate their tax burdens. Chichikov encounters a motley crew of characters along the way – from suspicious townsfolk and gullible nobility to corrupt officials. These interactions offer insight into the diverse facets of *19th-century Russian society* and its moral fabric. Dead Souls is a critique of a flawed system and an exploration of various aspects of human nature. It explores the themes of greed, corruption, societal façade, and grotesque. The work was planned as a trilogy by Gogol: Chichikov's arrival in the provincial town of N.; his journeys through the countryside persuading landowners; and his abrupt departure under mysterious circumstances. However, only the first part was completed and published in 1842. The second part was left incomplete, and the third part was never written.

Gogol's adeptness at blending social commentary with comedic undertones results in a work that is as thought-provoking as it is entertaining. The story of Chichikov's audacious plan and the range of characters he encounters on his journey create a realistic panorama of Russian life.

181.   Fear and Trembling (Søren Kierkegaard, 1843)

> *"Faith is the highest passion in a human being.*
> *Many in every generation may not come that far,*
> *but none comes further."*

—— *Søren Kierkegaard, Fear and Trembling*

Fear and Trembling is considered one of the most significant works of existentialist and religious philosophy due to its exploration of the tension between faith in God and reason. Kierkegaard introduces the concept of the *Knight of Faith,* an individual who places complete trust in God, even when societal and ethical norms oppose their actions. The Knight of Faith embodies a person who lives in faith, fearlessly navigating the paradoxes of existence. Kierkegaard examines this concept through the biblical story of Abraham, whom he considers the perfect Knight of Faith due to his unwavering obedience to God's command to sacrifice his son Isaac. Another important subject discussed by Kierkegaard is the *teleological suspension of the ethical.* This term describes the belief that religious duty can sometimes supersede ethical obligations. Kierkegaard uses the term *teleological* to signify that everything has a purpose or end goal (*telos* in Greek). For Abraham, the *telos* was to obey God, and this religious duty was considered higher than any ethical responsibility, resulting in the *suspension of ethics.* This controversial notion suggests that actions typically deemed unethical can be justified if they are committed out of religious duty.

Through an in-depth analysis of the biblical story of Abraham and Isaac, Kierkegaard argues that faith necessitates going beyond reason and moral law to attain true spiritual greatness. Fear and Trembling prompts readers to examine their own beliefs about morality through self-reflection, exploring the idea that, at times, we may have to choose between our moral convictions and the obligations imposed by society or our higher power, such as God.

182.   The Count of Monte Cristo (Alexandre Dumas, 1844)

"The difference between treason and patriotism is only a matter of dates."

— *Alexandre Dumas, The Count of Monte Cristo*

The novel follows the story of Edmond Dantes, a young and accomplished sailor who is falsely accused of treason just before his marriage to his beloved Mercedes. The plot against him is orchestrated by three individuals driven by jealousy, ambition, and fear: Fernand Mondego, who desires Mercedes for himself; Danglars, a coworker envious of Dantes' success; and Villefort, a self-serving prosecutor who sacrifices justice for personal gain and to preserve his social status. Unjustly imprisoned in the grim Chateau d'If, a fortress off the coast of Marseille, Dantes endures mental and physical torment for fourteen years. During his captivity, he forms a friendship with a fellow prisoner named Abbe Faria, who imparts knowledge and teaches him various subjects. Before his death, Faria reveals the location of a hidden treasure on the island of Monte Cristo to Dantes. Following a daring escape from Chateau d'If, Dantes retrieves the treasure, which grants him immense wealth and the means to enact his elaborate revenge. Assuming the persona of the Count of Monte Cristo, he embarks on an intricate quest for revenge against those who conspired against him. Dantes infiltrates Parisian society, exploiting his enemies' greed, corruption, and ambition to ensure they suffer consequences similar to his despair. However, Dantes undergoes moments of self-reflection and doubts the morality of his actions, recognizing the destructive nature of his cycle of vengeance. It is a nuanced transformation that Dumas skillfully portrays, emphasizing the conflict between justice and revenge. Dantes learns that true liberation lies in freeing himself from the chains of the past.

Dumas' captivating narrative has impacted literature, inspiring numerous adaptations in film and television due to its compelling plot and enduring themes.

183.   The Three Musketeers (Alexandre Dumas, 1844)

"All for one and one for all, united we stand, divided we fall."

— *Alexandre Dumas, The Three Musketeers*

The Three Musketeers is a thrilling adventure set in the early 1620s France during the *reign of Louis XIII*. The story follows the journey of d'Artagnan, a young and ambitious man who leaves his provincial home to join the King's Musketeers in Paris to serve the king. There, he forms an unbreakable bond with three seasoned Musketeers – Athos, Porthos, and Aramis. Together, they embody bravery, loyalty, and honor, united by their motto: "All for one and one for all." Their path is filled with danger, much of it orchestrated by the seemingly villainous Cardinal Richelieu. Although an antagonist, Richelieu's actions are driven by his desire to consolidate the power of the French monarchy, often conflicting with the Musketeers' efforts. Constance Bonacieux, d'Artagnan's love interest, plays a significant role in the plot. Her involvement in the Queen's affairs and her connections to the Musketeers are crucial elements of the story. The quartet also faces the cunning and vengeful Milady de Winter, whose complex history with Athos adds intrigue to the narrative. Milady stops at nothing to seek revenge, further complicating the Musketeers' mission. The heroic quartet embarks on perilous assignments, including rescuing Queen Anne from a political scandal, foiling assassination attempts on the King, and safeguarding crucial documents for the future of France. Despite the odds, the Musketeers emerge victorious, and their triumphs are rooted in their unwavering teamwork and camaraderie.

Dumas masterfully blends action, adventure, and wit, presenting vibrant and multifaceted characters. His expert combination of historical events and fictional narratives creates an engaging saga of friendship, courage, and political intrigue that continues to captivate readers for generations.

The Three Musketeers

184.   The Raven (Edgar Allan Poe, 1845)

> *"And the silken sad uncertain rustling*
> *of each purple curtain thrilled me*
> *—filled me with fantastic terrors never felt before."*

> —— *Edgar Allan Poe, The Raven*

The poem is set on a bleak December night, where a desolate and forlorn narrator is immersed in ancient books, seeking solace from the heartache of losing his beloved Lenore. As the narrator is about to fall asleep, he is startled by a gentle tapping at his door. Half-afraid and half-expecting, he tells himself it must be a visitor and nothing more. When he opens the door, there is nothing but darkness. His name, whispered by the wind, tricks him into believing it might be Lenore, and his heartache is rekindled. Upon returning to his chamber, the tapping continues at his window. Opening it, in flies a stately raven. It perches on the bust of Pallas Athena, the goddess of wisdom, which symbolizes the knowledge the narrator seeks in his grief. What transpires next is a tense conversation between the man and the raven. The man, intrigued by the bird's ability to speak, albeit only a single word, begins questioning it. His queries range from the raven's origins to inquiries about the afterlife and his dearly departed Lenore. The term *nevermore* echoes through the room more and more, and the narrator's initial fascination turns to irritation, desperation, and despair. As the poem concludes, the raven remains unmoving, and its shadow is cast upon the floor. The narrator's descent into madness symbolizes the encompassing power of grief and mourning, and the raven can be seen as an embodiment of his torment or a messenger from the afterlife.

The Raven's haunting atmosphere, lyrical quality, and dark motifs are a testament to Edgar Allan Poe's genius. His mastery of manipulating language and rhythm while evoking emotional intensity and psychological complexity has established this poem as a timeless literary work.

185.   Wuthering Heights (Emily Bronte, 1847)

> *"I have dreamt in my life,*
> *dreams that have stayed with me ever after, and changed my ideas;*
> *they've gone through and through me, like wine through water,*
> *and altered the colour of my mind."*

> —— *Emily Bronte, Wuthering Heights*

Wuthering Heights is an intense, atmospheric novel set on the Yorkshire moors. The narrative centers around two families: the Earnshaws of Wuthering Heights and the Lintons of Thrushcross Grange. The orphan Heathcliff, adopted by the Earnshaw family, develops a deep, passionate love for his foster sister Catherine Earnshaw. However, despite their mutual affection, Catherine chooses to marry the wealthy and refined Edgar Linton for his social status, leading to heartbreak and turmoil. Following Catherine's marriage, her health deteriorates, and she passes away shortly after giving birth to her daughter Cathy Linton. Consumed by grief and bent on revenge, Heathcliff eventually gains control of Wuthering Heights and begins a reign of terror on the remaining inhabitants. He manipulates and destroys the lives of the children – Cathy Linton and his own son Linton Heathcliff, whom he had with Edgar's sister Isabella Linton. The novel also explores the relationship between Cathy Linton and Hareton Earnshaw, the son of Hindley Earnshaw and the nephew of Catherine. Unaware of the bitter history and dark legacy of Wuthering Heights, Cathy and Hareton gradually fall in love despite their initial hostility and vast social differences. Their relationship, in stark contrast to that of Catherine and Heathcliff, offers a glimmer of redemption and the possibility of breaking the cycle of revenge that Heathcliff set in motion.

Wuthering Heights has been widely praised for its innovative narrative structure, utilizing multiple narrators and interwoven stories to create a complex tale. The raw emotional intensity, the examination of social constraints, and the exploration of love have made it a classic of literature.

186.   Vanity Fair (William Makepeace Thackeray, 1848)

> *"If a man's character is to be abused,*
> *say what you will,*
> *there's nobody like a relative*
> *to do the business."*

> — *William Makepeace Thackeray, Vanity Fair*

Vanity Fair (subtitled *A Novel without a Hero*) is a sweeping tale of two distinct women navigating the societal expectations and stratification of early *19th-century England*. The novel primarily revolves around Rebecca 'Becky' Sharp, an ambitious and cunning woman from a poor background, and Amelia Sedley, a gentle and naive woman of higher social standing. The intelligent and determined Becky uses her charm and manipulative abilities to improve her social class, primarily through her marriage to Rawdon Crawley. She navigates the treacherous waters of English high society with a ruthless determination to rise above her lowly status, regardless of the moral cost. In stark contrast, Amelia, born into a wealthy family, is a gentle and good-hearted individual, albeit somewhat naive. Her life takes a drastic turn when her father loses his fortune, and her husband George Osborne is killed in the *Napoleonic Wars* at the *Battle of Waterloo*, which is a significant event in the novel. Despite her hardships, she continues to hold on to her ideals and love for her husband George. Throughout the novel, she is consistently supported by William Dobbin, a loyal and selfless man who harbors an unrequited love for her.

Thackeray masterfully depicts a society obsessed with wealth and status, where morality often takes a backseat to ambition and desire. His engaging narrative style and biting social commentary make Vanity Fair a powerful exploration of human vanity, ambition, and morality. The novel's lasting success is attributed to its innovative narrative structure and insightful portrayal of Victorian society. The novel's success also changed how authors approached writing longer works – particularly the narrative structure.

187.   The Manifesto (Karl Marx and Friedrich Engels, 1848)

> *"The proletarians have nothing to lose but their chains.*
> *They have a world to win.*
> *Working men of all countries, unite!"*

— *Karl Marx and Friedrich Engels, The Manifesto*

The Manifesto outlines the basic principle, its objectives, and its strategies for achieving a *communist society* through a *proletariat revolution*. The first section discusses the ongoing struggle between the *bourgeoisie* and the *proletariat*. The second outlines the principles of communism. The third critiques contemporary socialist movements and theories. The final section calls for unity among proletarians against the bourgeoisie. It begins by affirming that "the history of all hitherto existing societies" has been one characterized by class struggles: between owners and nonowners, enslavers and slaves, the bourgeoisie (*capitalists*), and the proletariat (*workers*). These *class antagonisms* lead to revolutionary moments when those exploited finally rise against their oppressors. Marx then analyzes capitalism – its development from *feudalism* through *mercantilism* to *free competition* – and argues that it inevitably leads toward revolution due to its inherent contradictions between capitalism's need for more profit and greater exploitation of workers. Following this analysis is a brief overview of communism: what it stands for (*abolition of private property* and *equality among people* regardless of gender and nationality), how it will be achieved (*through working-class solidarity*), and what kind of society would result from such a transformation (*one without classes* or *state oppression*). Marx calls upon proletarians everywhere against capitalist exploitation to achieve freedom from oppressive economic circumstances through collective action.

The Manifesto of the Communist Party advocates for the revolutionary overthrow of the capitalist system and its replacement with communism, aiming to establish a classless society. It has dramatically shaped the development of economic, social, and political ideologies for over 150 years.

188.   Annabel Lee (Edgar Allan Poe, 1849)

> *"For the moon never beams without bringing me dreams*
> *of the beautiful Annabel Lee."*
>
> —— *Edgar Allan Poe, Annabel Lee*

Annabel Lee is a poem about the narrator's love for his beloved. The two were childhood sweethearts who shared a deep and passionate love. Despite their young age, they had an intense connection that was so strong it was envied even by angels in Heaven. The narrator recalls how they would sit together under the sea-side cliffs and talk of their undying love until one fateful night when the cold wind forever took her away from him. The *cold wind* metaphorically represents the forces of fate or mortality that separate the narrator from his beloved. It implies that her death was unexpected, perhaps due to illness, accident, or other unforeseen events. He believes this was done out of jealousy, as no one could match their bond or intensity of feeling. The poem ends with the narrator declaring that although Annabel has passed on to Heaven, he will never forget her and still loves her just as much as he did when she was alive: "For the moon never beams without bringing me dreams/ Of the beautiful Annabel Lee./ And the stars never rise, but I feel the bright eyes/ Of the beautiful Annabel Lee." He says that his soul can still visit hers at night while dreaming: "And all the night-tide, I lie down by the side/ Of my darling – my darling – my life and my bride." This powerful poem speaks deeply to anyone who has experienced true love and loss. It serves as a reminder of how powerful our emotions can be when we open ourselves up to them entirely.

Annabel Lee is a testament to eternal love. Its rhythmic and melodic qualities have inspired subsequent poets to experiment with similar techniques to evoke emotion and create mood. Its dark romanticism has been a touchstone for Gothic and romantic writers, who have drawn on Poe's themes of love, loss, and the supernatural.

189.   The Scarlet Letter (Nathaniel Hawthorne, 1850)

> *"On this unhappy being,*
> *selfishness and hate had bestowed a kind of evil alchemy,*
> *transmuting to poison the kindlier qualities of his nature;*
> *even as the same dark passions, in other children of Adam,*
> *have been the death of many a sweet and pleasant faculty."*

— *Nathaniel Hawthorne, The Scarlet Letter*

Hester Prynne is a woman condemned by her *Puritan community* for bearing a child out of wedlock, a visible evidence of her adultery. As penance, she must wear a *scarlet letter A* on her chest, signifying her sin. Despite the public shaming, Hester remains steadfast, refusing to reveal the father's identity of her illegitimate child Pearl. Hester's former husband, who adopts the pseudonym Roger Chillingworth, arrives in town. Disguising his true relationship with Hester, he integrates himself into the community. By calculated manipulations, Chillingworth discovers that the highly-respected Reverend Arthur Dimmesdale is Pearl's father. He then becomes obsessed with exacting revenge on Dimmesdale. Dimmesdale grapples with guilt and self-inflicted torment due to his secret sin. His psychological anguish begins to take a physical toll on his health, making him increasingly frail. This provides Chillingworth, posing as a physician, an opportunity to be closer to Dimmesdale under the pretext of offering medical care. Hester's strength and resilience form the novel's backbone as she endures her punishment with dignity. She finds solace in her work as an embroiderer and her life with her daughter Pearl, who grows into a fiercely independent young girl. As the novel nears its climax, the fates of Hester, Dimmesdale, and Chillingworth collide in a dramatic culmination. Hester earns a modicum of acceptance within the community, and Pearl finds solace in the love shared between her parents.

The Scarlet Letter stands as an early exploration of feminism in American literature by focusing on sin, guilt, and repression from a female perspective.

190.   David Copperfield (Charles Dickens, 1850)

> *"Whether I shall turn out to be the hero of my own life,*
> *or whether that station will be held by anybody else,*
> *these pages must show."*

— *Charles Dickens, David Copperfield*

The story begins with David's childhood and early years spent under the care of his cruel stepfather Mr. Murdstone, who sends him to work in a warehouse after the death of his mother and continues through the character's life into adulthood. Throughout the book, we follow David through various hardships and struggles, including poverty and being cheated out of an inheritance by Uriah Heep, whose manipulative actions play a crucial role in the narrative as he cunningly tries to gain control over the Wickfield estate, posing a significant obstacle in David's life. We also see how he meets several people who help him along his journeys, such as Peggotty, Agnes Wickfield, and Betsey Trotwood, all of whom become close friends or family to him during different stages in his life. The novel shows us how important friendship can be in times of difficulty but also illustrates themes such as justice versus injustice and social class distinctions which were very relevant during the times Dickens wrote this book. David Copperfield initially marries Dora Spenlow, who unfortunately passes away. Following her death, David eventually recognizes his feelings for his longtime friend, Agnes Wickfield. David's eventual career as a successful writer mirrors Charles Dickens' journey, adding an autobiographical dimension to the novel's plot.

David Copperfield offers readers an intimate view into the lives of ordinary people during Victorian England. Dickens' use of language is particularly noteworthy; his writing style often employs a rich vocabulary and complex syntax to convey emotion and atmosphere. Additionally, he uses satire to criticize societal conventions surrounding marriage and gender roles.

191.   Moby Dick (Herman Melville, 1851)

> *"Whenever I find myself growing grim about the mouth;*
> *whenever it is a damp, drizzly November in my soul;*
> *whenever I find myself involuntarily pausing before coffin warehouses*
> *and bringing up the rear of every funeral I meet;*
> *and especially whenever my hypos get such an upper hand of me,*
> *that it requires a strong moral principle to prevent me from deliberately stepping*
> *into the street, and methodically knocking people's hats off —*
> *then, I account it high time to get to sea as soon as I can."*

—— *Herman Melville, Moby Dick*

The story starts from the perspective of Ishmael, a philosophically inclined seaman, who signs onto the whaling ship Pequod for an adventurous voyage led by the enigmatic Captain Ahab. The Pequod's crew is diverse seafarers, including the thoughtful first mate Starbuck, the jolly second mate Stubb, the third mate Flask, and the formidable, Polynesian harpooner Queequeg. As Ishmael gradually discovers, the ship's mission is not merely commercial whaling but a quest driven by Ahab's personal vendetta against Moby Dick, an albino sperm whale of formidable size and ferocity. In a previous encounter, Moby Dick had cost Ahab his leg, which has since been replaced by a prosthesis made from a whale's jawbone. Consumed by his vengeful obsession, Ahab is hell-bent on hunting down the whale. Despite various omens and Starbuck's repeated pleas to abandon the reckless pursuit, Ahab remains resolute in his desire for vengeance. The story climaxes in a dramatic confrontation with Moby Dick, a disastrous battle that underscores the destructive power of Ahab's monomania. In his pursuit of revenge, Ahab in the end leads himself and his crew to their doom.

Herman Melville's powerful characters, philosophical digressions, intricate plot, and potent symbols contribute to its enduring status as a cornerstone of American literature. The novel's motif of man versus nature echoes in many contemporary narratives, influencing works as 'Jaws' and 'Life of Pi.'

192.   Uncle Tom's Cabin (Harriet Beecher Stowe, 1852)

> *"Our friend Tom, in his own simple musings,*
> *often compared his more fortunate lot,*
> *in the bondage into which he was cast,*
> *with that of Joseph in Egypt; and, in fact, as time went on,*
> *and he developed more and more under the eye of his master,*
> *the strength of the parallel increased."*

— *Harriet Beecher Stowe, Uncle Tom's Cabin*

Uncle Tom's Cabin depicts the journey of a slave who is forcibly separated from his loved ones and sold to settle his owner's debts. Along his path, he encounters various characters representing different facets of enslaved life; some exhibit compassion, others embody cruelty. Hereafter, he finds himself in the possession of Augustine St. Clare, whose daughter Eva develops an immediate fondness for him. However, tragedy strikes when Augustine passes away, and Uncle Tom is sold to Simon Legree, a notorious and abusive plantation owner infamous for his mistreatment of enslaved individuals. Cassy, another enslaved person on Simon Legree's plantation, plans an escape with a young woman named Emmeline. Unfortunately, Uncle Tom does not escape and faces a tragic fate under Simon Legree. Throughout the narrative, the novel unflinchingly portrays the harsh realities of the time, where human beings were commodified and subjected to inhumane treatment. Nonetheless, amidst this grim backdrop, moments of hope emerge, such as Eliza's courageous escape with her son at significant personal risk or George's eventual purchase of his own freedom, emphasizing the resilience and inner strength individuals can summon even in the direst circumstances.

Uncle Tom's Cabin serves as both a powerful reminder about how cruel slavery was while also providing us all with lessons on how we can strive towards freedom and no matter our situation, through powerful storytelling techniques that evoke strong emotions from readers.

193.   Madame Bovary (Gustave Flaubert, 1856)

> *"In the immensity of this future*
> *that she conjured for herself,*
> *nothing specific stood out:*
> *the days ... were as near alike as waves are."*

—— *Gustave Flaubert, Madame Bovary*

Madame Bovary dreams of more excitement and happiness than she can find in her marriage to the dull Charles Bovary. To fill the void, she begins seeking extramarital affairs with men like Rodolphe and Leon. Rodolphe is a wealthy and sophisticated landowner. She is initially drawn to his charm, charisma, and the excitement he represents. Leon, on the other hand, is a young law clerk whom Emma encounters during her visits to the town of Rouen. Leon possesses a poetic and romantic nature that seduces Emma's imagination. Both Rodolphe and Leon offer her temporary respite from the monotony of her provincial life and the disillusionment she experiences with Charles. Emma's spending habits soon become excessive in an attempt to maintain her new lifestyle, leading her into debt and ruining herself and Charles. Her desperate attempt at escaping reality only causes further distress when it becomes clear that none of these relationships will bring her true fulfillment or lasting happiness. Despite all this suffering, Emma never fully comes to terms with the consequences of her actions. In a state of desperation due to her insurmountable debts, she ultimately takes her own life. Madame Bovary exemplifies how destructive romanticism can be if taken too far without any real understanding or appreciation for its consequences.

Madame Bovary explores themes such as love and marriage, class conflict, and gender roles in 19th-century France, and its use of realism is portrayed by characters with depth, complexity, and nuance rather than stereotypes or caricatures. Many modern authors have drawn inspiration from Flaubert's style when crafting their own stories.

194.   On Liberty (John Stuart Mill, 1859)

> *"The only purpose for which power*
> *can be rightfully exercised*
> *over any member of a civilized community,*
> *against his will,*
> *is to prevent harm to others."*

— *John Stuart Mill, On Liberty*

On Liberty argues that individuals should be free to pursue their interests as long as they do not harm others. To this end, Mill proposes a *harm principle*, which states that government interference with an individual's freedom should only be justified if it can be shown that such interference is necessary to prevent harm to others. Mill argues for the importance of intellectual and moral diversity in society, claiming that different perspectives are essential for progress and development. He also defends freedom of thought and expression, arguing against censorship and against the imposition of ideological control over what people think or say. Moreover, he claims that even opinions that many find objectionable should still have an opportunity to be expressed without fear of suppression by authorities. In addition, Mill emphasizes the importance of individuality within society; he believes each person has unique talents and abilities that must be respected and nurtured for human flourishing. As such, he advocates for greater tolerance towards those different from us, so we can all benefit from their contributions to our collective well-being. Finally, Mill encourages us to take responsibility for our actions rather than relying solely on external authority figures like governments or religious institutions when deciding how we live our lives.

John Stuart Mill's On Liberty is one of the most influential works on personal liberty and freedom and is considered a milestone in the development of human rights. This work provides an essential framework from which modern conceptions of civil liberties are derived.

195.   Oblomov (Ivan Goncharov, 1859)

> *"And he was as intelligent as other people,*
> *his soul was pure and clear as crystal;*
> *he was noble and affectionate – and yet he did nothing!"*

— *Ivan Goncharov, Oblomov*

Ilya Ilyich Oblomov is a landlord and member of the nobility known for his extraordinary indolence. Living in St. Petersburg, Oblomov spends most of his time on his sofa, shrouded in his robe, contemplating life but seldom participating. He is caught in what becomes known as *Oblomovism*, a term coined from this book, which refers to extreme inertia, lack of will, and avoidance of life's responsibilities. The first part of the novel reveals Oblomov's daily life in detail, where even the mere thought of getting out of his bed seems insurmountable. His loyal servant Zakhar, though critical of his master's laziness, takes care of him. Amid this stagnation, Oblomov's childhood friend Andrey Schtoltz tries encouraging him to be more active and engaged with life. Schtoltz, an energetic and industrious man who starkly contrasts with Oblomov, introduces him to Olga, a cultured and lively young woman from an aristocratic family. Oblomov, against his nature, falls deeply in love with Olga, and for a time, it seems like her influence might draw him out of his idleness. However, despite his deep affection for Olga and her patient attempts to motivate him, Oblomov's fear of change and his inborn lethargy prevent him from capitalizing on this relationship. Growing frustrated with Oblomov's perpetual inaction, Olga eventually leaves him and marries Schtoltz. Desolate, Oblomov retreats further into his inertia, and despite his deteriorating health and dwindling finances, he clings to his sedentary lifestyle, tragically leading to his premature death.

Goncharov paints a tragic picture of a man trapped by his own passivity and offers a stark commentary on the declining nobility of 19th-century Russia.

196.   On the Origin of Species (Charles Darwin, 1859)

> *"I have called this principle,*
> *by which each slight variation,*
> *if useful, is preserved,*
> *by the term of Natural Selection."*

— *Charles Darwin, On the Origin of Species*

On the Origin of Species presented a revolutionary idea, suggesting that species evolved over time through *natural selection*. Darwin's theory proposed that all life forms are related and have descended from common ancestors. He argued that variations within species arise naturally due to environmental pressures and *survival of the fittest*, which enabled them to adapt and become better suited for their environment. Darwin used evidence from geology, geography, comparative anatomy, and embryology to support his claim that living organisms were not created separately but evolved through descent with modification from ancestral forms. He also provided detailed observations on how artificial selection could be used to change domesticated animals, such as dogs or pigeons, into different varieties with distinct traits. This challenged traditional religious beliefs about the immutability of species since it implied humans shared a common lineage with other animals instead of being specially created by God, as previously believed at the time. In addition, he discussed extinction as an essential factor in evolution – something which was initially controversial due to its implications for human mortality – suggesting some extinct species may have been replaced by newer ones arising out of evolutionary adaptation processes over time.

The Origin of Species by Charles Darwin is considered to be a groundbreaking scientific work as it introduced his theory of evolution and natural selection – ideas that revolutionized our understanding of life on Earth and its development over time, fundamentally changing biology and other fields such as anthropology and paleontology.

On the Origin of Species

197.   Great Expectations (Charles Dickens, 1860)

> *"I loved her against reason, against promise,*
> *against peace, against hope, against happiness,*
> *against all discouragement that could be."*

> — *Charles Dickens, Great Expectations*

The tale follows the life of Pip, an orphan residing with his sister and brother-in-law in rural England. The story begins when young Pip encounters a fugitive named Magwitch in the marshes and selflessly aids him in evading capture. This compassion sets off a chain of events shaping Pip's future. Soon after, Pip is introduced to the enigmatic Miss Havisham, a wealthy recluse who was abandoned on her wedding day. Raised in the decaying grandeur of Satis House, Miss Havisham molds Pip's impressionable mind while using her ward Estella to exact revenge on men. Pip, deeply infatuated with Estella's beauty, becomes entangled in a web of unrequited love and personal transformation. As Pip grows older, he leaves behind the simplicity of his country life and ventures to the bustling metropolis of London. There, he commences an apprenticeship as a blacksmith and receives unexpected financial support from a mysterious benefactor. Believing Miss Havisham to be the source of his newfound fortune, Pip is later shocked to discover that it is, in fact, Magwitch, the convict he aided in his youth. The narrative takes unexpected twists as Pip unravels the secrets of his past and the interconnectedness of the characters. Pip's journey ultimately leads him to confront his assumptions and prejudices, challenging his perception of wealth, social status, and personal integrity. The story's climax arrives when Pip visits Magwitch in prison, where the truth is revealed in a poignant confession. Magwitch's passing leaves Pip with profound remorse for his past actions and a desire to reconcile with his sense of morality.

The characters are complex and often have conflicting motivations, which add to the plot's drama.

198.   Les Misérables (Victor Hugo, 1862)

> *"To love another person*
> *is to see the face of God."*
>
> — *Victor Hugo, Les Misérables*

The narrative begins with the release of Jean Valjean from a lengthy prison term of 19 years for stealing bread to feed his sister's starving children and for subsequent attempts to escape prison. As he tries to reintegrate into society, he confronts the harsh reality of prejudice and alienation due to his criminal history. However, a transformative encounter with Bishop Myriel offers Jean Valjean a glimmer of hope and sets him on a path toward redemption. Adopting a new identity, Jean Valjean becomes a successful businessman and the mayor of a small town, all the while being haunted by the relentless pursuit of Inspector Javert, an unwavering law enforcer who believes in the impossibility of personal transformation. Amidst this pursuit, Jean Valjean assumes responsibility for Cosette, the daughter of Fantine, an impoverished woman forced into desperation to support her child. Fantine's tragic story is one of the pivotal elements in the novel. Jean Valjean and Cosette eventually escape to Paris. Meanwhile, there is growing political unrest in France, and the book introduces several characters that represent the students and workers of Paris. One of these students, Marius Pontmercy, falls in love with Cosette. Their love story becomes intertwined with the June Rebellion, a historical uprising in Paris. In the final scenes, Jean Valjean saves Marius's life, ensuring that Cosette's happiness is secured even as his future remains uncertain. Unfortunately, Jean Valjean must face the consequences of his past actions when his identity is finally revealed.

Les Misérables paints a realistic and intricate picture of life in 19th-century France, touching on social injustice, redemption, love, and the human spirit's resilience.

199.   Fathers and Sons (Ivan Turgenev, 1862)

"I don't see why it's impossible to express everything that's on one's mind."

— *Ivan Turgenev, Fathers and Sons*

The narrative centers around Arkady Kirsanov, a young man from a gentry family who returns to his family estate after completing his university studies. He is accompanied by his close friend Bazarov, a fervent nihilist who rejects conventional values and social institutions. Arkady's father Nikolai Kirsanov and his uncle Pavel Petrovich represent the older generation. They are more traditional and have trouble understanding the radical views of the younger men. Bazarov, in particular, becomes a source of conflict due to his outspoken nihilism. His disdain for social conventions and aristocratic traditions clashes with the values of Arkady's family, especially Pavel, who sees Bazarov's views as a threat to the established social order. Arkady and Bazarov visit the town where they meet Anna Sergeyevna Odintsova, a sophisticated widow. Bazarov falls in love with her, but his feelings are not reciprocated, which causes him emotional turmoil. Simultaneously, Arkady's father Nikolai has entered into a relationship with Fenichka, a former servant in their household, and they have a son together. This relationship also symbolizes the changing social dynamics of the time. As the characters' relationships evolve, the novel explores the tension between the progressive ideas of the younger generation and the more conservative values of the older generation. Arkady, initially influenced heavily by Bazarov, begins to distance himself from nihilism as he matures. The novel concludes with Bazarov's tragic death, which symbolizes his nihilistic philosophy's ultimate limitations and human cost.

Fathers and Sons explores the social and philosophical dilemmas of 19th-century Russia. The intricate psychological depth of its characters draws readers into a compelling narrative of generational conflict and tensions between traditional norms and emerging progressive values.

200.   Journey to the Center of the Earth (Jules Verne, 1864)

> *"As long as the heart beats, as long as body and soul keep together,*
> *I cannot admit that any creature endowed with a will*
> *has need to despair of life."*

— *Jules Verne, Journey to the Center of the Earth*

The novel follows Professor Otto Lidenbrock, his nephew Axel, and their guide Hans as they embark on a daring expedition to the Earth's core. The story begins in Hamburg, Germany, where Professor Lidenbrock discovers a cryptic message in an ancient runic manuscript. The deciphered message, written by a 16th-century Icelandic alchemist, suggests a passage to the center of the Earth through the Snæfellsjökull volcano in Iceland. Lidenbrock, an impulsive and ambitious geologist, decides to attempt this incredible journey and sets off for Iceland with his reluctant nephew Axel. After recruiting an Icelandic guide named Hans, the trio descends into the volcano. They face various challenges, including darkness, hunger, and labyrinthine passages. As they delve deeper, they encounter a subterranean world complete with an underground ocean called the Lidenbrock Sea and prehistoric creatures such as mastodons and marine reptiles. They witness astounding geological formations and natural phenomena. As the travelers continue their journey, they face perils, including storms in the underground ocean and a near encounter with an erupting geyser. The group continues their journey, but they do not reach the actual center of the Earth. Instead, after realizing that they must return to the surface, an underwater volcanic eruption propels them through an extinct volcanic chimney, and they emerge from the Earth in southern Italy.

Jules Verne's most famous works is considered a classic in the science fiction genre. The novel is notable for its combination of scientific knowledge of the time with adventurous imagination, and it has inspired numerous adaptations in films and other media.

201.   Alice's Adventures in Wonderland (Lewis Carroll, 1865)

> *"It takes all the running you can do,*
> *to keep in the same place."*

> — *Lewis Carroll, Alice's Adventures in Wonderland*

Alice is a young girl who falls down a rabbit hole and finds herself in an enchanted world filled with strange creatures. She meets many peculiar characters throughout her journey, including the White Rabbit, the Mad Hatter, the March Hare, and the Cheshire Cat. She also attends the Queen of Hearts' chaotic croquet game, where she must play against impossible odds to avoid being beheaded. Along the way, Alice discovers many lessons about growing up, such as learning to think for herself and not accepting everything at face value. With each new character she meets throughout her travels, Alice learns something valuable that helps shape her into a mature person. The story has become one of literature's most beloved tales because it speaks to children and adults alike, teaching us all important life lessons while entertaining us with its whimsical charm. Lewis Carroll's classic Alice's Adventures in Wonderland tale is enchanting and full of wit, wisdom, imagination, and fun. It serves as an enduring reminder that sometimes you must take risks or go on wild adventures to learn more about yourself and the world around you.

Alice's Adventures in Wonderland offers readers an imaginative escape into another world. Through its whimsical dialogue and memorable characters such as the Cheshire Cat and White Rabbit, it provides thoughtful insight into moral and philosophical questions about life and growing up. Readers have praised the novel for its imaginative use of language to create dream-like scenes that capture their imagination. In addition to being widely recognized as a literary masterpiece, Alice's Adventures in Wonderland has become an iconic part of popular culture.

Alice's Adventures in Wonderland

202.   Crime and Punishment (Fyodor Dostoevsky, 1866)

"It takes something more than intelligence to act intelligently."

— *Fyodor Dostoevsky, Crime and Punishment*

Crime and Punishment plunges the reader into the mind and life of Raskolnikov, an impoverished former student living in the grim and crowded St. Petersburg, Russia. Burdened by poverty and desperation, Raskolnikov develops a theory that extraordinary individuals are permitted to commit heinous acts for the greater good. He tests his theory by planning and executing the murder of a callous pawnbroker and her innocent sister Lizaveta, who becomes an accidental victim. Raskolnikov soon becomes tormented by guilt, paranoia, and fear of discovery. His inner struggle becomes a pivotal point of the novel, laying bare the profound psychological consequences of his actions. Raskolnikov's journey is further complicated by his interactions with various compelling characters. Sonya, a virtuous prostitute who cares for her destitute family, becomes a beacon of hope for Raskolnikov. Porfiry Petrovich, the investigative magistrate, presents another significant character. Although he has no solid proof against Raskolnikov, Porfiry's penetrating and psychological insights lead him to suspect Raskolnikov's guilt. He irrationally battles with Raskolnikov, manipulating him to confess voluntarily rather than confronting him with hard evidence. Their intellectual duels form some of the most engaging parts of the narrative. Additionally, the novel includes a diverse cast of secondary characters. Among them is Lebezyatnikov, a minor character who embodies the progressive and liberal ideas of the time, contrasting Raskolnikov's radical theories.

Crime and Punishment is more than a tale of crime and its repercussions. It is a deep dive into the human psyche, examining moral dilemmas, free will, and the dichotomy between 'ordinary' and 'extraordinary' individuals. It grapples with guilt, redemption, and the nature of punishment in society.

203.   War and Peace (Leo Tolstoy, 1869)

> *"We can know only that we know nothing.*
> *And that is the highest degree of human wisdom."*
>
> — *Leo Tolstoy, War and Peace*

War and Peace intricately weaves the destinies of three noble families – the Rostovs, the Bolkonskys, and the Bezukhovs – against Napoleon's invasion of Russia in 1812. The story commences in the high society of St. Petersburg, Russia, with a conversation between members of the Russian aristocracy, setting the stage for the central conflict that propels the narrative forward: *Napoleon's audacious ambition to conquer Moscow.* As the French army advances, the characters respond diversely – some fighting to resist the invaders, while others seek refuge or remain indifferent to the events unfolding. At the center of this sprawling epic are Pierre Bezukhov, an illegitimate son grappling with his identity amidst the chaos of war and societal transformation, and Andrei Bolkonsky, a principled and heroic figure who seeks meaning in the war. From his humble beginnings as an illegitimate child, Pierre unexpectedly inherits a fortune, which thrusts him into the upper echelons of society. Among the other notable characters is Natasha Rostova, a vivacious and charming young woman who initially becomes engaged to Andrei Bolkonsky. However, during Andrei's absence, she becomes infatuated with Anatole Kuragin and breaks her engagement. Anatole's subsequent betrayal plunges Natasha into despair. She turns towards religion and finds solace. After the turmoil of war and personal struggles, Natasha and Pierre Bezukhov find comfort in each other and marry. Andrei Bolkonsky meets a tragic end on the battlefield.

Tolstoy's masterpiece is a profound philosophical and historical epic. Through complex characters reminiscent of Shakespearean figures, Tolstoy paints a fresco of a society in upheaval, inquiring the interplay between the individual and the flow of history, the nature of freedom, and the role of fate.

204.   The Adventures of Tom Sawyer (Mark Twain, 1876)

> *"Well, everybody does it that way, Huck.*
> *Tom, I am not everybody."*

— *Mark Twain, The Adventures of Tom Sawyer*

The story is set in the fictional village of St. Petersburg, Missouri, and follows the escapades of a mischievous and imaginative boy named Tom Sawyer. Tom lives with his Aunt Polly, half-brother Sid, and cousin Mary. Tom is notorious for getting into trouble, whether skipping school to go swimming or tricking other boys into whitewashing a fence for him. One of Tom's most daring adventures occurs when he and Huck witness a murder in a graveyard at night. The two boys swear not to tell anyone what they saw, but they find themselves in a moral dilemma when Muff Potter, an innocent man, is accused of the crime. Meanwhile, Tom experiences the pangs of young love with Becky Thatcher, the new girl in town. Their innocent romance faces ups and downs, as Tom's antics and knack for trouble sometimes get in the way. As the story progresses, Tom and Huck go on thrilling adventures, including escaping to become pirates to search for buried treasure. When Tom and Becky get lost in a cave, they stumble upon Injun Joe, the real murderer they had seen in the graveyard. After a harrowing getaway from the cave, Tom becomes a local hero. Tom and Huck seek out the treasure they believe Injun Joe has hidden. After a series of daring escapades, they find the treasure in the cave where Tom had earlier encountered Injun Joe. The boys become rich, and the Widow Douglas decides to adopt Huck, which he reluctantly agrees to after Tom convinces him that he can still have adventures even if he becomes respectable.

This timeless tale brilliantly portrays the joys and challenges of boyhood. Through Tom's emprises, Mark Twain illustrates the importance of friendship, courage, and moral integrity while offering an endearing and humorous look at life in a small American town during the 19th century.

205.   Anna Karenina (Leo Tolstoy, 1877)

> *"All happy families resemble one another,*
> *each unhappy family is unhappy in its own way."*
>
> — *Leo Tolstoy, Anna Karenina*

The novel captures an era in which the Russian nobility is steeped in tradition, but the winds of change are sweeping across the land during Tsar Alexander II's reforms, which aimed to modernize and liberalize aspects of Russian society. At the heart of the narrative is the tragic figure of Anna Karenina. Married to the stern and upright government official Alexei Karenin, Anna finds herself in a life devoid of passion. This void is filled when she meets the charismatic Count Vronsky, and a whirlwind romance consumes them. However, their affair becomes a source of scandal and leads to Anna's isolation from the society she was once part of. Torn between her lover, her son, and a culture that demands propriety, Anna's inner turmoil intensifies as she wrestles with her choices. In contrast to Anna's story, Tolstoy presents the earnest Konstantin Levin, a thoughtful landowner seeking a purposeful existence and yearning to understand the deeper meanings of life and labor. Levin's love for the young Kitty Shcherbatskaya, who initially has her heart set on Vronsky, is pure and symbolizes hope and renewal. Their eventual marriage serves as a counterpoint to Anna's deteriorating relationship with Vronsky. The novel also features other characters, each meticulously detailed. Among them is Dolly, Kitty's older sister, who endures a marriage marred by infidelity, and her husband Stiva, whose carefree attitude contrasts with Levin's depth of character. Finally, Anna's life spirals into despair, and Tolstoy examines her psychological turmoil.

Anna Karenina is an epic tale where traditional morality holds sway, yet individuals like Anna search for freedom from societal norms, even if it means going against convention.

206.   The Brothers Karamazov (Fyodor Dostoevsky, 1880)

> *"Above all, don't lie to yourself.*
> *The man who lies to himself and listens to his own lie*
> *comes to such a pass that he cannot distinguish the truth within him,*
> *or around him, and so loses all respect for himself and for others."*

— *Fyodor Dostoevsky, The Brothers Karamazov*

The tale revolves around the intriguing lives of Fyodor Pavlovich Karamazov's three sons: Dmitri, Ivan, and Alyosha – each representing different facets of humanity. The *impulsive* Dmitri, the *intellectual* Ivan, and the *spiritual* Alyosha navigate through tumultuous relationships, existential questions, and moral struggles to find meaning in a troubled world. After spending some time abroad, Dmitri returns home only to find himself entangled in a love triangle with his father, both vying for the affection of the same woman Grushenka. This rivalry threatens to obliterate his personal aspirations and thrusts him into a dangerous world of deception and violence. Ivan wrestles with his inner demons, deeply questioning the existence of God and contemplating the very nature of morality itself. Amid these conflicts, Alyosha emerges as a compassionate mediator, endeavoring to reconcile his warring brothers despite their stark differences while simultaneously seeking solace in his unwavering faith. The narrative reaches its climactic zenith in a gripping courtroom drama, where each brother must confront the other over accusations surrounding their father's murder. It is within this crucible that unexpected truths are unveiled, demonstrating that even amidst tragedy, compassion can triumph, mending the fractures and illuminating the transformative nature of the human connection.

Dostoevsky incorporates thought-provoking theological and philosophical discussions, exploring the personal and the universal. The novel probes the nature of good and evil, the burden of free will, and the power of grace through adversity.

207.   I Malavoglia (Giovanni Verga, 1881)

"Why is the sea sometimes green and sometimes turquoise,
sometimes white and sometimes as black as lava?
Why is it never just the colour of water? Alessi asked.
It's God's will, his grandfather said.
That way the sailor knows when he can go out to sea
and when it's best to stay on shore."

— *Giovanni Verga, I Malavoglia*

The novel follows the story of the Malavoglia family, who live in a small fishing village on the coast of Sicily. The patriarch, Padron 'Ntoni Malavoglia, is an old man whose family struggles to make ends meet. The novel focuses on the challenges faced by Padron 'Ntoni and his family, including his grandson 'Ntoni. The family incurs a debt to buy a cargo of lupins, but the ship carrying the lupins is wrecked, losing the precious cargo. This event leads to the economic ruin of the Malavoglias. The novel explores the poverty and hardship faced by those, particularly fishermen, living in rural communities. Through a series of tragic events – including deaths and the struggles of the younger 'Ntoni – we see how difficult life can be for these people as they wrestle against fate and misfortune. Despite this adversity, however, there is a sense of hope as love and loyalty within the family help them endure and potentially overcome difficult circumstances. The book also vividly portrays Sicilian life during this period; its culture, customs, and traditions are explored through descriptions of everyday activities such as fishing trips and festivals, which bring together members from different parts of society regardless of class or wealth differences.

I Malavoglia captures historical accuracy along with emotionally intriguing characters. The novel serves as an insightful commentary on class relations at the time, demonstrating how inequality can shape one's experience while remaining rooted in hope and solidarity amongst oppressed communities.

208.   So Spoke Zarathustra (Friedrich Nietzsche, 1883)

"You must be ready to burn yourself in your own flame;
how could you become new, if you had not first become ashes?"

—— *Friedrich Nietzsche, So Spoke Zarathustra*

Zarathustra, a revered prophet who emerges from solitude in the mountains, proclaims the disappearance of God and advocates the self-creation of human values and morality. The central thesis is the idea of the *Übermensch* or *Overman*, representing the individual who transcends human limitations and creates their own values and meaning. Zarathustra delivers his radical message to an ever-expanding audience with unwavering determination, challenging individuals to forge their existence independent of traditional religious dogmas and social norms. Although met with perplexity and even hostility, Zarathustra persists in guiding people toward a life imbued with meaning beyond the confines of conventional thought structures. On his journey of transformation, he encounters a myriad of symbolic figures representing various aspects of the human experience: Death personified as a skeleton, a wise elder embodying wisdom, women as epitomes of beauty, children exemplifying innocence, and animals as reflections of human nature. Kings denote power, merchants exemplify greed, and so on. By interacting with these different characters and spreading his teachings, Zarathustra steadily ascends toward enlightenment. Eventually, he retreats to the mountains, leaving only his profound wisdom for others to interpret and assimilate according to their understanding. The ultimate message of Zarathustra can be seen as an invitation for each individual to discover their truth and create their values, liberated from conventional beliefs and societal constraints.

One of Nietzsche's most important works, due to its exploration into themes such as nihilism, existentialism, and free will vs. determinism, is somewhat unique in its poetic and aphoristic style.

209. Pinocchio (Carlo Collodi, 1883)

> *"Most unfortunately, in the lives of puppets*
> *there is always a 'but' that spoils everything."*
>
> — *Carlo Collodi, Pinocchio*

The story of Pinocchio begins in the quaint Italian village where Geppetto, an old woodcarver, carves a puppet out of a magical piece of wood. He is astounded when the puppet comes to life and exhibits a mischievous and willful demeanor. Geppetto names him Pinocchio and nurtures a fatherly affection for him. Pinocchio embarks then on whimsical and often perilous adventures. Along the way, he meets a colorful cast of characters, including the Talking Cricket, who offers sage advice that Pinocchio often ignores; the cunning Fox and Cat, who exploit his gullibility; and the Blue Fairy, who protects and guides him with maternal love. The story's central leitmotif is Pinocchio's long nose, which grows whenever he tells a lie. This serves as a metaphor for the consequences of dishonesty and the importance of integrity. Through a series of misfortunes, many of which are consequences of his own choices, Pinocchio undergoes profound changes. He is transformed from a rebellious puppet into a compassionate and responsible individual. One of the most dramatic episodes occurs when Pinocchio and Geppetto are swallowed by The Terrible Dogfish. Within the belly of the sea creature, Pinocchio and Geppetto reunite, and Pinocchio realizes the importance of family and self-sacrifice. This experience is pivotal in Pinocchio's maturation. As the story concludes, Pinocchio's transformation is complete when the Blue Fairy rewards his excellent heart by turning him into a real boy.

Pinocchio is a rich allegory of the trials of growing up, the consequences of one's actions, and the everlasting bond between parent and child. Collodi's masterpiece has continued to fascinate readers and has been adapted into various forms, from film to theater, underscoring its timeless appeal.

210.   The Adventures of Huckleberry Finn (Mark Twain, 1884-1885)

"All right, then,
I'll go to hell."

— *Mark Twain, The Adventures of Huckleberry Finn*

The Adventures of Huckleberry Finn follows its protagonist – Huck – as he escapes from his abusive father and joins Jim, an escaped slave. Together, they embark on a journey toward freedom, traveling down the Mississippi River on a raft. During their expeditions, they encounter various characters who challenge their beliefs about race, morality, and family dynamics. They make their way southwards on the river, surrounded by dangers such as criminals and slave hunters looking for Jim or anyone else that stands out from *normal society* at the time – including Huck himself because he is not civilized enough according to others' standards. As Huck continues to run into different people along his adventure, he learns valuable lessons while also trying to help protect Jim in any way he can so that, eventually, both can find peace and safety far away from danger. Conclusively, despite knowing the risks and the legality of freeing enslaved people, Huck decides to help free Jim. This act demonstrates the power of true friendship, showing that it transcends laws and societal expectations. Huck's choice highlights the importance of loyalty and compassion, emphasizing that our bonds with others are more significant than any external constraints or judgments imposed upon us.

The Adventures of Huckleberry Finn offers readers insight into themes such as race relations, class issues, and personal identity struggles, all within a historical context. Furthermore, this novel powerfully demonstrates how friendship has the potential power to break through any barrier regardless of differences in background.

The Adventures of Huckleberry Finn

211.   Beyond Good and Evil (Friedrich Nietzsche, 1886)

"In every real man a child is hidden that wants to play."

— *Friedrich Nietzsche, Beyond Good and Evil*

Beyond Good and Evil is a hammer shattering long-held beliefs about morality and truth. This trailblazing philosophical treatise dares to question the binary nature of good and evil, peering beneath the surface to expose the raw power dynamics that shape our moral compass. Nietzsche is audacious and unabashed, unmasking traditional morality as a façade, a clever tool that powerfully wields to keep the masses in check. But Nietzsche does not stop at morality. With a piercing gaze, he turns towards religion, tearing down the curtains to reveal it as another instrument of control. He paints religious doctrines as irrational veils that obscure reality. It is a provocative challenge, forcing the reader to question whether objective truth is an illusion and if our firmest beliefs are merely fragile constructs. Amidst this whirlwind, Nietzsche introduces the concept of the *will to power*, asserting that this intrinsic force genuinely drives human actions and ambitions. He calls for a *master morality* that venerates strength, creativity, and individualism over submission and conformity. He warns of the traps of dogmatic thinking and makes a robust case for art that transcends mere moral judgments. Nietzsche is not just giving you an alternative lens to view the world; he is handing you a chisel and asking, "What will you carve out of the monolith of established beliefs?" Through his insightful and, at times, jarring reflections, he implores individuals not to meekly accept what they are told but to scrutinize, dissect, and construct their own edifices of understanding.

Beyond Good and Evil is a rebellion in the form of philosophy. It is a call to intellectual arms. This groundbreaking work has left an indelible mark on philosophy, setting the stage for existentialism and forever changing the way we think about morality, power, and the nature of human existence.

212.   The Strange Case of Dr. Jekyll and Mr. Hyde (Robert Louis Stevenson, 1886)

> *"All human beings, as we meet them, are commingled out of good and evil: and Edward Hyde, alone, in the ranks of mankind, was pure evil."*

—— *Robert Louis Stevenson, The Strange Case of Dr. Jekyll and Mr. Hyde*

Set against the backdrop of Victorian London, the narrative unfolds through the investigative endeavors of the principled solicitor Gabriel John Utterson. The plot unveils an enigmatic connection between Utterson's venerable friend Dr. Henry Jekyll and the malevolent figure Edward Hyde. As the narrative progresses, Stevenson shows the complex relationship between these central characters. Through meticulous investigation, Utterson uncovers the disquieting truth of Jekyll's scientific experiments, which aimed to dissociate the aspects of good and evil within the human psyche. Jekyll's concoction allows for a physical manifestation of his dark impulses through Edward Hyde. A pivotal moment in the narrative is the brutal demise of Sir Danvers Carew, a paragon of virtue within the community. This atrocious act symbolizes the unbridled malevolence of Hyde and catalyzes the unraveling of Jekyll's clandestine endeavors. The tension escalates as the authorities, initially searching for Hyde, redirect their attention to Jekyll. The culminating revelations depict a tragic figure in Jekyll, who faces insurmountable consequences after losing control over his *alter-ego*. The novel is a complex and layered examination of identity, morality, and the societal constraints of Victorian England. The dichotomy between Jekyll and Hyde represents the internal struggle between civility and primality.

Stevenson's work invites a scholarly discourse on the implications of duality and the ethical considerations regarding scientific experimentation on the human psyche. The novel has been instrumental in establishing the horror genre, with the character of Edward Hyde becoming an archetypal representation of malevolence.

213.   The Picture of Dorian Gray (Oscar Wilde, 1890)

"To define is to limit."

— *Oscar Wilde, The Picture of Dorian Gray*

Dorian is a young man of exceptional beauty and charm. His life takes a significant turn when he crosses paths with Lord Henry, an alluring gentleman who becomes his guide into a world of extravagance and indulgence. Under Lord Henry's influence, Dorian becomes increasingly enamored with his physical appearance. Longing for eternal youth, he wishes that his portrait, to be painted by his talented friend Basil Hallward, should bear the burden of aging and the consequences of his actions while he remains eternally youthful. As the portrait takes shape, capturing Dorian's young perfection, a profound transformation occurs within him. Emboldened by the realization that his external beauty will never fade, Dorian plunges headlong into a life of hedonism, chasing pleasure and gratification with reckless abandon. Time passes, and as Dorian indulges in more passionate and immoral pursuits, his hidden secrets and sins start unraveling. The portrait, reflecting the true nature of his soul, becomes increasingly grotesque and corrupted, bearing the weight of his transgressions. Yet, to the outside world, Dorian remains unchanged: his youthful visage is a mask concealing the darkness within. Haunted by the portrait's twisted reflection of his moral degradation, Dorian descends into profound despair. He is tormented by the juxtaposition of his eternal youth and the vile acts he has committed. Seeking liberation from the portrait's curse, Dorian sets out on a path of attempt at atonement, only to find that the consequences of his actions are inescapable.

Oscar Wilde's masterpiece warns against vanity and sharply critiques Victorian society. The author's wit and eloquence are on full display as he explores aestheticism and the notion that art should be appreciated for its beauty alone.

THE FIRST WORLD WAR ERA

THE FIRST WORLD WAR ERA

From 1900 to 1930, the literary world underwent seismic shifts, stirred by myriad forces: the spirit of *modernism*, the severe impact of *World War I*, and the burgeoning influence of women writers.

The early years of this period pulsed with innovation and audacious experimentation as novelists and poets rose to challenge the entrenched conventions of the post-romantic era. H.G. Wells' utopian studies kindled the flames of this era, characterized by a heady blend of radicalism and romanticism and fueled by fresh ideas in anthropology, psychology, philosophy, political theory, and psychoanalysis.

But the thunderous outbreak of *World War I* in 1914 sounded the death knell for this initial phase of the modernist revolution. The cataclysmic war left Anglo-American modernists acutely aware of the chasm between their lofty ideals and the chaos that engulfed the present. Modernist and more conservative writers felt the war's impact, particularly the poets who witnessed its horrors firsthand. Virginia Woolf, a luminary of the modernist and feminist ranks, saw her perspective as an antidote to the destructive egocentrism she believed lay at the heart of the male mind, a force she held responsible for the war's devastation. Her works excavated subjectivity, time, and history in fiction and fostered a growing sense among her contemporaries that traditional literary forms were no longer adequate vessels for expression.

At the core of the ensuing crisis lay the catastrophic global economic collapse of the late 1920s and early 1930s, a calamity that plunged humanity into the abyss of despair and uncertainty. The *Great Depression*, as it came to be known, inflicted untold suffering upon countless individuals and families; their lives mired in poverty, unemployment, and an all-pervasive despondency. The economic upheaval cast an elongated shadow over the decade, sowing seeds of doubt in the very fabric of society. Concurrently, the specter of fascism loomed menacingly, casting a pall of fear and foreboding. Across Europe, totalitarian regimes seized power, disseminating hatred, intolerance, and aggressive ideologies.

T.S. Eliot, a significant figure during this period, ignored conventional poetry rules. He skillfully used myths and symbols to deeply explore the concept of individual and collective *rebirth through self-sacrifice*.

In his fiction, James Joyce illuminated the personal toll exacted by the sexual and imaginative repression of life in Ireland. His sweeping novel *Ulysses* – a veritable tapestry of creative richness – stood as a provocative counterpoint to the more orthodox works of the era.

The 1920s and early 1930s crises served as crucibles, fostering introspection, encouraging artistic exploration, and birthing new voices and perspectives that would shape the cultural landscape. Amid the maelstrom of turmoil and uncertainty, glimmers of resilience, creativity, and hope emerged. Artists, writers, and intellectuals sought solace and inspiration amidst the chaos, striving to extract meaning from adversity.

214.   The War of the Worlds (H.G. Wells, 1898)

> *"It is still a matter of wonder how the Martians are able to slay men so swiftly and so silently."*

> — *H.G. Wells, The War of the Worlds*

The novel opens with a series of strange occurrences: astronomers observe a series of explosions on the surface of Mars, and shortly after, cylindrical objects plummet from the sky near Woking, Surrey. The cylinders turn out to be Martian spacecraft, and from them emerge alien creatures with technology far surpassing that of humankind. They construct towering three-legged fighting machines known as *tripods* and unleash destruction with heat rays and chemical weapons. Panic and chaos ensue as the Martians advance, leaving a trail of destruction. As the narrator navigates through a landscape where humanity is on the brink of annihilation, he encounters other survivors. The Martians continue their campaign of terror, and along with their destruction, a red weed – an alien plant that they brought with them – begins to proliferate and alter Earth's ecology. However, the Martians succumb to infections caused by Earth's bacteria, against which they have no immunity. One of the novel's central points at issue is the critique of imperialism and colonialism. By placing the British, who were at the time the dominant colonial power, in the role of the colonized, Wells raises questions about the consequences of imperialism. Furthermore, the book contains a message about the humbling power of nature. Despite their advanced intellect and technology, the Martians are defeated not by human ingenuity but by microscopic organisms, underlining the vulnerability of even the most formidable powers to nature.

The War of the Worlds is widely regarded as one of the foundations upon which modern science fiction was built. Its innovative use of realistic detail in depicting an alien invasion was groundbreaking and set a template for countless future works in the science fiction genre.

215.   The Interpretation of Dreams (Sigmund Freud, 1899)

> *"The interpretation of dreams*
> *is the royal road to a knowledge*
> *of the unconscious activities of the mind."*

— *Sigmund Freud, The Interpretation of Dreams*

The Interpretation of Dreams analyzes dream symbolism and suggests that dreaming is related to subconscious desires and experiences overlooked or suppressed during conscious life. One of the core tenets of Freud's dream theory is that dreams serve as a form of *wish fulfillment*, especially of unfulfilled desires rooted in childhood and sexuality. He distinguishes between the *manifest content* of dreams, which is what a person remembers and experiences during the dream, and the *latent content*, which represents the underlying, hidden wishes and meanings. Freud explains various mechanisms through which the mind disguises and protects itself from the latent content, which include *repression, displacement, condensation,* and *symbolization.* He illustrates these concepts through case studies from his psychoanalytic practice and anecdotes from acquaintances and strangers. He believed that by analyzing dreams properly, one can reveal the inaccessible parts of our unconscious and gain valuable insights into various aspects of human psychology, such as sexuality, mortality, and anxiety. Freud posits that addressing the hidden layers of the unconscious through dream analysis can contribute to resolving mental health issues. While Freud's ideas around dream interpretation and the role of the unconscious mind in shaping behavior remain significant, they have also been subject to critique and are considered controversial by some in psychology.

Freud's Interpretation of Dreams seeks to break through to the unconscious. His theories about the role of dreams in shaping our behavior remain influential to this day, and ideas around dream symbolism continue to be studied and discussed.

The Interpretation of Dreams

216.   Lord Jim (Joseph Conrad, 1900)

"How does one kill fear, I wonder?
How do you shoot a specter through the heart,
slash off its spectral head, take it by its spectral throat?"

— *Joseph Conrad, Lord Jim*

The narrative is primarily structured as a *frame story*, with the Captain Charles Marlow recounting Jim's saga to an attentive audience. Jim is a young British sailor who dreams of being a hero. However, when faced with a storm and the belief that his ship is sinking, he abandons the ship and its passengers, betraying his heroic ideals. The ship, however, does not sink, and Jim's action is publicly exposed, leading to his disgrace and revocation of his seaman's certificates. Haunted by his ignominious past, Jim wanders through Southeast Asia, taking up obscure posts. Through this odyssey of penance, he eventually finds himself in Patusan, a remote village beleaguered by internal strife and external threats. In Patusan, Jim's inherent valor surfaces as he employs his talents and leadership in aiding the villagers. He has conferred the title *Lord Jim* and integrates into their community, achieving a sense of belonging and respect that had eluded him. The novel takes an intricate turn when a nefarious character Gentleman Brown confronts Jim about his past. This encounter is not merely the dissemination of rumors, but a more profound clash embodying Jim's past and present. His death is a consequence of a chain of events set in motion by the arrival of the group of pirates led by Gentleman Brown. Jim meets his end through an act of atonement that reinforces his regained honor and integrity.

Lord Jim is a profound exploration of the human psyche and the perennial conflict between idealism and reality. The novel interrogates the constructs of heroism and the scrutiny individuals undergo within societal frameworks. Above all, it delves into the relentless pursuit of absolution within one's conscience.

217.   Buddenbrooks (Thomas Mann, 1901)

"We are most likely to get angry and excited in our opposition to some idea when we ourselves are not quite certain of our own position, and are inwardly tempted to take the other side."

— *Thomas Mann, Buddenbrooks*

Set in the 19th century in Lübeck, Germany, the novel chronicles the life and eventual decline of the prosperous Buddenbrook family throughout four generations. The story begins with the elder Johann Buddenbrook, the senior patriarch of the family's successful grain trading business. He passes on the industry to his son Thomas, who is depicted as an ambitious character, embodying the ethos of the patrician class. Parallel to Thomas's narrative, the novel explores the life of his sister Antonie (Tony). Tony's story is marred by marital disappointments: her marriages, arranged to maintain and elevate the family's social standing, end up in failures, reflecting the family's underlying fragility. The focus then transitions from Thomas to his son Johann, affectionately known as Hanno. Unlike his forebears, Hanno is a sensitive and artistic soul with a particular affinity for music. His physical frailty and lack of interest in mercantile pursuits symbolize the erosion of the values and vigor that had sustained the family's prominence. The family's trajectory is adroitly interwoven with broader societal changes, including economic transformations, the rise of a new bourgeoisie, and shifts in cultural values. Another poignant theme is the decay of physical and mental health through the generations. The Buddenbrooks' gradual decline in health is symbolic of the degeneration of the family as a whole. The novel culminates in the fall of the Buddenbrook house, literally and metaphorically. The family's estate is eventually sold, and the once-proud family name fades into obscurity.

Through his elegant prose and narrative complexity, Mann has created an enduring portrayal of the decline of a family intricately bound to the vicissitudes of history and societal evolution.

218.   The Hound of the Baskervilles (Arthur Conan Doyle, 1901-02)

> *"It is an old maxim of mine that when you have excluded the impossible, whatever remains, however improbable, must be the truth."*

— *Arthur Conan Doyle, The Hound of the Baskervilles*

The story is set on the desolate moors of Devonshire, where the Baskerville family is allegedly haunted by a monstrous hound due to an ancient curse. The novel begins with Dr. James Mortimer consulting Sherlock Holmes about the mysterious death of his friend Sir Charles Baskerville. Mortimer is concerned for the safety of the new heir Sir Henry Baskerville, who has arrived from Canada to claim his inheritance. Sir Charles's death and sightings of a large, spectral hound revive the legend of the cursed Baskerville family. Holmes sends Dr. Watson to Baskerville Hall to protect Sir Henry and gather information. Watson observes the strange behavior of the estate's residents and neighbors, including the butler Barrymore and the naturalist Stapleton. In the meantime, Holmes secretly arrives on the moor and conducts his investigation in disguise. Holmes's astute deductive reasoning reveals that the hound is not supernatural but a real dog made to appear ghostly. He uncovers that Stapleton, posing as a neighbor, is, in fact, a Baskerville relative seeking to murder Sir Henry to inherit the Baskerville wealth. Holmes and Watson orchestrate a plan to catch Stapleton red-handed. In a dramatic climax on the moor, they save Sir Henry from the ferocious hound, which is shot dead. Stapleton meets his end in the grim marshes while fleeing.

The Hound of the Baskervilles is celebrated for its atmospheric setting, compelling plot, and ingenuity of Sherlock Holmes in debunking superstition through logical deduction. The novel adeptly employs gothic elements, suspense, and a meticulously constructed mystery, enchanting readers and solidifying Sherlock Holmes's status as a timeless detective.

219.   The Immoralist (André Gide, 1902)

"Nothing thwarts happiness so much as the memory of happiness."

— André Gide, *The Immoralist*

The novel is structured as a confessional letter, wherein Michel reveals his inner turmoil to his close friends. Initially, Michel is portrayed as a conforming intellectual, recently married to Marceline, a kind and dutiful woman. His seemingly predictable life takes a turn when he falls severely ill on their honeymoon in North Africa. During his convalescence, Michel becomes enamored with the vivacity and simplicity of the cultures he encounters. The lush landscapes, the candidness of the people, and the absence of societal restrictions begin to erode his formerly steadfast morals. As Michel's health rebounds, so does his appetite for life, but not in the conventional sense. He develops an insatiable craving for sensual and hedonistic experiences, progressively alienating him from his responsibilities and wife. One of the significant influences on Michel's transformation is his acquaintance with Ménalque, an audacious and enigmatic figure that becomes a friend and a mentor to Michel, guiding him further into the depths of hedonism. Throughout this period, Marceline remains steadfast in her love for Michel but is tormented by his increasing indifference and recklessness. She is also plagued by her failing health. Michel's inattentiveness towards Marceline culminates in tragedy when her condition worsens, and she succumbs to her illness. Haunted by guilt and sorrow, Michel attempts to find solace in artistic and intellectual endeavors. However, he struggles to reconnect with a sense of purpose. His self-indulgence has led to a chasm that he cannot bridge, and he is left emotionally and socially isolated.

Gide's nuanced portrayal of Michel's journey offers a sharp critique of societal constraints while illuminating the potentially destructive nature of unbridled self-indulgence.

220. The Call of the Wild (Jack London, 1903)

> *"His development (or retrogression) was rapid.*
> *His muscles became hard as iron,*
> *and he grew callous to all ordinary pain."*

— *Jack London, The Call of the Wild*

The Call of the Wild follows the gripping tale of Buck, a large St. Bernard-Scotch Shepherd mix. Initially living a comfortable life on a California estate, Buck is suddenly uprooted and sold as a sled dog during the Klondike Gold Rush. The novel follows Buck's transformation as he adapts to the brutal conditions of the Yukon. Underfed, overworked, and often mistreated by his human masters, Buck learns to rely on his primal instincts to survive. As he adjusts to his new life, Buck begins to hear the call of the wild, the beckoning of his ancestral lineage that urges him to revert to his primitive instincts. He becomes more independent, fierce, and astute in navigating the challenges of his environment. Buck develops a deep bond with John Thornton, a kind and empathetic gold prospector who saves him from mistreatment. Through this relationship, Buck experiences genuine affection and loyalty. However, when a tragic event takes Thornton's life, Buck's ties to the human world are severed. He responds to the call that haunts him, shedding the last vestiges of his domesticated self. Buck becomes a creature of the wild, eventually leading a wolf pack, embracing his ancestral past, and finding true freedom and fulfillment in the wilderness.

The Call of the Wild is a poignant exploration of nature, survival, and the inherent instincts that lie within. Through Buck's eyes, the novel examines themes such as the clash between civilization and the wild, the importance of adaptation for survival, and the unbreakable bonds of loyalty and friendship. Jack London's evocative prose brings the harsh landscapes of the Yukon to life, immersing the reader in an unforgettable journey of self-discovery and transformation.

The Call of the Wild

221.   Three Essays on the Theory of Sexuality (Sigmund
  Freud, 1905)

"The sexual life of adult women is a 'dark continent' for psychology."

— *Sigmund Freud, Three Essays on the Theory of Sexuality*

In the essays, Sigmund Freud, one of the pioneers of psychoanalysis, lays the foundation for modern theories of sexuality and its connection to psychology. This groundbreaking work, published in 1905, was revolutionary for its time and continues to be influential in psychology and the study of human sexuality. The first essay *The Sexual Aberrations* tackles what were considered sexual perversions at the time, such as fetishism, sadism, and masochism. Freud challenges prevailing perceptions, arguing that these behaviors are not solely inherent but developed through biological drives and external influences, including upbringing and environment. In the second essay *Infantile Sexuality*, Freud posits that childhood experiences and fantasies play a crucial role in an individual's psychological development and sexual behavior in adulthood. This essay introduces the concept of psychosexual development, including the now-famous notions of the *Oedipus complex* and sexual stages in early childhood. The final piece *Transformations of Puberty* examines the changes in libido that occur during puberty and the resulting shifts in sexual behavior and preferences. Freud also explores the connection between neurosis and sexual development, suggesting new approaches for neurotic disorders based on his theories.

Three Essays on the Theory of Sexuality broke new ground by liberating the study of human sexuality from the constraints of moral and religious doctrine and by advocating for its scientific investigation. This work played a significant role in establishing psychoanalysis as a legitimate field of study, despite its controversy and criticism. Freud's insights into the complexities of human sexuality have had a lasting impact on both psychology and society.

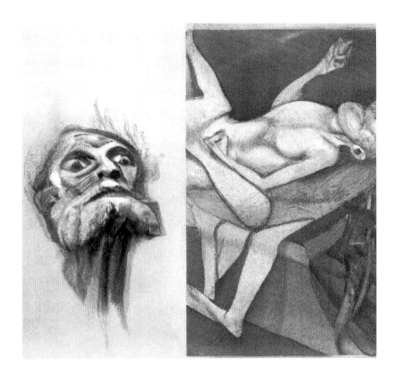

Three Essays on the Theory of Sexuality

222.   Alcools (Guillaume Apollinaire, 1913)

"All the words I have to say have turned into stars."

— *Guillaume Apollinaire, Alcools*

Alcools is a work often hailed as a cornerstone of *modernist literature* and a precursor to the *Surrealist movement*. One of the book's most notable features is its innovative approach to form and structure. Apollinaire's deliberate choice to omit punctuation marks from the poems adds an ethereal fluidity and openness to the text, making it feel boundless and open to various interpretations. A famous poem in the collection is *Zone*, a sprawling, energetic, and visionary piece that captures the essence of modern urban life. Apollinaire uses striking imagery and fragmented language to paint a vibrant picture of Paris. It is a poem where past and present coalesce, and the dizzying pace of modern life is depicted through a cascade of images and observations. Another highlight is *La Chanson du Mal Aimé* (*The Song of the Poorly Loved*). In this emotionally charged poem, Apollinaire inquires motives of unrequited love, isolation, and longing. This piece's melancholic tone and lyrical beauty take the reader through the depths of human emotion. Apollinaire's poetry is often noted for its interplay between tradition and innovation. While he uses classical forms such as the sonnet and pays homage to various historical references, he simultaneously injects his work with a distinctly modern dynamism. His poem *Rhénanes* is an example of this duality, as he utilizes the traditional French form of the *alexandrine* yet creates a contemporary portrayal of his travels along the Rhine River, evoking the juxtaposition between history and the present day.

Alcools pushed the boundaries of poetic form and explored the rapidly changing world of the early 20th century. Its influence can be seen in the modernist literature, particularly the Surrealist movement. Apollinaire's blend of lyrical intensity, formal innovation, and emotional depth solidifies his place as one of the most innovative poets of his time.

223. The Metamorphosis (Franz Kafka, 1915)

> *"As Gregor Samsa awoke one morning*
> *from uneasy dreams he found himself*
> *transformed in his bed into a gigantic insect."*

— *Franz Kafka, The Metamorphosis*

The Metamorphosis begins with a startlingly abrupt and inexplicable premise: a traveling salesman named Gregor Samsa wakes one day to find himself transformed into a monstrous, repugnant insect. The transformation is not just a physical one. It serves as an allegory for alienation, identity, and the cruel indifference of the world toward individual suffering. This grotesque metamorphosis leaves Gregor helpless, forced into confinement within his room, unable to go about his usual routine or provide for his family as he once did. Gregor's family reacts to his transformation with a complex mixture of horror, revulsion, pity, and pragmatism. The financial hardship that Gregor's condition imposes on his family leads them to resentment and neglect. As their disdain for Gregor's altered form increases, they sever all emotional ties, pushing Gregor further into isolation. Gregor's physical and emotional state deteriorates. He becomes less human in his behavior, losing his ability to speak and even his taste for human food. His room, once a human bedroom, gradually turns into a storage area filled with dust and unused items, symbolizing the garbage heap his life has become. The novel reaches its tragic end when Gregor succumbs to neglect, starvation, and despair, dying lonely and sad. His family, far from grieving, experiences relief. They quickly move on, with a feeling of liberation.

Kafka masterfully weaves a tale that forces us to confront the alienation, dehumanization, and isolation that profound personal changes can bring about. It challenges our understanding of identity, humanity, and the meaning of life itself. The Metamorphosis is an enduring testament to Kafka's genius, making it one of the greatest pieces of literature of all time.

224.   The General Theory of Relativity (Albert Einstein, 1916)

> *"According to this theory, the metrical qualities of the continuum of space-time differ in the environment of different points of space-time, and are partly conditioned by the matter existing outside of the territory under consideration."*

— *Albert Einstein, The General Theory of Relativity*

The Theory of Relativity is a groundbreaking scientific framework that reshaped our comprehension of gravity and space-time. According to this theory, gravity arises from the *curvature of space-time*, a phenomenon triggered by the presence of mass and energy. Einstein's equations, which elegantly describe the behavior of gravity, serve as *field equations* that elucidate the intricate geometry of space-time surrounding any object possessing mass or energy. These equations also offer predictions regarding various cosmological effects. They unveil phenomena such as *time dilation* caused by *gravitational fields* and the *redshift* experienced by light traversing through them. When coupled with *quantum mechanics*, the Theory of Relativity provides insights into the vast cosmos on a grand scale (although the unification of General Relativity and quantum mechanics is still an open problem in physics). The implications of the theory extend far beyond unraveling the interplay between matter and the fabric of space-time. This theory led to the prediction of the black holes, before their later discovery. Its transformative influence enters also into cosmology and navigation. Today, we rely on its principles to power essential technologies like *GPS* navigation systems.

The General Theory of Relativity is one of humanity's most remarkable achievements. Its far-reaching implications span numerous scientific disciplines, and its foundations have been fortified by extensive experimental evidence throughout history. Undoubtedly, this revolutionary piece within modern physics forever altered our perception of reality, leaving an indelible mark on the landscape of scientific knowledge.

225.   Tractatus Logico-Philosophicus (Ludwig Wittgenstein, 1921)

"Whereof one cannot speak, thereof one must be silent."

— *Ludwig Wittgenstein, Tractatus Logico-Philosophicus*

The Tractatus Logico-Philosophicus is characterized by its succinct, aphoristic style and profound depth. It is composed of seven main propositions, which are further elucidated through sub-propositions and commentary. Wittgenstein's primary concern in this work is to explore the intricate relationship between language, thought, and reality. Central is Wittgenstein's assertion that *language's logical structure reflects the world's logical structure*. He contends that language should be employed to create clear and analytical representations of the world. Beginning with the first proposition, "The world is all that is the case," Wittgenstein maintains that *the world consists of facts*, which can be articulated through logical propositions. Wittgenstein then introduces the concept of *picturing*, elucidating how language propositions can depict states of affairs in the world. Wittgenstein's famous sixth proposition demarcates what can be articulated in language from what can only be shown. He argues that attempting to verbalize certain aspects that are inherently beyond language's expressive capacity results in nonsensical or meaningless utterances. He contends that *logical truths do not disclose deep metaphysical realities but are merely by-products of language's structure*. This perspective challenges traditional philosophical pursuits for profound metaphysical truths. The Tractatus played an influential role in the development of *logical positivism*; however, Wittgenstein himself later distanced himself from some interpretations of his work by logical positivists.

The Tractatus Logico-Philosophicus is an intellectually demanding yet invaluable piece of philosophical literature. In addition to its philosophical ramifications, the Tractatus has implications in fields such as linguistics, cognitive science, and artificial intelligence.

226.   In Search of Lost Time. Remembrance of Things Past.
(Marcel Proust, 1913-27)

> *"The real voyage of discovery consists not*
> *in seeking new landscapes, but in having new eyes."*
>
> —— *Marcel Proust, In Search of Lost Time*

In Search of Lost Time is a multi-volume work, each dealing with different aspects of the narrator's life. A common leitmotif is *the passage of time and how it affects perception and memory*. Set in France during the late 19th and early 20th centuries, the novel begins with the unnamed narrator's childhood experiences in the bucolic town of Combray. Proust introduces the concept of *involuntary memory* epitomized by the famous *Madeleine* episode, where the taste of a small cake dipped in tea evokes a flood of memories for the narrator. As the narrative progresses, the protagonist moves to Paris and becomes entwined with its rich and complex society. Through the narrator's experiences and relationships, Proust explores love's capricious nature, friendship's intricacies, and desire's fleeting nature. Characters such as the manipulative Odette, the charming Gilberte, the passionate Albertine, the aristocratic Robert de Saint-Loup, and the art connoisseur Charles Swann are intricately developed, each contributing to the narrator's ever-evolving perspective on life. Of particular note is Proust's portrayal of the *impermanence of social status* and the shifting sands of societal norms. Through elaborate and introspective prose, Proust examines the way memory shapes identity. He challenges the notion of a *fixed self* and posits that *our identities are constantly reconstructed through our memories* and experiences. Proust's writing style itself is noteworthy. His sentences are often incredibly long and intricate, mirroring the complexity of thought and memory, making the novel both rewarding and challenging.

Proust meditates on the nature of human consciousness, the relativity of time, the power of memory, and its role in immortalizing human experience.

227. Six Characters in Search of an Author (Luigi Pirandello, 1921)

"Less real, perhaps; but more true!"

— *Luigi Pirandello, Six Characters in Search of an Author*

The play blurs the lines between fiction and reality. This *avant-garde drama* takes place in a theater. The routine of the acting company is disrupted by the unexpected intrusion of six mysterious individuals who claim to be characters from an *unfinished* play. The six characters, consisting of a Father, a Mother, a Stepdaughter, a Son a Boy and a Child, are in distress. They explain that their creator, an author, has left them unfulfilled and unfinished. Trapped in limbo, they yearn for their stories to be told and to achieve a sense of existence through the completion of their narrative. As the six characters reveal the complexities of their lives, which include themes of estrangement, betrayal, and passion, the theater manager is initially incredulous but eventually agrees to stage their story. The theater's actors are assigned to portray the characters, but tensions arise as the *actual* characters critique the actors' representations of them. The boundary between reality and fiction becomes increasingly porous as the characters and actors interact. Despite being fictional, the six characters convey emotions and histories that seem more genuine and consistent than those of the tangible actors. This raises questions regarding the nature of existence, identity, and the relationship between artists and their creations. Tragic events occur in the play's final act: the Child drowns, and the Boy commits suicide. The Stepdaughter flees, leaving the Son, Mother, and Father on the scene. The play ends with the director questioning the reality of events and lamenting the loss of a day's work.

Pirandello created a meta-theatrical work that stimulates the audience to reflect on the nature of reality, the constancy of identity, the limits of art, and the more general Pirandellian concept of the "relativity of truth."

228.   Siddhartha (Hermann Hesse, 1922)

*"Everyone can perform magic, everyone can reach his goals,
if he is able to think, if he is able to wait, if he is able to fast."*

—— *Hermann Hesse, Siddhartha*

Siddhartha is a young man born into nobility in ancient India. Driven by an insatiable thirst for knowledge and understanding, Siddhartha forsakes his aristocratic life to seek *enlightenment*. Accompanied initially by his devoted friend Govinda, he explores asceticism with a group of *Samanas* but finds this path wanting. As his journey continues, he crosses paths with the enlightened Gotama Buddha. While Govinda is drawn to Gotama's teachings and chooses to follow him, Siddhartha respectfully disagrees, believing that true enlightenment must be found through *personal experience* rather than doctrine. Venturing further, he experiences the sensual and material world with Kamala, a courtesan, and learns lessons in love and attachment. However, the emptiness within him persists. In the next phase of his life, Siddhartha is drawn to a tranquil river where he meets Vasudeva, the ferryman. Vasudeva's silent wisdom and the *eternal river* become instrumental in Siddhartha's self-discovery. The river symbolizes the unity and oneness of all things, and it is here that Siddhartha learns to listen deeply to the sounds of the river, which reflect the sorrows and joys of existence. Years pass, and as Siddhartha harmonizes with the natural world, he begins to realize the cyclical nature of life and how suffering and happiness are inherently connected. His accumulated experiences culminate in a profound enlightenment that transcends words – a realization of the interconnectedness of all life and the impermanence of the self.

Siddhartha is an elegant tale that explores an individual's quest for meaning beyond societal norms and the wisdom attained through meditation and life experiences. It is a poignant reminder that actual knowledge is personal and often beyond the realm of words.

229.   The Waste Land (T.S. Eliot, 1922)

"April is the cruelest month."

— *T.S. Eliot, The Waste Land*

The Waste Land is a monumental modernist poem, dense with allusions and imagery, embodying the disillusionment and despair of the *post-World War I* era. The opening line, "April is the cruelest month," sets the tone by contrasting the traditional association of April with spring and rebirth with the stark reality of a spiritually barren society. The poem is fragmented, consisting of five sections: *The Burial of the Dead, A Game of Chess, The Fire Sermon, Death by Water*, and *What the Thunder Said*. In The Burial of the Dead, Eliot references diverse literary works, including Dante's Inferno, to evoke a sense of decay and death that permeates contemporary life. This section introduces the motif of failed rebirth in a devastated land. A Game of Chess illustrates emotional emptiness by depicting tormented relationships. It is replete with references to Shakespeare and Ovid, revealing the superficiality and despair underlying societal engagements. The Fire Sermon alludes to the Buddha's sermon against physical desire, juxtaposing the spiritual against the decadence of modern life. Eliot portrays a world consumed by lust and void of meaningful connections. In Death by Water, Eliot employs mythological references to describe the inevitability of death. The image of a drowned sailor symbolizes the decay and demise of civilizations. Finally, What the Thunder Said is a cacophonous climax that draws on Hindu mythology. Speaking in Sanskrit, the thunder imparts wisdom that suggests the potential for spiritual redemption.

Throughout the poem, Eliot employs a kaleidoscope of references to mythology, history, and literature, creating a multi-layered landscape of the world's confusion, disillusionment, and yearning for meaning. Its rich allusions and striking imagery make it a touching portrayal of a society struggling to find grounding in the wake of a shattered worldview.

230.   Ulysses (James Joyce, 1922)

> *"Think you're escaping and run into yourself.*
> *Longest way round is the shortest way home."*
>
> — *James Joyce, Ulysses*

Ulysses is a monumental modernist novel that chronicles a single day, June 16th, 1904, in Dublin, through the experiences of its central characters Stephen Dedalus and Leopold Bloom. Employing a *stream-of-consciousness technique*, Joyce explores their inner thoughts, feelings, and reflections. The novel is structured into eighteen episodes, each with a distinct style and form, drawing parallels with Homer's *Odyssey*. Stephen Dedalus, a young writer, is still reeling from the death of his mother and is struggling to find his place in the world. Leopold Bloom, a middle-aged Jewish advertising canvasser, wanders through life, pained by his wife Molly's infidelity. As the day grows, the paths of Stephen and Bloom cross, providing a deep exploration of their psyches. Bloom's day begins with preparing breakfast and meandering through Dublin, where he attends a funeral and reflects on various aspects of life and society. In the meantime, Stephen, teaching in a school, ponders philosophically and later engages in intense discussions with friends about art and nationalism. As the night descends, Stephen and Bloom's paths converge more closely. After a nightmarish, hallucinatory experience in a brothel, they share a moment of companionship and reflection at Bloom's home. Though they part ways, this interaction forms the novel's crux, symbolizing their search for kinship and understanding in a *fragmented world*. The story closes with a famous soliloquy by Molly Bloom, Leopold's wife, which provides an intimate and uninhibited insight into her character.

Ulysses is renowned for its experimental narrative style, dense allusions, and linguistic innovation. Joyce's mastery of weaving the personal with the mythic has elevated his work to one of the most influential and celebrated novels of the 20th century, revolutionizing narrative structure and language.

231.   The Prophet (Kahlil Gibran, 1923)

> *"And ever has it been
> that love knows not its own depth
> until the hour of separation."*
>
> — *Kahlil Gibran, The Prophet*

The Prophet consists of twenty-six lyrical essays crafted in profound and emotional language that transcends time and culture barriers, impacting readers worldwide for nearly a century. The narrative takes place on the eve of Almustafa's return to his homeland after spending twelve years in the foreign city of Orphalese. As he prepares to board the ship that will carry him back home, the people of Orphalese approach him, seeking his wisdom on the core elements of human life. The remaining narrative takes the form of a series of enlightening discourses that Almustafa provides in response to their inquiries. Almustafa's teachings dig into a myriad of topics central to human existence. No aspect of life is left untouched, from love, marriage, and children to work, freedom, and death. Each discourse reveals profound wisdom about the human condition, delivered in rich, evocative language that resonates deeply with readers. They guide a life of virtue and a broader philosophical perspective on the universal human experiences of joy and sorrow, struggle, and triumph. Gibran's exquisite storytelling is characterized by his masterful use of poetic prose and symbolic imagery, enhancing the narrative's emotional depth. Almustafa, the compassionate and enlightened prophet, emerges as a symbol of universal wisdom, a spiritual guide who helps us navigate our experiences and emotions.

The work is a philosophical exploration of the complexities and richness of life. Its universal themes and timeless wisdom have made it a beloved classic worldwide. Beyond providing spiritual guidance, The Prophet also offers a profound appreciation for the beauty of language and the power of poetry, making it an invaluable treasure in world literature.

232.   The Magic Mountain (Thomas Mann, 1924)

"We come out of the dark and go into the dark again,
and in between lie the experiences of our life.
But the beginning and end, birth and death, we do not experience;
they have no subjective character,
they fall entirely in the category of objective events, and that's that."

— *Thomas Mann, The Magic Mountain*

Hans Castorp, a young and naive engineer from Hamburg, sets out on a three-week visit to his cousin Joachim at a tuberculosis sanatorium in the Swiss Alps. The charming atmosphere of the sanatorium, the endless dialogues, and the alluring presence of other patients lure him into extending his stay to seven years. In this microcosm away from the everyday world, time seems to lose its meaning, and Hans becomes submerged in an ocean of introspective exploration. At the sanatorium, Hans is drawn into the philosophical and ideological debates between the humanist Settembrini and the fanatic Naphta, which are a backdrop to European tensions on the brink of *World War I*. Additionally, Hans experiences a romantic and intellectual awakening through his infatuation with Clawdia Chauchat, another patient. Through Hans's eyes, the reader is invited to explore the critical junction in human history, where old certainties were crumbling, and the horrific wars would soon redefine humanity. In a profound and introspective journey that questions the certainties of culture, religion, and progress, Hans Castorp emerges as a transformed individual, still uncertain about the future but deeply affected by his experiences on The Magic Mountain.

The Magic Mountain is a symbolic and psychological study of the individual and society in the decadent period of European culture before the war. Thomas Mann masterfully uses the elevated and isolated sanatorium as a metaphor for the sickness and the intellectual and spiritual state of Europe. The novel serves as an allegory, with a wealth of metaphors, of the ailments and tensions of the 20th century.

233.   The Trial (Franz Kafka, 1925)

> *"Someone must have traduced Joseph K.,*
> *for without having done anything wrong*
> *he was arrested one fine morning."*

— *Franz Kafka, The Trial*

The story follows Josef K., who is inexplicably arrested on his thirtieth birthday for a never-specified crime. Throughout the novel, Josef K. grapples with a nightmarish legal maze as he tries to understand the charges against him and seeks a way to defend himself. As he navigates the judicial labyrinth, Josef K. encounters an array of bizarre characters, including court officials, lawyers, and other accused individuals, each of whom seems to be as entangled in the incomprehensible system as he is. The courts are shrouded in obscurity, the legal procedures are absurd and frustrating, and the process appears arbitrary and indifferent to the human spirit. Kafka's portrayal of this bewildering world is rich in allegory, serving as a profound critique of the dehumanization and irrationality of modern bureaucracy. The novel is emblematic of *Kafkaesque*, a term derived from the author's name, characterizing life's illogical, oppressive, and dreadful qualities within complex and uncontrollable social systems. The narrative is permeated by a sense of existential anxiety as Josef K. struggles with realizing his own impotence in the face of forces that he cannot comprehend or influence. A central motif is the desperate quest for clarity and justice in an indifferent world. In a bleak conclusion, Josef K.'s trial culminates in his execution by two enigmatic agents without any resolution or understanding of the case against him. His final moments are tinged with desperation and surrender.

Kafka crafted an iconic novel that combines psychological depth with a scathing indictment of the alienating structures of modern society. It remains a definitive exploration of the struggle for meaning in a bewildering world.

234.   The Great Gatsby (F. Scott Fitzgerald, 1925)

"You can't live forever; you can't live forever."

— *F. Scott Fitzgerald, The Great Gatsby*

Set in the fictional towns of West Egg and East Egg on Long Island, the story is narrated by Nick Carraway, who has recently moved to New York to work in the bond business. Nick's humble abode is overshadowed by the sprawling mansion of Jay Gatsby, a mysterious millionaire notorious for his extravagant parties. As Nick gets acquainted with Gatsby, he becomes a witness to the enigmatic millionaire's infatuation with Daisy Buchanan, who is not only married to the wealthy but arrogant Tom Buchanan but is also Nick's cousin. Gatsby's luxurious lifestyle emerges a facade erected in the pursuit of his unattainable dream – rekindling his past romance with Daisy, whom he had loved before leaving to fight in *World War I*. The plot thickens as Daisy and Gatsby's secret liaison intensifies. Concurrently, Tom has an affair with Myrtle Wilson, whose husband George is unaware of her infidelity. The intertwined web of deceit and forbidden love unravels as tensions mount. The climax is reached during a heated confrontation at a New York City hotel, where secrets are laid bare. Tom lashes out at Gatsby, belittling him and his love for Daisy. In the tragic denouement, Myrtle is killed in a hit-and-run accident by Gatsby's car, which Daisy was driving. Gatsby takes the blame, and in the aftermath, George Wilson, believing Gatsby to be the culprit, shoots him before taking his own life. The tragedy leaves the characters bereft and defeated, with the unattainable *American Dream* shattered.

The novel explores the disintegration of the American society drowning in decadence and opulence. Through eloquent prose, Fitzgerald paints a somber picture of the pursuit of wealth and status and the ultimate hollowness accompanying their attainment. The story remains a critique of a society where dreams are as fragile as the promises that build them.

235.   Mrs. Dalloway (Virginia Woolf, 1925)

> *"Mrs. Dalloway said*
> *she would buy the flowers herself."*
>
> — *Virginia Woolf, Mrs. Dalloway*

The novel takes us into the world of Clarissa Dalloway, an affluent woman residing in *post-World War I* London. The book describes her preparations for a soirée she will be hosting that evening while also delving into her reflections on her past and present existence. Throughout the day, we are introduced to other characters who intersect with Clarissa's life, such as Septimus Warren Smith, a traumatized war veteran grappling with PTSD; Peter Walsh, an old friend from Clarissa's past; Sally Seton, a former companion; and Richard Dalloway, Clarissa's husband. Through their interactions and experiences in post-war England, these characters reveal different facets of their personalities, illustrating that despite outward disparities, shared experiences can foster connections. The novel employs a stream-of-consciousness style to unearth Mrs. Dalloway's inner thoughts while also shedding light on broader social issues of the time, including class divisions and gender roles. It also explores themes of mental health struggles, examining how society deals with such challenges without adequately considering individual stories and experiences. By juxtaposing internal and external perspectives, Virginia Woolf weaves a multilayered narrative that allows readers to comprehend the characters' motivations and emotions surrounding their own lives.

Virginia Woolf's Mrs. Dalloway is a profound exploration of identity, trauma, memory, love, death, and mental health – all set against the backdrop of post-World War I London. Its emphasis on human connection and compassion is a poignant reminder that, despite our disparities, we are all intricately connected.

236.   The Sun Also Rises (Ernest Hemingway, 1926)

*"You can't get away from yourself
by moving from one place to another."*

— *Ernest Hemingway, The Sun Also Rises*

The Sun Also Rises is a novel about the *Lost Generation* of post-WWI Europe. The story follows Jake Barnes and his group of friends as they travel from Paris to Spain for the annual Festival of San Fermín. Along with Jake is Lady Brett Ashley, an Englishwoman who has been divorced multiple times; Robert Cohn, a Jewish American writer; Bill Gorton, a fellow expatriate; Mike Campbell, who is engaged to Brett; Pedro Romero, a young bullfighter; and Count Mippipopolous. The characters' relationships are complex and entwined with their personal struggles. Jake loves Brett but cannot consummate his love due to an injury he sustained during *World War I* that renders him impotent. Robert falls desperately in love with Brett, but she does not return his affections, leading him into bouts of depression and jealousy throughout the novel. The themes explored include anti-Semitism – represented by Robert's character – the effects of war on individuals' lives, and how people cope with trauma through alcohol consumption or other forms of escapism such as bullfighting or promiscuity. The novel ends ambiguously when Brett leaves for England after her relationship with Pedro ends abruptly due to pressure from both society and religion. Jake remains in Spain, where he receives a telegram from Brett asking for his help, and despite losing the woman he loved so deeply, he seems to find contentment.

In The Sun Also Rises, Ernest Hemingway portrays life among post-WWI Europeans whose lives were irrevocably changed forever by war – exploring the disillusionment felt by many members of the Lost Generation. Through his characters' experiences, Hemingway explores identity and purposelessness in life – topics still relevant today.

237.   Steppenwolf (Hermann Hesse, 1927)

> *"I am in truth the Steppenwolf that I often call myself;*
> *that beast astray that finds neither home nor joy nor nourishment*
> *in a world that is strange and incomprehensible to him."*

— *Hermann Hesse, Steppenwolf*

Steppenwolf takes us into the complex world of Harry Haller, an intellectual in his middle age who has grown weary and disillusioned with the mundaneness and constraints of societal life. He perceives himself as an outcast, a lone *Steppenwolf* (a prairie wolf), struggling vehemently to reconcile his refined human intellect with his primitive *wolf-like* instincts and desires. This fierce inner conflict propels him on a mystical and spiritual odyssey for inner peace, wholeness, and a deeper understanding of himself. The novel intricately follows Haller's encounters with a captivatingly diverse cast of characters, including the enigmatic Hermine, the free-spirited Pablo, the alluring Maria, and the classical genius Mozart. Through these enlightening interactions, Haller undergoes a metamorphosis as he realizes that true contentment and liberation lie in introspective self-reflection and embracing his dual nature rather than repudiating it. A pivotal and transformative moment in his journey is his venture into the *Magic Theater*, a surreal space that transcends the conventional boundaries of existence. It is not a physical place but a psychological *state of mind* where the boundaries of reality and imagination become indistinguishable in symbolic performances that force him to confront his deepest fears, desires, and illusions. Through the enigmatic Magic Theater, Haller discovers the intrinsic beauty in the ordinary moments of life, gaining a newfound appreciation for the multifaceted nature of human existence.

Steppenwolf masterfully combines elements of philosophy, mythology, spirituality, and symbolism, offering a deep exploration of existential themes and the intricacies of human psychology and self-discovery.

238.   To the Lighthouse (Virginia Woolf, 1927)

"A light here required a shadow there."

— *Virginia Woolf, To the Lighthouse*

The novel is a poignant exploration of a British family's life on the Isle of Skye during the early 20th century, encompassing the tumultuous years of *World War I* and the evolving dynamics of different generations. The novel delves into its characters' hopes, dreams, and struggles as they navigate personal desires and societal expectations. Mr. Ramsay, an aging scholar, grapples with his longing to leave a lasting intellectual legacy while facing the inevitability of passing time. Meanwhile, Mrs. Ramsay is deeply invested in securing her children's future and maintaining the unity of their fragile family, especially during challenging times. Their son James yearns for the symbolic journey of sailing to a nearby lighthouse with his father, a cherished aspiration that embodies their shared bond. On the other hand, their daughter Cam wrestles with the conflict between her desire for independence and the pressure to conform to the traditional role her mother embodies. Throughout the story, a pivotal event unfolds as the family debates whether to embark on the sailing trip, uncertain about the weather conditions. Tragically, Mrs. Ramsay passes away just before they can fulfill their plans, leaving a profound sense of loss. However, her enduring spirit and resilience in the face of adversity inspire hope for future generations to surpass limitations previously imposed upon them.

To the Lighthouse by Virginia Woolf is an ambitious and complex novel that explores the depths of human emotion through a family's journey to a lighthouse set against the backdrop of the Isle of Skye. Woolf's writing style has been praised for its lyrical beauty and ability to evoke powerful emotions from readers. Themes such as mortality, self-discovery, and artistic expression are explored in detail throughout this classic work.

To the Lighthouse

239.   Gypsy Ballads (García Lorca, 1928)

> *"At the forge the gypsies*
> *cry and then scream*
> *The wind watches, watches,*
> *the wind watches the Moon."*

— *García Lorca, Gypsy Ballads*

García Lorca's Gypsy Ballads is a collection of poems that celebrates the spirit and culture of Spain's Gypsy people. The first poem in the collection sets up a powerful theme: the contrast between the beauty and freedom of nature with society's attempts to contain and control it. Throughout the book, Lorca uses the images of birds, mountains, rivers, stars, and other elements from nature to evoke an atmosphere filled with longing for something greater than what can be found within human civilization. Most of these poems were inspired by traditional Spanish folklore and personal experiences from Lorca's travels through Andalusia. He also draws on his own feelings about love and death throughout many pieces in this work. He sometimes employs surrealist techniques such as dream-like images to tap into the realm of the subconscious, allowing his inner emotions to flow freely onto the pages. This abstract language heightens the intensity of his poetic expressions and evokes a more resounding emotional response in the reader. Lorca was deeply committed to preserving Spanish culture through literature. Gypsy Ballads is no exception. Through glowing imagery, he paints a picture not only of gypsies but also of rural life in general during this period in history. By celebrating their joys and sorrows, he brings attention to their plight and admires their tenacity.

Gypsy Ballads is a landmark of poetry. It captures the spirit of Gypsy culture throughout its lyrical storytelling and paints an evocative portrait of Spain's vibrant gypsy community during its time.

240.   The Threepenny Opera (Bertolt Brecht, 1928)

"First comes food, then morality."

— *Bertolt Brecht, The Threepenny Opera*

The Threepenny Opera is a groundbreaking *play with music* featuring a sharp, satirical edge and incisive social commentary. Accompanied by a memorable and innovative score composed by Kurt Weill, the work is celebrated for blending a wide array of musical styles, from jazz to ballads, with an astute critique of capitalism. Set in a seedy underworld of Victorian London, the story tracks the escapades of Macheath, commonly known as *Mack the Knife*, a charismatic and notorious criminal with a magnetic charm. Macheath enters into a marriage with Polly Peachum, invoking her parents' ire. Her father Jonathan Peachum is a man who has built his fortune by controlling and exploiting the city's beggars; he is depicted as an avaricious, unprincipled character who capitalizes on the misery of others. Mr. Peachum is adamant about bringing Macheath to the gallows, and to accomplish this, he enlists the assistance of his ally Police Chief Tiger Brown. However, Macheath is resourceful and wily. He manages to evade capture, and during his escapades, he becomes entangled with another woman, Lucy Brown, the daughter of Tiger Brown. She aids him in breaking out of prison, but his freedom is short-lived as he is captured once more and sentenced to hang. At the end, in a mocking twist that parodies conventional happy endings, Macheath is surprisingly saved by an improbable royal pardon and, ludicrously, is bestowed with a title and pension. This *deus ex machina* ending serves as a critique of the arbitrary nature of society and justice.

In The Threepenny Opera, Brecht employs the 'epic theatre' technique, encouraging the audience to critically engage with social issues rather than simply identifying with the characters. The songs in the play, like "Mack the Knife," have transcended the work and become classics.

241.   The Sound and the Fury (William Faulkner, 1929)

> *"It's not when you realise that nothing can help you*
> *— religion, pride, anything —*
> *it's when you realise that you don't need any aid."*

> —— *William Faulkner, The Sound and the Fury*

Set in early 20th-century Mississippi, the novel chronicles the disintegration of the Compson family, former *Southern aristocrats* struggling to come to terms with societal changes. The book is divided into four sections, each narrated from a different perspective, and employs a *stream-of-consciousness style* and *non-linear timeline*, which can make the narrative challenging yet rewarding. The first section is described by Benjy Compson, who is intellectually disabled. His narrative is filled with sensations and memories, and through his eyes, the readers get glimpses of his family members, especially his beloved sister Caddy. The second section is from Quentin Compson, the most introspective and tormented of the siblings. Quentin is obsessed with the idea of *Southern honor* and is particularly troubled by Caddy's perceived promiscuity, which he views as tarnishing the family's honor. His section reflects his mental state with fragmented, tortured introspection as he approaches a tragic end. The third section follows Jason, the cynical and embittered brother, whose greed and selfishness starkly contrast with his brothers. His section focuses more on the present and the economic struggles of the Compson family. The fourth and final section is narrated in the third person and focuses on Dilsey, the black servant of the Compson family. Through Dilsey's eyes, we witness the final downfall of the Compsons. While Caddy Compson does not have her own section, she is pivotal to the novel. Each of the narrators' sections revolves around their reactions to her actions, which form a central plot point.

The Sound and the Fury uses an innovative narrative style to explore the decline of the Old South and the inexorable nature of time, with the Compson family's story serving as a microcosm of larger societal changes.

242. The Man Without Qualities (Robert Musil, 1930-42)

> *"And what would you do, ...*
> *if you could rule the world for a day?*
> *I suppose I would have no choice but to abolish reality."*

> — *Robert Musil, The Man Without Qualities*

Musil's work is an unfinished, modernist, labyrinthine, satirical, and philosophical work that critiques the declining *Austro-Hungarian Empire* and the crisis of values in modernity. The novel follows Ulrich, a man of intellect but seemingly devoid of the driving qualities that define a person's role in society. Ulrich is called back to Vienna to participate in the *Parallel Campaign*, a nationalist cultural movement celebrating the 70th year of Emperor Franz Joseph's reign, which aims to assert the grandeur of his Empire. The movement's hollowness mirrors Ulrich's inner emptiness. Ulrich interacts with various characters representing different strata of Viennese society, including his hedonistic cousin Diotima, the pragmatic Count Leinsdorf, and the nihilistic murderer Moosbrugger. Through these interactions, Musil critiques the crumbling social order, political opportunism, and the banality of the era's intellectual movements. The narrative is rich with philosophical digressions as Ulrich contemplates the role of individuality, morality, and identity in a rapidly changing world. A significant shift in the novel occurs when Ulrich's estranged sister Agathe arrives. Through their intense and ambivalent relationship, Musil switches the narration to mysticism, duality, and the search for a *transcendental* form of existence.

The Man Without Qualities is an extensive critical analysis of society at the brink of collapse, seeking meaning at a time when traditional values and social constructs are disintegrating. Its fragmented and unfinished state adds to its mystique, reflecting the inconclusiveness of the moral dilemmas it explores. The richness and complexity of this work make it both challenging and rewarding for readers seeking depth in literary exploration.

243.   Maigret and the Madwoman (Georges Simenon, 1931)

"I'm relying on you. I trust you."

— *Georges Simenon, Maigret and the Madwoman*

Chief Inspector Jules Maigret of the French police is approached by an elderly woman named Léontine Antoine. Léontine is convinced that someone has been entering her apartment and moving objects around, but her complaints are initially dismissed by many as the ramblings of a paranoid old lady. Maigret, known for his compassionate nature and keen intuition, is inclined to believe her and promises to look into her concerns. Tragically, before Maigret can investigate further, Léontine is found murdered in her apartment. This ignites Maigret's to solve the case. During his investigation, Maigret uncovers that Léontine was not as unassuming as she appeared. He finds a slip of paper with gun grease in her apartment, which, although puzzling at first, turns out to be a critical clue pointing toward an old family secret. As Maigret explores Léontine's past, he focuses on her niece Angèle Louette and her boyfriend Le Grand Marcel, known to have criminal ties. The astute detective senses that Angèle, a woman with a strong personality and manipulative tendencies, is hiding something. When Maigret confronts Marcel regarding the case, he takes off for Toulon after a falling out with Angèle. Maigret continues his investigation, painstakingly unearthing a network of relationships around Léontine. Through this exploration, he learns of the deep-seated motives behind the mysterious break-ins at Léontine's apartment and the reasons for her murder.

Maigret and the Madwoman is a gripping detective novel that showcases Georges Simenon's mastery of creating atmospheric settings and rich, complex characters. With a well-crafted plot, the story goes beyond the typical detective narrative and delves into the psychological aspects of its characters. Maigret's astute observation and understanding of human nature make this novel a standout piece.

Maigret and the Madwoman

244.   Brave New World (Aldous Huxley, 1932)

> *"The more stitches, the less riches."*
>
> — *Aldous Huxley, Brave New World*

Brave New World, is set in a technologically advanced future London in the year 2540, referred to as *632 After Ford* (AF). This society is characterized by mass production, consumerism, and scientific conditioning, and is governed by the *World State*. Citizens are stratified into a rigid *caste system* consisting of Alphas, Betas, Gammas, Deltas, and Epsilons. The World State utilizes scientific techniques, including *genetic engineering* and *hypnopaedia* (sleep-teaching) to condition individuals from birth to conform to societal norms and accept their preordained roles. A drug called *soma* is widely used to suppress negative emotions and maintain social harmony. The story primarily follows Bernard Marx, an intelligent *Alpha* who feels alienated due to a physical defect. Lenina Crowne, a *Beta*, becomes a romantic interest for Bernard. They embark on a trip to a *Savage Reservation*, where people live outside the World State's control. At the Savage Reservation, Bernard and Lenina encounter John, born to a woman from the World State. John's upbringing, during which Shakespeare's works heavily influenced him, provides him with a value system that sharply contrasts with the World State. Seeing an opportunity, Bernard returns John to the World State, hoping to gain attention and challenge societal norms. However, as John is exposed to the sterile and dehumanized lifestyle of the World State, his deeply ingrained humanistic values clash with its citizens' emotion-suppressed contentment. His inability to reconcile the two worlds culminates his disillusionment and ultimate tragedy.

The novel is a thought-provoking critique of the relentless pursuit of technological progress at the expense of human values. Through the lens of a society where stability is maintained through emotional suppression, Huxley questions the definition of a utopian society.

245.   The General Theory of Employment, Interest, and
Money (John Maynard Keynes, 1936)

> *"The ideas of economists and political philosophers,*
> *both when they are right and when they are wrong,*
> *are more powerful than is commonly understood.*
> *Indeed the world is ruled by little else."*

— *J. M. Keynes, The General Theory of Employment, Interest, and Money*

Published amid the *Great Depression*, this work responded to the
catastrophic economic events that classical economics failed to
explain or address effectively. Central to Keynes's theory is the
idea of *aggregate demand* – the total spending in an economy – and
its crucial role in determining employment levels and economic
output. In contrast to *classical economics*, which held the idea that
supply creates its demand (often referred to as *Say's Law*) and that
markets would *naturally adjust* to achieve full employment,
Keynes argued that during economic downturns, pessimistic
expectations could lead to reduced spending, which in turn
would lead to unemployment and underutilization of resources.
Keynes introduced several essential concepts, such as *liquidity
preference*, which explains why people might hoard cash during
uncertain times instead of investing it. He also emphasized the
marginal propensity to consume, demonstrating that when
individuals receive additional income, they do not spend all of
it and how this can affect overall demand. A central tenet of
The General Theory is the advocacy for *government intervention* in
the economy. Keynes argued that during recessions, when
private spending declines, the government should step in to
offset this decline by increasing public spending or cutting taxes.
This intervention would avoid prolonged economic downturns.

*The General Theory represents a monumental shift in economic thinking
and led to the emergence of Keynesian economics. Its insights, particularly
regarding the role of government in moderating economic cycles through fiscal
policy, have had a lasting impact on economic policies around the globe.*

THE SECOND WORLD WAR ERA

The Library of Humanity

THE SECOND WORLD WAR ERA

In the tumultuous era of *World War II*, literature emerged as an indelible reflection of the experiences and thoughts that defined an era culminating in war, genocide, and political upheaval in which totalitarian regimes rose to power. The terrible truth of the Holocaust became manifest, and the destructive force of the atomic bomb left an indelible scar on human history. Within this crucible, the voices of writers and thinkers captured the essence of the postwar landscape, shaping the cultural fabric of a new era.

Among these voices, Ernest Hemingway witnessed the war, having served as a correspondent. Drawing on his first-hand encounters, he gave life to his novel *For Whom the Bell Tolls*. Set during the *Spanish Civil War*, the narrative chronicles the struggles of a group of rebels against fascist forces. Through a lifelike description, Hemingway explored the depth of emotions and moral dilemmas faced by those who dared to challenge oppression. The reader is transported into a world where the burdens of individual choices collide against the backdrop of ruthless conflict.

George Orwell, another exemplary author of this era, drew on his own wartime experiences to develop powerful political and social critiques. In works such as *Animal Farm* and *Nineteen Eighty-Four*, Orwell deftly revealed the insidious dangers of totalitarianism and propaganda. His narratives served as cautionary tales, illuminating the imperative of individual resistance in the face of oppressive systems. These seminal works continue to be a rallying cry, challenging us to question authority, safeguard personal freedoms, and remain steadfast guardians of truth and justice.

On the other hand, from the philosophical and social reflection perspective, the Austrian Karl Popper delved into the philosophical and political implications of war. In his influential tome *The Open Society and Its Enemies*, Popper argued for the value of individual freedom and addressed the danger of the allure of totalitarian ideologies. He extolled the virtues of democracy and critical thinking as essential tools for dismantling oppressive systems and safeguarding the rights of every individual.

Primo Levi, an Italian writer and Holocaust survivor, witnessed the unimaginable horrors of the Nazi concentration camps. His memoir *If This is a Man* provided a stark account of the human capacity for evil while celebrating the indomitable spirit of survival and hope. Levi's writings have become a powerful testament to the Holocaust, begging to be remembered and stimulating contemporary discussions of genocide and human rights.

Collectively, the literature of the *World War II* era paints a picture of resilience, heroism, sacrifice, and the individual's unwavering power to find meaning amid chaos and oppression. The writers and thinkers of this era wielded their pens as weapons, fearlessly critiquing the social and political forces that shaped their times. Their works are guiding beacons, reminding us of the eternal significance of compassion, courage, and the tireless pursuit of truth and justice, even in the saddest of circumstances. Their literary legacy serves as a testament to the resilience of the human spirit, which always yearns for freedom and justice, even in the face of the darkest and most inexplicable shadows of evil.

246.   Nausea (Jean-Paul Sartre, 1938)

> *"Through the lack of attaching myself to words,*
> *my thoughts remain nebulous most of the time.*
> *They sketch vague, pleasant shapes and then are swallowed up;*
> *I forget them almost immediately."*

> — *Jean-Paul Sarte, Nausea*

Set in the dreary, fictional French town of Bouville, the novel is woven with brooding, atmospheric prose that reflects Roquentin's tormenting sensations of *nausea*, his intense disgust, and alienation as he confronts the raw, absurd essence of existence. Roquentin, a historian, finds himself plagued by a visceral sense of revulsion towards the mundane objects and affairs of daily life. This *nausea* is emblematic of his profound disorientation and despair as he grapples with the idea that life may lack inherent meaning or purpose. His diary entries, which form the bulk of the novel, chronicle his terrifying epiphanies and relentless search for meaning beyond societal constructs. As the bleakness of Bouville envelops him, Roquentin's thoughts often dissolve into nebulous forms. This reflects his indecisive struggle between finding solace in pleasant illusions or confronting the possibly meaningless void. His interactions with other characters, such as the Self-Taught Man or Anny, further sharpen his existential crisis. They are mirrors reflecting different facets of human coping mechanisms and the desperate quest for significance in a seemingly indifferent world. In the climax of his despair, Roquentin undergoes a catharsis. He realizes freedom lies in embracing the absurdity and creating one's essence through action. Through a final, somewhat liberating revelation, he perceives the sheer contingency of existence and assumes the responsibility of carving his path without needing external validations.

Nausea reminds us that our lives may fundamentally lack inherent meaning. Still, we can construct our identities and find purpose by embracing our freedom and taking responsibility.

247.   The Theatre and Its Double (Antonin Artaud, 1938)

> *"The true theater, because it moves and makes use of living instruments, continues to stir up shadows where life has never ceased to grope its way."*

— Antonin Artaud, *The Theatre and Its Double*

The Theatre and Its Double is a manifesto that reimagines the very fabric of theatre. Evoking the rawness of human emotions and the underlying currents of society, Artaud heralds a call to awaken the dormant power of *theatrical performance*. For Artaud, the theatre transcends mere entertainment. It can potentially be a *sanctuary* where reality is deconstructed and rebuilt, casting away the shadows of the societal façade. Unlike the traditional theatre that he deemed superficial and ensnared in spectacle, Artaud championed the *Theatre of Cruelty*. However, this term should not be misconstrued. The cruelty Artaud refers to is not sadism or an embrace of violence for its own sake but instead an unflinching encounter with the raw, unadulterated aspects of existence. In the *Theatre of Cruelty*, senses are assailed, perceptions challenged, and the psyche shattered and remolded. Through visceral images, thundering sounds, and piercing lights, the theatre becomes an alchemical reaction where the boundaries of consciousness dissolve. Words, though present, do not reign supreme; instead, the language of the body, space, and sensory stimuli articulate the unutterable. Artaud also addresses the role of the actor, who is not just a character but a conduit. Through physicality, voice, and communion with the audience, the actor embodies the primal forces that the *Theatre of Cruelty* seeks to unleash. It is a *mutual metamorphosis* – the actor changes within the crucible, and the encounter transforms the audience.

This seminal work forever altered the theatre landscape, enriching it with a depth and urgency that continue reverberating through contemporary performance art.

248.   The Grapes of Wrath (John Steinbeck, 1939)

"If you're in trouble or hurt or need
– go to poor people.
They're the only ones that'll help
– the only ones."

— *John Steinbeck, The Grapes of Wrath*

This powerful novel describes the struggles of the Joad family during the *Great Depression*. Like thousands of others known as *Okies*, the family is forced to abandon their farm in the Dust Bowl of Oklahoma due to environmental devastation and economic despair. Steinbeck captures the essence of desperation as the Joads embark on an arduous journey along *Route 66*, with a flicker of hope towards the promises of California, a land rumored to be flowing with opportunities. The book depicts the physical hardships they endure and the emotional toll as their dreams are repeatedly crushed. Steinbeck's narrative is masterful. He weaves the Joads' personal journey with broader social and economic issues. Though symbolic, the Grapes in the title bitterly manifest in the lives of the Joads and their fellow migrants as fruits of hope that are continually soured by the harsh realities they face. Along their journey, the resilience and unity of the Joad family are tested. Steinbeck meticulously details how their struggles symbolize the collective hardships countless families faced during this era. However, as the Joads arrive in California, they are met not with the abundance they envisioned but with disdain, exploitation, and squalor. They find themselves trapped in a cycle of poverty, with scant opportunities for employment and a system rigged against the working poor.

The Grapes of Wrath is a cultural outcry. Steinbeck's evocative prose and compelling characters starkly depict the sheer tenacity of the human spirit amid insurmountable adversities. The author's use of symbolism and imagery helps to bring his characters' struggles to life.

249.   And Then There Were None (Agatha Christie, 1939)

> *"There were, I considered,*
> *amongst my guests, varying degrees of guilt.*
> *Those whose guilt was the lightest should, I considered,*
> *pass out first, and not suffer the prolonged mental strain and fear*
> *that the more cold-blooded offenders were to suffer."*

> — *Agatha Christie, And Then There Were None*

And Then There Were None introduces us to an intriguing tale that takes us on a secluded island off the coast of Devon, England. Burdened by guilt over their past crimes, eight strangers gather under the assumption of a mysterious host's presence. However, it becomes apparent that their host is absent, leaving them isolated and vulnerable. As they begin to realize that each guest is being systematically murdered, panic rises, and a desperate fight for survival ensues. The tension escalates with each death, leaving only Vera Claythorne and Dr. Armstrong as the last survivors. In a shocking revelation, the mastermind behind the killings is exposed as Justice Wargrave, a former judge who staged his death to execute his twisted form of *private justice*. In a cruel twist of fate, both remaining individuals meet their demise through suicide or exhaustion, having been stranded on the island without sustenance. Agatha Christie's And Then There Were None is a testament to her remarkable storytelling prowess, intricately woven plot, and gripping writing style that keeps readers on edge until the final pages.

Since its publication, this timeless murder mystery has captivated readers worldwide, thanks to its skillful use of red herrings and unexpected plot twists. It remains a cherished classic in the realm of literature, offering not only a thrilling narrative but also insights into morality and justice within society. Christie's deft characterization and climactic setting further enhance the depth of this intricate masterpiece, making it a must-read for mystery genre fans.

250. For Whom the Bell Tolls (Ernest Hemingway, 1940)

"There's no one thing that's true. It's all true."

— *Ernest Hemingway, For Whom the Bell Tolls*

The novel focuses on Robert Jordan, an American College professor who volunteers to join the *Republican forces* of the *Spanish Civil War* in 1937. He is on a dangerous mission to destroy a bridge critical to the *Nationalists*, aided by a motley group of guerilla fighters. As Jordan immerses himself in the mountainous landscape and the lives of the guerilla fighters, he faces not just the external strife of war but an internal struggle. He grapples with the nature of conflict, human life's values, and evolving perceptions of duty. The rugged Spanish terrain and the relentless atmosphere of war serve as the backdrop for Jordan's journey. A central element of the story is the bond that Jordan forms with Maria, a young woman scarred by the atrocities of war. Their love blossoms amid the chaos, offering a glimpse of hope and solace. This romance is interwoven with the harsh realities of war, painting a stark contrast between the fragility of human connection and the brutality of the conflict. Through camaraderie among the guerilla fighters, we witness glimpses of resilience and sacrifice. However, internal divisions within the group, especially the wavering loyalties of their leader Pablo, add tension. The novel reaches its climax as Jordan executes his mission to blow up the bridge. However, the toll of the war is exacted on the battlefield *and* also on the soul. As Jordan lies injured, waiting for the final confrontation with death, he reflects on the interconnectedness of humanity.

For Whom the Bell Tolls is an eloquent examination of war and the human condition. Hemingway's terse prose and the intricate interplay of themes like love, loyalty, and sacrifice make it an enduring classic. The novel captures the essence of John Donne's words that "no man is an island," emphasizing that each man's demise diminishes humanity, and when the bell tolls, it tolls for all.

251.   The Tartar Steppe (Dino Buzzati, 1940)

"In the dream, there is always something absurd and confusing,
and one never gets rid of the vague feeling that it is all false,
that one fine moment one will have to wake up."

— *Dino Buzzati, The Tartar Steppe*

At the heart of this tale is Giovanni Drogo, a young officer whose eager anticipation for glory leads him to a desolate fortress perched on the border of an ominous expanse known as the *Tartar Steppe*. The atmosphere at the fort is soaked in an eerie stagnation. The men there await an enemy that might never come, and Drogo's initial enthusiasm for adventure and heroism gradually turns to despair and disillusionment as the days melt into one another. Buzzati masterfully conjures an otherworldly mood that seems like a thick fog, reflecting Drogo's internal struggle with his self-imposed exile and the unrelenting passage of time. As seasons fall away, Drogo's yearning for meaning refuses to subside. His life becomes a metaphor for the human condition. His wait is emblematic of the existential desire for purpose and fulfillment that often eludes our grasp. The barren steppe outside the fort symbolizes a physical wilderness and an emotional and spiritual void. Drogo ventures into the steppe in a desperate attempt to break free from the shackles of his monotonous existence. But instead of adventure, he finds a desolate emptiness that mirrors the void within him. A revelation ensues. In all its vast indifference, the steppe forces him to confront the arbitrary nature of his dreams. Returning to the fort, Drogo finds solace not in the heroic endeavors he once imagined but in the bonds forged with his fellow soldiers and the realization of life's intrinsic value.

Through beautiful prose and haunting imagery, Buzzati challenges the reader to consider the fragile human pursuit of meaning amidst the inexorable passage of time, highlighting existential themes universal to the human condition.

The Tartar Steppe

252.   The Stranger (Albert Camus, 1942)

"I may not have been sure about what really did interest me,
but I was absolutely sure about what didn't."

— *Albert Camus, The Stranger*

The protagonist Meursault, is a French-Algerian who epitomizes indifference and emotional detachment. The story unfolds in Algiers, beginning with Meursault attending his mother's funeral without displaying any emotion. This lack of grief sets the stage for his perpetual disconnection from society and its norms. Meursault lives in the present moment, indulging in sensory experiences without contemplating future consequences or adhering to societal expectations. This is not out of apathy but stems from his *refusal to ascribe conventional moral categories* to his emotions and actions. His detachment becomes a defining trait that isolates him, making him a stranger among his peers. When Meursault commits murder by impulsively shooting an Arab man, his subsequent trial becomes less about the crime and more about his character. The court is disturbed not just by his violent act but also by his *lack of conventional emotional responses*, refusal to conform to social norms, and apparent rejection of any deeper meaning in life. Meursault's ultimate conviction reflects society's inability to tolerate an individual who does not conform to its expectations. In the final moments, as Meursault awaits execution, he has an internal reckoning. He does not find traditional meaning or redemption but embraces the *indifferent nature of the universe*. He accepts the randomness of existence and the absence of cosmic order and, in doing so, accepts his fate without any plea for sympathy or divine intervention.

The Stranger is a stark philosophical exploration of existentialism. Camus invites the reader to confront the unsettling notion that life might be devoid of inherent meaning. Meursault's audacious embrace of his authenticity makes him a quintessential antihero.

253.   Being and Nothingness (Jean-Paul Sartre, 1943)

> *"If existence really does precede essence,*
> *there is no explaining things away*
> *by reference to a fixed and given human nature."*

— *Jean-Paul Sartre, Being and Nothingness*

Being and Nothingness is a monumental work that has become a cornerstone of existentialist philosophy. One of the critical concepts is the idea that *existence precedes essence*. This notion challenges the traditional view that there is a fixed human nature or essence that determines our actions and values. Instead, Sartre posits that individuals are *radically free* and must create their own identity through their choices and actions. This freedom, according to Sartre, is double-edged. On the one hand, it empowers individuals by recognizing their capacity to shape their destiny. On the other hand, it leads to a profound sense of anguish, as it comes with the realization that there are no inherent values or meanings in the world to guide our choices. A central concept is the notion of *nothingness*, which Sartre believes is at the heart of human consciousness. He associates nothingness with *negation* and argues that *consciousness differentiates itself from the external world through the process of dissolution.* The negation associated with nothingness allows for this freedom, allowing individuals to envision alternatives, question the status quo, and thus exercise freedom. Sartre also introduces the notion of *bad faith*. This concept refers to the psychological phenomenon where individuals deceive themselves into believing they are not free and, therefore, not responsible for their actions. According to Sartre, bad faith is a form of self-denial that leads to *inauthentic living* and unhappiness.

Being and Nothingness is a philosophically dense and intellectually challenging work that delves into the nature of human existence, freedom, and responsibility. It encourages readers to embrace the possibilities and burdens of their liberty and strive for authenticity.

254.   The Little Prince (Antoine de Saint-Exupéry, 1943)

> *"It is only with the heart that one can see rightly;*
> *what is essential is invisible to the eye."*

— *Antoine de Saint-Exupéry, The Little Prince*

Antoine de Saint-Exupéry crafts a literary gem that is part allegory, part philosophical treatise. The story unfurls through the recollections of an aviator who finds himself marooned in the vastness of the Sahara Desert. Here, he is graced by the enigmatic presence of a young boy, the eponymous Little Prince, whose tales are woven with the ardor of a cosmic odyssey. The Little Prince, an interstellar wayfarer, hails from an asteroid and is on a quest to fathom the complicated nature of the adult world. His celestial sojourns have led him to meet a motley assembly of characters, each embodying myopia and foibles of adulthood. A tyrannical king bereft of subjects, a lugubrious drunkard, and a man consumed by vanity are but a few of the souls he encounters. These vignettes serve as a mirror, reflecting the perplexities and contradictions inherent in the human experience. As the aviator is drawn into the Little Prince's sagas, he becomes cognizant of the sagacity beneath the boy's naïve façade. The journey takes on a poignant hue as the Little Prince's ultimate longing is revealed: a singular rose he cherished and left behind on his asteroid. This rose epitomizes the ineffable essence of love and connection, elements that transcend material possessions and societal accolades. Through their shared experiences, the aviator and the Prince discern the verities underpinning existence: "What matters most in life isn't what we have or where we go but rather whom we choose to love."

With lyrical prose and ethereal illustrations, The Little Prince is an ode to the wonderment of childhood, the pursuit of meaning, and the bonds that animate the human spirit.

The Little Prince

255.　　Ficciones (Jorge Luis Borges, 1944)

> *"A book is not an isolated being:*
> *it is a relationship, an axis of innumerable relationships."*
>
> —— *Jorge Luis Borges, Ficciones*

Ficciones is a compilation of short stories that are woven with the threads of magical realism and an undercurrent of philosophical introspection. The anthology is divided into two sections, each an exquisite tapestry of narrative innovation. The first, *The Garden of Forking Paths*, is suffused with a dreamlike aura where characters navigate symbolic and allegorical landscapes. The reader traverses a multilayered maze with a Chinese scholar, who, upon unearthing an ancient manuscript of labyrinthine narratives, is led to believe in his ability to shape destiny. The phantasmagoric stories of this section, layered with enigmas, beckon the reader into an otherworldly realm where logic often gracefully bows to the unfathomable. The second section, *Artifices*, continues the exploration with a more pronounced philosophical tinge. *The Library of Babel* envisages a universe as an interminable library brimming with books that possess every conceivable permutation of letters. This seemingly boundless realm epitomizes the inscrutability of existence and knowledge. In *Death and the Compass*, a detective's methodical quest to untangle a murder unravels into a metaphysical journey that transcends human agency. *Tlön, Uqbar, Orbis Tertius* is a formidable exploration of a clandestinely conceived universe molded by ideational constructs, which threatens to supersede our reality.

With his alchemy of poetic language and erudition, Jorge Luis Borges constructs a mesmerizing universe. His storytelling challenges conventional temporal and spatial constructs and embraces the paradoxical and the arcane. Allegories, parables, and metaphysical contemplation invite readers to step across the threshold into a world where boundaries dissolve and reality is iridescent with infinite possibilities.

256.   Gigi (Sidonie-Gabrielle Colette, 1944)

"It's delightful when your imaginations come true,
isn't it?"

— *Sidonie-Gabrielle Colette, Gigi*

Gigi is a spirited and ambitious young woman living in early 20th-century Paris under the watchful care of her grandmother Madame Alvarez and her great-aunt Alicia. Born into a family of courtesans, Gigi is meticulously groomed to follow in their footsteps. The novel contrasts youth's vivacity and innocence with the time's rigid societal norms. Gigi's life takes a turn when she starts spending time with Gaston Lachaille, a wealthy Parisian playboy and family friend who is weary of his empty, high-society lifestyle. Their interaction sparks a genuine connection that takes both by surprise. As Gaston starts to appreciate Gigi's unpretentious nature, Gigi herself becomes more aware of her feelings toward him. As her family pressures her into becoming Gaston's courtesan, Gigi defies expectations. She refuses to be bound by the constraints of society, asserting herself and expressing her desire for an honest and committed relationship if they are to be together. Through vibrant descriptions and witticism, Colette captures the essence of Parisian culture and the strict societal codes of the *Belle Époque* period. Gigi's character embodies youthful exuberance, wit, and a willful nature that challenges the established norms. The narrative also exposes the underlying currents of gender roles and the commodification of relationships within society.

Colette weaves an enchanting tale of growth, self-determination, and the strength to forge one's path. Through Gigi's audacious character and journey, the novella continues to resonate as a timeless exploration of love, social expectations, and the indomitable spirit of youth.

257.   Animal Farm (George Orwell, 1945)

> *"All animals are equal,*
> *but some animals are more equal than others."*
>
> —— *George Orwell, Animal Farm*

Animal Farm is an allegorical novel that deftly depicts the consequences of a *revolution that leads to totalitarianism.* The story is set on a farm owned by Mr. Jones, a neglectful farmer who frequently fails to fulfill his responsibilities and mistreats his animals. One night, the animals assemble to listen to Old Major's speech in which the old boar speaks about the need to rebel against human oppressors and establish an *egalitarian society.* Following Old Major's death, two pigs named Snowball and Napoleon step up to lead the revolt. They succeed in ousting Mr. Jones and take control of the farm. The animals establish a system of beliefs known as *Animalism*, which asserts that all animals are equal. Despite this principle, disagreements between Snowball and Napoleon on governance lead to conflict. Napoleon uses guard dogs as enforcers to seize control, and Snowball is driven from the farm. Napoleon, now a dictator, along with Squealer, who serves as his propagandist, alters and manipulates the Seven Commandments of Animalism to justify his increasingly oppressive rule. As the novel progresses, the pigs become more human-like in their behavior and governance, eroding the initial ideals of the revolution. Among the animals, an aged and cynical donkey named Benjamin remains skeptical. He sees through the propaganda and understands the corrupt nature of the new leadership, holding pessimistic views regarding positive change.

Animal Farm is a sharp critique of totalitarian regimes, particularly focusing on the Soviet Union under Joseph Stalin. Through his storytelling, George Orwell illustrates how noble ideals can be perverted and manipulated by unscrupulous individuals seeking power. The novel serves as a cautionary tale, highlighting the dangers of concentrated power and manipulation.

258.   The Open Society and Its Enemies (Karl Popper, 1945)

"Unlimited tolerance must lead to the disappearance of tolerance."

—— *Karl Popper, The Open Society*

The Open Society and Its Enemies is an influential two-volume work that engages in an incisive analysis of the philosophy of science, politics, and history. Popper suggests that there are two main types of societies: *closed* and *open*; the closed ones rely on authority, tradition, and blind faith; the open ones accept criticism as part of their culture, allowing them to progress further than closed societies over time. In the first volume *The Spell of Plato*, Popper examines Plato's political philosophy. He argues that Plato's call for a *utopian society* with a rigid hierarchical structure was a reaction to the perceived decay of the tribal culture and that his philosophical positions were fundamentally totalitarian. The second volume *The High Tide of Prophecy: Hegel, Marx, and the Aftermath* focuses on the historicism in Hegel's and Marx's theories. Popper contends that their dialectical method and deterministic approach to history are antithetical to the principles of the open society. He criticizes Marx's *historical materialism* and predicts the eventual collapse of the Marxist social structure due to its internal contradictions. Popper's advocacy for an open society is rooted in his belief in the necessity of critical discourse, individual freedom, and the evolutionary development of social institutions. He opines that communities should be amenable to reform without violence or revolution, and he underlines the significance of piecemeal social engineering, which calls for implementing small changes to address social issues.

The Open Society and Its Enemies is an erudite, meticulously researched work that stands as a bastion for democratic values and human freedom. It is not merely a critique of historicism but an impassioned plea for continuously examining our societal constructs through critical rationalism.

259.   Man's Search for Meaning (Viktor Frankl, 1945)

"Everything can be taken from a man but one thing:
the last of the human freedoms to choose one's attitude
in any given set of circumstances, to choose one's own way."

— *Viktor Frankl, Man's Search for Meaning*

Viktor Frankl was an Austrian neurologist and psychiatrist, and Holocaust survivor. The book is divided into two parts: the first recounts Frankl's harrowing experiences in Nazi concentration camps during *World War II*; while the second introduces his psychotherapeutic method called *logotherapy*, centered on the human pursuit of *meaning*. In the first section, Frankl does not merely describe the brutalities he faced, but instead, he delves into the psychological impact and the spiritual experiences that arose from them. He depicts the agony, the intermittent moments of reprieve, and the mental fortitude required to withstand the unimaginable. Frankl posits that even in the direst circumstances, the individual retains the ability to choose their attitude and find meaning in suffering. The second section, focusing on logotherapy, establishes that life's primary motivational force is the *search for meaning*. Frankl critiques the Freudian notion that pleasure is the central pursuit of human life. He asserts that meaning can be found in three ways: by creating or doing something, experiencing love or connection, and preparing ourselves for unavoidable suffering. One of the key strengths of the book is Frankl's ability to combine personal narrative with psychotherapeutic insights. His experiences provide a visceral understanding of his theoretical propositions.

Man's Search for Meaning is an indomitable work that explores the darkest depths of human experience and emerges with a message of hope and purpose. Its combination of autobiography and psychological theory offers readers a unique lens through which to examine their lives. Frankl's work is a testament to the resilience of the human spirit and the relentless pursuit of meaning that defines our existence.

260.   Paroles (Jacques Prévert, 1946)

"Our Father who art in heaven
Stay there
And we'll stay here on earth"

— *Jacques Prévert, Paroles*

Paroles includes poems about the beauty and fragility of life, as well as its hardships and sorrows. The opening quote is a good representation of Prévert's style and reflects Prévert's inclination to challenge traditional norms and often be irreverent. In many of his pieces, Prévert explores themes such as love, death, loneliness, nature, and freedom. The first poem, *Dans le vieux parc solitaire et glacé* (In the old solitary and icy park), starts with a lonely man who takes a walk through an empty park at night. He reflects on how time passes quickly while he feels as if he were standing still. Other poems explore topics such as childhood memories (*Les enfants qui s'aiment*), joys of life (*La joie de vivre*), and dreams for the future (*Le rêve*). The issue of mortality is explored in several works, including *Chanson d'automne*, which speaks of the inevitability that one day we will all die; however, this should not stop us from enjoying our lives now while we can. Another piece, *Rien n'est plus beau que la vie* (Nothing is more beautiful than life), celebrates life's joys despite its fragility and fleeting. Prévert also writes about social issues such as poverty (*Vendredi Saint à La Salpêtrière*) and war (*Lumières de lune sur les ruines*). His work emphasizes that even during troubling times, there can be moments of lightness or hope if people choose to see them.

Jacques Prévert's Paroles is a poetic masterpiece that offers a thought-provoking look at the human condition. Through his masterful use of imagery and metaphor, Prévert paints expressive pictures of inner turmoil and longing for companionship, capturing life's beauty and tragedy. His clever wordplay brings to life the struggles each person faces in their search for meaning in the world around them.

261.   A Streetcar Named Desire (Tennessee Williams, 1947)

"Whoever you are,
I have always depended on the kindness of strangers."

— *Tennessee Williams, A Streetcar Named Desire*

The Pulitzer Prize-winning play is set in the vibrant *French Quarter* of *post-World War II* New Orleans. The play immerses us in the life and turmoil of Blanche DuBois, a woman from a declining aristocratic family in the *American South*. Blanche arrives in New Orleans to stay with her sister Stella and her brutish husband Stanley Kowalski, who is of Polish descent and represents the rising working class. Blanche's cultured and refined demeanor contrasts sharply with Stanley's coarse and primal nature. Blanche's seemingly aristocratic poise masks a life of desperation and loss, including the loss of the family estate Belle Reve. She also harbors a fragile mental state, exacerbated by a series of tragic events in her past. Stanley, deeply suspicious of Blanche, uncovers the truth about her past and takes aggressive steps to expose her, leading to an escalating tension. Meanwhile, a romantic relationship begins to blossom between Blanche and Stanley's friend Mitch. This relationship represents a glimmer of hope for Blanche but crumbles under the weight of her secrets and Stanley's relentless antagonism. The quote at the beginning reflects her vulnerability and her tragic dependence on others for validation and support, often from strangers. As the story reaches its climax, Blanche's grip on reality weakens. The culmination of her fractured relationship with Stanley leads to a harrowing confrontation scene. Eventually, Blanche is committed to a mental institution, signifying her final descent into a world divorced from reality.

The play is a masterful exploration of the clash of social classes, mental health fragility, and relationships' complex nature. Tennessee Williams' richly drawn characters and the play's atmospheric setting create a powerful and haunting commentary on loss and the human capacity for destruction.

262.   The Diary of a Young Girl (Anne Frank, 1947)

"Think of all the beauty still left around you and be happy."

— Anne Frank, *The Diary of a Young Girl*

The Diary is a touching chronicle of a young Jewish girl forced into hiding with her family and friends in an attic in Amsterdam during the harrowing years of *World War II*. On July 6th, 1942, her family retreats into the concealed refuge that will become their world of enforced silence during daylight hours, trepidation whenever footsteps approach, and desperate concealment whenever visitors arrive. Anne forms deep connections with her companions in confinement, forging a particularly profound bond with Peter Van Pels. Amidst the monotony of their seclusion, rays of hope pierce the darkness when they receive precious gifts from Miep Gies, the courageous office secretary who assists in their concealment. While the ever-present fear of discovery plagues Anne's thoughts, she finds solace in the world of literature, immersing herself in books, especially those that transport her to the peaceful realm of nature. Her pen becomes an instrument of respite, crafting poems and stories that envision a future where freedom reigns. As the grip of war tightens, 1944 heralds a chilling turn of events. The increasing peril faced by Jews across Europe casts a shadow of dread over Anne and her companions, intensifying their fears of being discovered. In the heart-wrenching month of August, their worst fears are realized when German police unveil their hidden place, condemning all eight occupants to the clutches of concentration camps. None survive, except Anne Frank's father Otto Frank and Miep Gies, who discovers Anne's diary after their departure, preserving it as a testament that refuses to be silenced.

The Diary is a powerful testament of courage, hope, and resilience even in times of darkness; it stands today as an undeniable reminder that no matter how bleak things may seem, there is always hope.

263. If This Is a Man, Survival in Auschwitz (Primo Levi, 1947)

"I am constantly amazed by man's inhumanity to man."

— *Primo Levi, If This Is a Man*

Levi's haunting memoir bears witness to his harrowing journey as an Italian Jew deported to Auschwitz. His words paint heartbreaking pictures of the inescapable realities endured by prisoners, from the grueling labor imposed upon them to the relentless and capricious beatings inflicted by their captors. The memoir unflinchingly lays bare the stark deprivation of sustenance, clothing, and medical aid, as prisoners fight valiantly to preserve their lives amidst the barren wasteland of suffering. Yet, amidst the desolation, Levi's unwavering spirit shines through, illuminating the indomitable human capacity for resilience and dignity. His poignant recollections witness the devastating toll inflicted upon those who lost hope or succumbed to illness. Cruelty bore no rationale within the camp's confines, and Levi's observations unveil the arbitrary and unpredictable nature of suffering. As the tides of war shift, liberation arrives, though not without its own set of trials. Soviet forces discover Auschwitz, largely abandoned by German forces, with the remaining prisoners, including Levi, in a state of grave illness. They provide much-needed medical aid and begin the arduous process of recovery for the survivors. Levi's memoir concludes with reflections on the resounding impact of his experiences as he contemplates the meaning of life in the aftermath of such immense suffering.

Levi's memoir is a testament to the indomitable human spirit forged amidst the darkest corners of history. His words are a solemn reminder that even in the face of unimaginable darkness, the human spirit possesses an unwavering capacity to seek solace, find meaning, and emerge triumphant. His reflective approach to his horrific experiences not only narrates personal survival but also serves as an enduring critique of totalitarianism and anti-Semitism.

THE POST-WAR ERA

THE POST-WAR ERA

The post-war literary landscape of the 1950s and 1960s reverberated with a profound sense of disillusionment and alienation forged in the crucible of the devastating *Second World War*. Emerging from the ashes of destruction, this era bore witness to a remarkable confluence of transformative movements, including *Existentialism*, the *Beat Generation*, and the *Civil Rights Movement*, resounding through the veins of literature and culture.

Within this literary landscape, one eminent figure stood tall: Samuel Beckett, an Irish playwright and novelist whose name became synonymous with the existential angst and nihilism that permeated the post-war ethos. Beckett's magnum opus, *Waiting for Godot*, epitomizes the human condition in the wake of cataclysmic events, as his characters find themselves caught in the clutches of absurdity and the futility of existence.

Alongside Beckett, another indelible voice resonated throughout the era: Jack Kerouac, an emblematic figure of the Beat Generation. Kerouac's iconic novel, *On the Road*, unfurled like a manifesto of freedom, rebellion, and unabashed non-conformity, encapsulating the yearning for liberation from the shackles of a rigid society. With a celebration of spontaneity, individualism, and a rejection of the mainstream, Kerouac's words kindled the flames of countercultural fervor.

Among the leading literary figures, J.D. Salinger shone brightly with his novel *The Catcher in the Rye* becoming an emblematic touchstone for disenchanted youth navigating a rapidly shifting world. Through the eyes of the iconic protagonist Holden Caulfield, Salinger painted a poignant portrait of a disaffected teenager desperately seeking authenticity and railing against the stifling expectations imposed by family and society. The novel is a permanent testament to the perennial struggle of coming of age and the quest for self-discovery.

Entrenched within these writers' somber tones and bleak narratives lies an echoic critique of their time's social and political structures. By plunging into the depths of individual experience, they laid bare the inherent meaninglessness and oppressive forces that afflicted society. Their words were a rallying cry, beckoning future generations to question the status quo, challenge oppressive systems, and strive relentlessly toward a more just and equitable world.

Amid desolation, these writers unearthed the shards of hope, infusing their works with a profound understanding of the human condition. Through their gripping narratives and cleverly employed rhetorical tools, they urged readers to confront the existential abyss, grapple with the complexities of their existence, and ultimately emerge with a renewed sense of purpose and a burning desire for a better tomorrow. Their literary contributions remain enduring beacons, illuminating the path toward a more compassionate and enlightened future.

264.   The Second Sex (Simone de Beauvoir, 1949)

"No one is more arrogant toward women,
more aggressive or scornful,
than the man
who is anxious about his virility."

—— *Simone de Beauvoir, The Second Sex*

The Second Sex is an analysis of the historical and social construction of women's oppression. In it, Beauvoir argues that women have been relegated to a secondary status by men throughout history. She claims that gender roles are imposed upon women from birth and reinforced through education and other institutions such as marriage and religion. Beauvoir outlines how patriarchy perpetuates itself by maintaining control over female sexuality through laws governing reproductive rights, abortion access, and contraception availability. She also discusses the ways in which traditional marriages limit personal freedom for both men and women while providing economic benefits for the husband only. She gives examples of historical figures such as Joan of Arc or Rosa Luxemburg, who exemplify the defiance of oppressive gender norms. Simone de Beauvoir powerfully argues that women must be liberated *from* their subordinate position if true equality is ever going to be achieved between genders; it is up to every individual person – man or woman – to fight against injustice wherever they see it within society so that future generations can enjoy greater freedoms than those currently enjoyed.

De Beauvoir argues that men have created a one-sided view of women as the "Other," which serves to gravely mistreat them through stereotypes based on false assumptions about biology, gender roles, and female sexuality. Beauvoir's groundbreaking use of existential philosophy to analyze women's oppression paved the way for subsequent feminist theories.

265.   Death of a Salesman (Arthur Miller, 1949)

"Sometimes...it's better for a man
just to walk away.
But if you can't walk away?
I guess that's when it's tough."

—— *Arthur Miller, Death of a Salesman*

Death of a Salesman is an iconic play about Willy Loman, an aging salesman who has worked the same job for over thirty years. He struggles to make ends meet, and his career prospects are bleak. His two sons, Biff and Happy, have grown up with their father's dreams of success but have yet to achieve any success in life themselves. Willy desperately clings to the belief that he can still make something out of himself through hard work and determination, even as he begins to slip into senility due to age-related issues such as memory loss and confusion. As his family struggles financially, Willy grows increasingly desperate, eventually resorting to drastic measures that lead him down a path of self-destruction. The play follows Willy's journey from hopeful optimism about providing for his family, despite all odds, to his eventual demise after repeatedly failing to reach his goal. At its core, Death of a Salesman is about how we define success – not necessarily by money or material possessions but rather by our relationships with those we love most deeply – and what happens when our dreams do not come true. Miller captures what it means for us when we fail at achieving our goals: sadness mixed with acceptance.

What makes Death of a Salesman especially gripping is its critical examination of the 'American Dream,' demonstrating the disillusionment of those chasing unattainable ideals. With its deep characterization and intense dialogue, this classic continues to be studied today for its insights into human nature and society.

266.   Nineteen Eighty-Four (George Orwell, 1949)

*"If you want a picture of the future,
imagine a boot stamping on a human face – for ever."*

—— *George Orwell, Nineteen Eighty-Four*

In this dystopian novel, we find ourselves immersed in the chilling future of Oceania, a fictional state governed by an omnipotent and malevolent entity known as *The Party*. Under its iron grip, citizens live ensnared in a web of oppression, subjected to ceaseless surveillance and mercilessly punished for the slightest deviation from orthodoxy. At the helm of this totalitarian regime stands the enigmatic figure of Big Brother, an object of veneration and dread. Our guide through this bleak landscape is Winston Smith, a seemingly obedient denizen of Oceania who dares to nurture subversive thoughts and dreams of liberation. Driven by an insatiable hunger for freedom, Winston embarks on a path of rebellion, ultimately encountering the clandestine resistance organization known as *The Brotherhood*. Here, he discovers a kindred spirit in Julia, a comrade who shares his yearning for liberation – their forbidden love blossoms amidst the suffocating shadows, a defiant act against the Party's strict control. But the walls have ears, and their audacity does not go unnoticed. The merciless agents of the Thought Police descend upon them, shattering their fragile oasis of rebellion. Desperate and broken, Winston's spirit withers as he succumbs to the Party's ruthless will. In a final act of betrayal, Winston denounces Julia, sacrificing their bond in a last-ditch effort to preserve himself.

Through the deft strokes of George Orwell's pen, Nineteen Eighty-Four unveils a haunting vision of a society consumed by totalitarianism. It compels us to confront the darkest corners of human nature and the fragility of our individuality in the face of oppressive regimes.

267.   The Labyrinth of Solitude (Octavio Paz, 1950)

"Love is an attempt to penetrate another being,
but it can only be realized if the surrender is mutual."

— *Octavio Paz, The Labyrinth of Solitude*

The Labyrinth of Solitude is a collection of essays examining
Mexican identity and culture. In these essays, Paz discusses the
influences of Spanish colonialism and Catholicism on modern
Mexico and its unique characteristics. He argues that Mexicans
have developed a sense of *duality* in their identity – a public face
they present to outsiders while maintaining an inner solitude
that only those close can see. Paz also examines how foreign
powers like Spain, France, and the United States have shaped
Mexican history. He explores concepts such as *death symbolism* in
art and traditional festivals like the Day of the Dead (*Día de los
Muertos*), where Paz uncovers the intricate symbolism behind
the colorful altars, marigolds, sugar skulls, and offerings,
revealing how they serve as powerful expressions of Mexico's
cultural identity and its unique relationship with death. Paz also
examines the pre-Columbian concept of *Mictlán*, the realm of
the dead in Aztec mythology. In his conclusion, Paz asserts that
despite all its complexities, Mexico remains full of hope for a
better future, where individuals can express themselves more
freely without sacrificing their cultural heritage or national
pride. As the world landscape continues to change, Paz
anticipates potential paths forward for the evolving identity of
this fascinating nation.

The Labyrinth of Solitude explores the cultural and psychological identity
of Mexican people. Through lyrical and philosophical prose, Paz reveals
how centuries of oppression by colonial and foreign powers have shaped the
nation's collective consciousness and sense of self-worth. He examines pre-
Hispanic cultures, emphasizing ritualized sacrifice, and post-Independence
movements which sought to redefine national identity in terms of modernity.

The Labyrinth of Solitude

268.   The Catcher in the Rye (J.D. Salinger, 1951)

"And I have one of those very loud, stupid laughs.
I mean if I ever sat behind myself in a movie or something,
I'd probably lean over and tell myself to please shut up."

— *J.D. Salinger, The Catcher in the Rye*

Kicked out from his prep school due to academic failures and a penchant for unruly behavior, Holden Caulfield ventures into the bustling landscape of New York City. Throughout this urban expedition, he stumbles across various individuals, each possessing unique perspectives and personal histories. He wrestles with a tumult of emotions, chiefly his apprehension and puzzlement regarding the enigmatic nature of adulthood. His introspection causes him to relentlessly question the *essence of existence and his place within it.* Holden grapples with a profound sense of isolation as his relationships with others fail to provide the deep connection he yearns for. His unsuccessful attempts at reaching out, whether to former teachers or casual acquaintances, only underscore his loneliness and the inaccessibility of genuine human connection. Amid his restless wanderings through the city, a peculiar fixation grips Holden – the ducks that inhabit Central Park and their mysterious whereabouts during the winter. This inquiry is more than mere curiosity; it symbolizes Holden's anxieties about change, transition, and adaptation. It is a metaphor for his fear of moving forward, transitioning from adolescence to adulthood. Holden's urban exploration reaches an emotional climax when he reunites with his beloved younger sister Phoebe, in the quiet seclusion of their parents' apartment. Phoebe is more than just a cherished sibling to Holden; she is a mirror reflecting his vulnerabilities and contradictions.

The novel's protagonist Holden Caulfield embodies the universal adolescent experience of alienation. The Catcher in the Rye is a sociological phenomenon that continues to inspire generations about the complexities of growing up.

269.   Memoirs of Hadrian (Marguerite Yourcenar 1951)

> *"He had reached that moment in life, different for each one of us,*
> *when a man abandons himself to his demon or to his genius,*
> *following a mysterious law which bids him*
> *either to destroy or outdo himself."*

— *Marguerite Yourcenar, Memoirs of Hadrian*

Memoirs of Hadrian is set in the second century AD and follows the life and thoughts of Roman Emperor Hadrian. The novel begins with a letter written to his adopted son Marcus Aurelius, as an attempt to provide him guidance on how to rule successfully. This letter gives readers insight into Hadrian's reflections on his reign and legacy as emperor. He recounts his travels throughout the empire and reflects upon its people, culture, history, and politics. Hadrian also shares stories from childhood that shaped him into the ruler he eventually became. He speaks at length about Antinous, whom he loved deeply but who died young due to mysterious circumstances while they were traveling together in Egypt. The novel culminates with a reflection on death itself – a topic that looms over much of the narrative as it progresses – and concludes with a solemn statement: "Death is no more than passing from one room into another...but there's a difference for me because I know I am going where you cannot follow." This serves as an acknowledgment that although death will inevitably take us all away from our loved ones eventually, those memories remain forever imprinted in our hearts even after we are gone. Marguerite Yourcenar's Memoirs of Hadrian explores what it means to be emperor and what it means to be human – to love deeply yet accept loss gracefully when it comes time for us all to leave this world behind.

Memoirs of Hadrian has been praised for its literary excellence and acclaimed as an innovative work that combines historical fiction with philosophical meditation on the nature and purpose of human life.

270.   The Conformist (Alberto Moravia, 1951)

> *"It's funny, though, you know?*
> *Everyone would like to be different from the others,*
> *but instead you want to be the same as everyone else."*

> —— *Alberto Moravia, The Conformist*

In The Conformist, we are introduced to Marcello Clerici, a man driven by a traumatic childhood incident to aspire to the perceived safety of absolute conformity. Marcello's desperate need for normalcy leads him to embrace the political ideologies of Fascist Italy and to marry Giulia, a woman who epitomizes the conventional life he desperately craves. Marcello's resolve to conform is tested when he accepts a mission to assassinate Professor Quadri, an anti-fascist intellectual who has fled to France. Executing the mission forces Marcello to grapple with the ethical implications of his choices and the price he pays for his obsession with normalcy. Marcello's determination is further challenged when he encounters Professor Quadri and his sensuous wife Lina. The intellectual and sensual freedoms embodied by the Quadris confront Marcello with a world outside his realm of conformity. Their influence awakens suppressed desires and leads him to question his life choices and dedication to obedience. The ensuing internal struggle adds complexity to Marcello's character, exposing the chasm between his public persona and inner self. Despite the intellectual and emotional turmoil stirred by his encounter with the Quadris, Marcello executes the assassination. His action reaffirms his unwavering commitment to conformity. The disturbing culmination of Marcello's mission underscores the devastating impact of his choices on his mental state.

Alberto Moravia's dark, atmospheric narrative is intricately woven with philosophical introspection and psychological depth. His deft character portrayal lures readers into Marcello's tormented psyche, offering a haunting exploration of conformity against the backdrop of a turbulent political era.

271.   The Origins of Totalitarianism (Hannah Arendt, 1951)

"The last century has produced an abundance of ideologies that pretend to be keys to history but are actually nothing but desperate efforts to escape responsibility."

—— Hannah Arendt, The Origins of Totalitarianism

Hannah Arendt examines the rise of totalitarianism in Europe during the 20th century and its unprecedented cruelty toward humanity. She argues that totalitarianism is a new form of government, distinct from other conditions such as despotisms or dictatorships, which relies on terror to control its citizens instead of depending on laws or customs. To explain why this type of government has arisen, she looks at three factors: imperialism, anti-Semitism, and racism. Arendt traces how imperialistic policies led to the creation of large states with diverse populations forced together without any sense of national identity; these people had no allegiance except to their rulers, who exploited them for their own gain while providing little protection against outside forces like invading armies or economic downturns. This created an atmosphere where fear became rampant. People began looking for scapegoats to blame for all their troubles. In many cases, they were Jews since they were often seen as *the other* due to their different religion and culture; thus, anti-Semitism became a powerful tool used by demagogues to manipulate public opinion and gain power through hate speech directed towards Jews (and other minorities). Racism played an essential role in creating an environment where it was acceptable for one group to dominate another based solely on skin color – this allowed political leaders like Hitler to target specific groups within society which he deemed inferior and begin his campaign against them with impunity.

The Origins of Totalitarianism is a seminal work in the field of political theory and shows us that similar horrors can easily be repeated if we ignore our history.

272.   Waiting for Godot (Samuel Beckett, 1953)

> *"Nothing happens.*
> *Nobody comes,*
> *nobody goes.*
> *It's awful."*
>
> — *Samuel Beckett, Waiting for Godot*

In Samuel Beckett's enigmatic play, an iconic piece of the *Theatre of the Absurd*, there are two weary protagonists named Vladimir and Estragon who find themselves in an endless wait for the mysterious Godot. Set in a barren landscape marked by a solitary, withered tree, their days are filled with rambling conversations that fluctuate between the trivial and the existential. They reminisce, jest, and even consider ending their lives, but inertia keeps them bound to their self-appointed task. The monotony is momentarily interrupted by a pompous man named Pozzo and his downtrodden servant Lucky. Their interactions offer bleak commentary on the human condition and social hierarchies. Twice, a young Boy arrives with messages from Godot, each time promising his arrival the following day. As the second act mirrors the first, it becomes evident that Vladimir and Estragon are trapped in a repetitive cycle where waiting takes precedence over action. The nature of Godot remains shrouded in mystery, and the protagonists' anticipations go unfulfilled. The play concludes with Vladimir and Estragon still waiting with their resolutions to leave or act eternally postponed. Waiting for Godot, steeped in absurdism and existential themes, forces the audience to grapple with the meaning of existence and the essence of human perseverance.

Waiting for Godot challenges us to reconcile with the enigmas of life, to find solace within the realms of the unknown, and to embrace the profound wisdom that lies within our limitations. Through the prism of relentless waiting, we confront the reality of the human condition, its absurdities, and the acceptance of the inexplicable.

273.   The Lord of the Rings (J.R.R. Tolkien, 1954-55)

> *"The world is indeed full of peril*
> *and in it there are many dark places."*
>
> — *J.R.R. Tolkien, The Lord of the Rings*

J.R.R. Tolkien transports us to the mythical world of Middle-earth, a realm inhabited by hobbits, elves, dwarves, and humans. The heart of the story lies with Frodo Baggins, a humble hobbit entrusted with a dangerous task - to destroy the One Ring. Created by the Dark Lord Sauron, the Ring's destructive power threatens to plunge the world into eternal darkness. Accompanied by his faithful friend Samwise Gamgee and fellow hobbits Peregrin Took and Meriadoc Brandybuck, Frodo undertakes a perilous journey across Middle-earth. They are joined by an assembly of diverse characters: the wizard Gandalf, whose wisdom guides their path; Aragorn, the ranger destined to reclaim his kingdom; the elf Legolas, a master archer; Gimli, a dwarf with indomitable spirit; and Boromir, a valiant warrior from Gondor. Their mission is fraught with danger, as they must cross treacherous landscapes, evade Sauron's relentless minions, the Nazgûl, and battle vast armies. Despite the odds, their goal remains – to cast the One Ring into the fires of Mount Doom, thus defeating Sauron and preserving the freedom of Middle-earth.

The Lord of the Rings series is a monumental achievement in fantasy literature, woven with intricate mythology, vibrant characterizations, and profound themes that resonate universally. Tolkien's erudition as a professor of Anglo-Saxon and English language and literature at Oxford University shines through his work, particularly in his creation of the Elvish languages, which were influenced by Finnish and Welsh. Some argue the influence of Romanticism in Tolkien's evocative descriptions of nature. Tolkien's contribution extends beyond literature, influencing artists, filmmakers, game designers, and linguists, and continues to generate scholarly and popular interest.

274.   Lolita (Vladimir Nabokov, 1955)

> *Life is short. From here to that old car you know so well*
> *there is a stretch of twenty, twenty-five paces.*
> *It is a very short walk. Make those twenty-five steps.*
> *Now. Right now. Come just as you are.*
> *And we shall live happily ever after.*

> — *Vladimir Nabokov, Lolita*

Vladimir Nabokov's masterpiece presents an unsettling narrative of Humbert, a middle-aged academic who is attracted to nymphets – young girls symbolizing an idealized notion of love. His obsession leads him to a quaint New England town, lodging with Charlotte Haze, a widow with a daughter named Dolores or *Lolita*. Drawn magnetically to Lolita, Humbert maneuvers his way into her life, even marrying Charlotte to stay close to the young girl. Tragically unaware of Humbert's lustful intentions for her daughter, Charlotte dies in an accident, clearing the way for Humbert to bring Lolita more fully into his sphere of influence. Following this, Humbert and Lolita embark on a nomadic journey across the country, constantly moving from one motel to the next to remain unnoticed. Eventually, they settle at Beardsley College, where Humbert returns to his academic pursuits and tightens his hold over Lolita. Despite Humbert's controlling grip, Lolita seeks freedom, connecting with her peers and eventually eloping with Clare Quilty, a man of advanced age with a questionable past. A desperate Humbert, traveling across America, unveils disturbing layers of Quilty's life but only reunites with a transformed Lolita years later – now pregnant and married – far removed from the innocent girl he had exploited.

Lolita is an iconic yet contentious literary work, navigating provocative themes that test the boundaries of ethical perspectives. Composing elegantly crafted prose with its grotesque narrative probes the complexity of human sexuality, merging the line between artistic brilliance and moral ambiguity.

275. Howl (Allen Ginsberg, 1956)

"Follow your inner moonlight, don't hide the madness."

— *Allen Ginsberg, Howl*

Structured in three sections, Howl paints a striking picture of the counterculture and the restless youth of *1950s America*. The opening lines immediately seize the reader's attention with a vivid description of "angel-headed hipsters burning for the ancient heavenly connection to the starry dynamo in the machinery of night," setting the stage for the tumultuous lives of individuals grappling with poverty, addiction, madness, and societal constraints in their search for meaning and enlightenment. Ginsberg pens some of the poem's most iconic lines in this first section, including "I saw the best minds of my generation destroyed by madness." The second section, imbued with a deep sense of personal connection, concentrates on Ginsberg's close friend, Carl Solomon, who was hospitalized due to mental health issues. The final section serves as a touching epilogue, reiterating the motives of the first two sections, such as the pursuit of liberation from societal shackles, and endows the poem with an undertone of hope with reference to love and human compassion. Howl is a poetic roller-coaster, pulsating with Ginsberg's distinctive voice that powerfully resounds against societal injustice and offers a hand of kinship to those trapped in the struggles of life. It is a clarion call for breaking free from conventional norms and channeling an authentic and liberating energy. Ginsberg connects with the reader through charged language and searing imagery and igniting a deep sense of empathy.

Howl is a cornerstone of post-World War II American poetry, and its influence has permeated through subsequent generations of poets who followed in its wake. The poem's raw emotion encapsulates the struggles many faced during that period, urging the reader to acknowledge and contemplate the social and personal hardships conveyed within its lines.

276.   On the Road (Jack Kerouac, 1957)

"Nothing behind me, everything ahead of me, as is ever so on the road."

— *Jack Kerouac, On the Road*

Jack Kerouac's novel is a vibrant chronicle of wanderlust, friendship, and the pursuit of the ineffable, inspired by the author's own cross-country adventures. The narrative is shared through the perspective of Sal Paradise, a character modeled on Kerouac himself. When Sal meets the ex-convict and irrepressible free spirit Dean Moriarty, an indelible bond is quickly formed, setting the stage for their series of meandering road trips across America. Introduced to each other by Sal's friend Carlo Marx, Sal and Dean become the axis around which a diverse group of *Beat Generation* eccentrics revolves. Their unquenchable thirst for new experiences takes them through the *postwar American landscape* – imbued with jazz, poetry, and the raw ardor of youth. Their travels carry them through the vast expanses of the western United States. In San Francisco, they encounter Dean's teenage wife, Camille, who is expectantly pregnant. From there, they move further, reaching Denver, where a reunion occurs between Dean and his estranged father. The itinerary eventually extends to Mexico City, providing an intoxicating, contrasting backdrop for their exploits. Their return to New York City is shadowed by stark realizations of change. But the siren call of the road is irresistible. Sal, the ever nomadic soul, sets off again, with the inimitable Dean joining him soon after. Sal's subsequent journeys sweep him across several more cities, eventually ending in San Francisco. The narrative culminates with Sal's introspective reflection on his multitude of transformative experiences and with his love for *life on the road* – his *freedom*.

On the Road captures an era and a sentiment. The novel's enduring themes of freedom, personal quest, and the embracement of life's myriad possibilities serve as a stirring exploration of self-discovery and authenticity.

On the Road

277.   Zazie dans le métro (Raymond Queneau, 1959)

> *"All she really wants to do is ride the metro,*
> *but finding it shut because of a strike,*
> *Zazie looks for other means of amusement."*

— *Raymond Queneau, Zazie dans le métro*

In this entertaining story, we discover the interesting escapades of a lively 12-year-old girl wandering the enchanting streets of Paris. Left in the care of her Uncle Gabriel while her mother spends time with her lover, Zazie is both delighted and dismayed by the bustling metropolis. Her paramount desire, however, is to explore the complex network of the metro, which, to her disappointment, is closed due to a strike. Undeterred, Zazie embarks on a series of adventures above ground, meeting a diverse array of eccentric characters ranging from nimble-fingered pickpockets to sagacious old ladies and diligent policemen. During these encounters, she finds herself in peculiar situations: a carriage swarming with clucking chickens or the precarious possibility of being arrested for ticket evasion. Through these events, Zazie draws a colorful picture of Parisian life, revealing its peculiarities and bringing to light hidden facets of her being. Narrated from Zazie's tender perspective, the narrative takes on a delightful point of view, allowing us to observe the world through her youthful eyes, where moments of hilarity mingle with poignant traces of melancholy. Queneau deftly weaves threads of popular culture throughout the novel, adding an extra layer of depth and wit, making it an engaging read for young and mature minds alike.

Zazie has become a classic in French literature, pioneering the use of unconventional narrative styles and influencing countless writers with its creative use of language and bright imagery.

278.   Rhinoceros (Eugène Ionesco, 1959)

"Childhood is the world of miracle and wonder;
as if creation rose, bathed in the light, out of the darkness,
utterly new and fresh and astonishing.
The end of childhood is when things cease to astonish us."

—— *Eugène Ionesco, Rhinoceros*

Ionesco mixes comedy and drama to illuminate the formidable force of groupthink and conformity, allegorically related to fascism. We meet Berenger, an ordinary man who is faced with a bewildering reality: his once familiar town is being overrun by the astonishing transformation of its inhabitants into rhinoceroses. As Berenger witnesses his friends and neighbors succumb, one by one, to this peculiar metamorphosis, his struggle to preserve his own identity intensifies amidst the rising wave of uniformity. Yet, his valiant efforts to retain his individuality face insurmountable odds as the collective mentality engulfs those around him. Amidst this chaotic whirlwind, a glimmer of hope emerges in the form of Daisy, another resolute human who stands steadfastly. However, ultimately, Daisy too succumbs to the rhinoceritis, leaving Berenger as the last human standing. Rhinoceros presents a metaphorical exploration of the overwhelming power of mob mentality when confronted with seemingly insurmountable challenges. Through this compelling narrative, we gain profound insight into the intricate motives that drive some individuals to align with the actions of others while others strongly defend their beliefs, unyielding in the face of adversity.

Rhinoceros urges readers to forge their path, challenge societal norms, and courageously think for themselves. It beckons us to stand firm in our convictions, defying the currents of conformity that threaten to sweep us away, ensuring the everlasting power of free thought and the preservation of our unique identities.

279.   Catch-22 (Joseph Heller, 1961)

> *"Just because you're paranoid*
> *doesn't mean they aren't after you."*
>
> — *Joseph Heller, Catch-22*

Catch-22 is a satirical war novel that follows the story of Yossarian, an American bombardier stationed in Italy during *World War II*. Yossarian is desperate to escape combat duty, but the military bureaucracy has created a *catch-22* which prevents him from doing so – if he requests to be released from duty due to insanity, this, however, proves his sanity as only someone sane would want to avoid danger; if he does not request discharge then he must stay on duty. Throughout the course of the novel, Yossarian meets a variety of characters with their own unique motivations for surviving or avoiding combat missions, including Milo Minderbinder, who creates a syndicate that profits off wartime supplies, and Major Major, who hides out in his office pretending not to be available. At the same time, everyone else goes off into battle. In addition to these characters are other soldiers, such as Clevinger and Dunbar, whose attempts at survival often fail miserably despite their best efforts. As the narrative advances, Yossarian finds it increasingly challenging to preserve his sanity amidst the surrounding chaos. Eventually, he concludes that regardless of his efforts, there is always another Catch-22 obstructing his path to safety. However, the novel ends on a hopeful note as Yossarian decides to rebel against the absurdity by deserting the army.

Catch-22 offers a scathing critique of bureaucracy and war through its dark humor and bizarre logic. The novel has become one of history's most widely read antiwar books, with its questions still relevant today. Heller's writing style has been praised for its wit and ability to capture both the absurdity and horror experienced by those involved in wartime conflict.

280.   The Structure of Scientific Revolutions (Thomas Kuhn, 1962)

> *"A scientific revolution is a non-cumulative developmental episode in which an older paradigm is replaced in whole or in part by an incompatible new one."*

> —— *Thomas Kuhn, The Structure of Scientific Revolutions*

The Structure of Scientific Revolutions is a landmark work in the history and philosophy of science. It proposes a revolutionary new theory on how scientific knowledge develops over time, challenging traditional assumptions about linear progress and absolute truth. Kuhn suggests that scientific progress is not a steady, cumulative process but occurs through *paradigm shifts* – fundamental changes in basic concepts and theories that occur when anomalies cannot be explained within existing paradigms. He argues that these paradigm shifts are often driven by social factors, such as power dynamics between different groups or interests, rather than purely intellectual ones. Kuhn also introduces several other key concepts, such as normal science, which describes research conducted within an accepted framework; revolutions, which occur when the old paradigm breaks down; and incommensurability, meaning two competing paradigms cannot be compared directly because they use different terms to describe reality. These ideas have immensely influenced many disciplines, including sociology, psychology, economics, and education. Kuhn provides an innovative perspective on how scientific understanding evolves – one that has been widely influential since its publication.

Kuhn introduced the concept that science does not progress steadily from one discovery to another but proceeds through periodic revolutions or paradigm shifts when accepted ways of thinking give way to new theories and ideas about how the world works.

281.   The Order of Things (Michel Foucault, 1966)

> *"As the archeology of our thought easily shows,*
> *man is an invention of recent date.*
> *And one perhaps nearing its end."*

— *Michel Foucault, The Order of Things*

The Order of Things scrutinizes the evolution and maturation of human sciences such as linguistics, economics, psychology, anthropology, and biology. Foucault posits that knowledge is inherently shaped by its historical context and is intertwined with power dynamics. He introduces three different epistemes, or frameworks, through which humans have interpreted reality over time: *The Classical Age, The Age of Man,* and *The Age of Discourse.* Foucault begins by dissecting the premodern episteme, *The Classical Age.* During this period, knowledge was organized based on resemblances between objects, independent of scientific methodologies. Transitioning to the modern episteme, *The Age of Man,* he details an era marked by scientific advancement through observation and experimentation. This period ushered in a deeper understanding of nature and birthed new forms of societal power. Finally, Foucault analyzes *The Age of Discourse,* in which language is pivotal in our perception of reality. This framework opens the door for questioning established norms and offers the potential to construct individual truths from diverse viewpoints. Throughout The Order of Things, Foucault illustrates how each epoch develops its unique lens of world comprehension yet remains interconnected with preceding eras through the persistence of shared concepts like reason and truth.

The Order of Things examines how society employs classification systems – language, science, and knowledge archives – to construct frameworks that shape individual actions and societal functioning. In turn, these structures yield profound insights into the nature of life itself.

282.   The Master and Margarita (Mikhail Bulgakov, 1967)

> *"Yes, man is mortal, but that would be only half the trouble.*
> *The worst of it is that he's sometimes unexpectedly mortal – there's the trick."*

— *Mikhail Bulgakov, The Master and Margarita*

Within The Master and Margarita, we enter a supernatural setting alongside the enigmatic Devil himself, known as Woland. The narrative begins with his arrival in Moscow, accompanied by his entourage, who together stir up a whirlwind of otherworldly adventures that cast a satirical eye on Soviet society. The entourage accompanying Woland includes a colorful array of characters, each possessing its peculiar allure. Among them, we encounter the eccentric and mischievous Behemoth, a diabolical cat who adds a touch of whimsy to their exploits. Behemoth's presence cannot be ignored as he playfully wreaks havoc with his devilish charm, leaving a trail of bewilderment and amusement in his wake. While Woland's arrival sparks chaos and astonishment among Moscow's citizens, his entourage further draws notice and fascination. Together, they form an enthralling ensemble, enchanting the curious and the skeptical with their supernatural abilities and charismatic allure. The intertwined stories of The Master and Margarita also come to the fore. The Master, an embattled writer, finds himself entangled in a web of persecution due to his controversial work centered around the encounter between Pontius Pilate and Jesus Christ. Margarita, yearning to break free from her mundane existence, meets Woland, and in a profound act of devotion to the Master, she becomes the hostess of Satan's grand spring ball, leading her on a captivating journey through the streets of Moscow.

The Master and Margarita casts a spell upon its readers, drawing them into a realm where the supernatural coexists with the ordinary and where the presence of Woland and his entourage leaves an indelible mark upon the fabric of Moscow's society.

283. One Hundred Years of Solitude (Gabriel García Márquez, 1967)

"It's enough for me
to be sure
that you and I
exist at this moment."

—— *Gabriel García Márquez, One Hundred Years of Solitude*

In this enchanting tale, we witness a fascinating journey through the lives of the Buendía family in the picturesque town of Macondo, nestled in the heart of Colombia. The story commences with the adventurous José Arcadio Buendía and his resilient wife Úrsula Iguarán, who found the town and from whose union are born two sons José Arcadio and Aureliano. Their descendants continue to hold these names, marking the cyclical nature of their family history. Their children and subsequent generations grow amidst Macondo's mesmerizing myths and magical realities. As time progresses, Macondo transforms from a paradisiacal, isolated settlement into a vibrant town that grapples with external influences, burgeoning technologies, and a cascade of socio-political upheavals. The Buendías, themselves a microcosm of human existence, wrestle with their inner demons, incestuous attractions, and prodigious talents, while remaining inexorably bound to the town's whimsical spirit.

Gabriel García Márquez masterfully employs the technique of "magical realism," a style of writing that he largely popularized. This style meshes the ordinary and the fantastical in a seamless blend, reflecting the realities of life with a touch of enchantment. Its commentary on the cyclical nature of history and the fatalistic perspective on progress and human behavior has been the subject of extensive literary criticism and interpretation. For his significant contributions to literature, García Márquez was awarded the Nobel Prize in Literature in 1982.

284.   The Double Helix (James Watson, 1968)

> *"The instant I saw the picture*
> *my mouth fell open*
> *and my pulse began to race."*

> — *James Watson, The Double Helix*

The Double Helix is a scientific account of the discovery of the DNA's structure. The book begins with an overview of the scientific community's understanding at the time regarding DNA, which was that it contained genetic information, but its exact structure was unknown. It then describes how Watson and Crick work together to uncover this mystery. Critically, it is essential to acknowledge the pioneering work of Rosalind Franklin, whose X-ray crystallography images were central to Watson and Crick's revelation that DNA is a double helix. Through experimentation and observation, they were able to determine that DNA is made up of two strands wound around each other in a double-helix shape. They also determined that these strands comprise four different types of nucleotides: adenine, thymine, guanine, and cytosine. The book explores how this discovery revolutionized biology as scientists now had a better understanding of genetics and how mutations can occur within genes over generations. It provides insight into the mechanics behind inheritance patterns and diseases that could be caused by mutations in specific cell genes. This groundbreaking work opened up many avenues for future research. Today, through molecular biology, we are getting closer to understanding life's enigmas, ranging from genetic codes to methods of preventing diseases.

The Double Helix documented one of the most significant scientific discoveries ever made – that DNA is a double helical structure that serves as genetic material for all living organisms on Earth. This discovery has revolutionized our understanding of biology and has become fundamental to modern medicine today.

THE CONTEMPORARY ERA

THE CONTEMPORARY ERA

The literature of the contemporary era, from the 1970s to the present day, is an incredibly diverse and vibrant collection that reflects the profound changes that have shaped our world over the past five decades. It is a living and breathing field, deeply impacted by the evolving global landscape, rapid technological progress, and the sweeping social movements that continue to expand before our eyes.

Among the myriad literary trends that have shaped this period, *Postmodernism* stands out. Originating in the mid-20th century, this movement gained significant momentum in the 1960s and 70s, breaking away from traditional narrative paradigms to espouse fragmentation, intertextuality – a concept referring to the interconnection between literary works, and metafiction – a form of narrative that self-consciously reflects upon itself as a work of art. Authors like Italo Calvino in *If on a Winter's Night a Traveler* and Salman Rushdie in *Midnight's Children* skillfully employed these techniques to challenge established norms and invite readers into a labyrinthine exploration of meaning and reality.

The contemporary era's literature is a tribute to the enduring relevance of literary expression. Authors continue to push the boundaries of language and form, offering fresh insights into the human experience and challenging dominant narratives. Through their works, they invite readers to critically examine the world we inhabit, interrogate power dynamics, and explore the intricacies of identity, love, loss, and resilience.

As we stand in 2023, we find ourselves surrounded by an abundance of contemporary literary works, both acclaimed and awaiting discovery. Navigating this vast landscape can be challenging, and the evaluation of these recent creations requires time, perspective, and critical judgment. Let us allow these works to settle and prepare for the discerning eyes of future generations, who will undoubtedly provide a more comprehensive understanding of the literary contributions of the early 2000s and beyond.

285.   Language and Mind (Noam Chomsky, 1972)

> *"The study of language and mind*
> *can be pursued for its own sake,*
> *as an aspect of the general problem*
> *of understanding man's place in nature."*

— *Noam Chomsky, Language and Mind*

Language and Mind is a seminal work by renowned linguist Noam Chomsky that transformed the field with his revolutionary ideas about *generative grammar*, which has become fundamental to modern linguistic theory today. With this book, he introduced his influential idea that humans possess an innate capacity for acquiring complex languages through a process called *transformational grammar* – something he referred to as *the human-language faculty* or *Universal Grammar* (UG). All human languages share a common underlying structure, which is innate to the human mind. He argued that UG provides all speakers with specific knowledge about their native language(s) from birth, enabling them to acquire any natural language quickly without having first been exposed to it before learning begins. This leads him to propose that structural elements are shared across all languages regardless if they have similar origins or not – thus showing universal properties among them all despite their differences in sound and lexicons, etc. Language and Mind also discussed topics such as semantics and meaning within context, along with other psycholinguistic aspects related to speech production, comprehension, and cognitive development in children through adulthood – providing readers with a comprehensive overview of the complexities surrounding human communication.

Chomsky made groundbreaking contributions to linguistics by introducing the concept of generative grammar. This idea revolutionized our understanding of how language works and is acquired, making Language and Mind one of the most essential books on language ever written.

286.   Invisible Cities (Italo Calvino, 1972)

> *"Cities, like dreams, are made of desires and fears,*
> *even if the thread of their discourse is secret,*
> *their rules are absurd, their perspectives deceitful."*

— *Italo Calvino, Invisible Cities*

Invisible Cities is a collection of tales that the great explorer Marco Polo shares with Kublai Khan. Through these stories, Polo attempts to describe the many cities he has visited and experienced during his travels. Each city is unique and presented in sharp detail: from its inhabitants' customs and traditions to their architecture, artistry, music, and food. As Polo tells Khan about each city he visits – some real, some imagined – the emperor begins to understand that all cities are connected through shared experiences of joys and sorrows alike; what makes them distinct are only minor details or nuances that make up their identities. Throughout the novel, there is an underlying tension between reality versus illusion which can be seen in how Calvino conveys different interpretations of life within each city's narrative arc – often blurring the lines between fantasy and fiction with reality and truth to illustrate how perception shapes our experience of any given place or situation. In Invisible Cities, readers come away with a greater appreciation for both tangible realities we inhabit as well as intangible ones we imagine – understanding that it takes both kinds of worlds for us to comprehend who we are at our core level indeed.

By skillfully combining mythology, philosophy, and travel into a narrative, Calvino presents a complex yet concise examination of human identity concerning our built environment. Themes such as memory, communication, and identity are explored through memorable descriptions of fantastic cities which exist in neither the past nor present but somewhere in between; this dynamic makes Invisible Cities one of the most influential works about imaginary cities ever written.

Invisible Cities

287.   The Gulag Archipelago (Aleksandr Solzhenitsyn, 1973)

"If only it were all so simple!
If only there were evil people somewhere
insidiously committing evil deeds,
and it were necessary only to separate them
from the rest of us and destroy them.
But the line dividing good and evil
cuts through the heart of every human being."

— *Aleksandr Solzhenitsyn, The Gulag Archipelago*

The Gulag Archipelago is an autobiographical work documenting the Soviet Union's forced labor camp system. The *Gulag system* was a vast network of scattered settlements in remote regions of the Soviet Union, often in harsh and inhospitable environments. Labor camps were the most common type of Gulag settlement. Other settlements included colonies or villages where exiles were forced to reside under close supervision. Conditions varied, but generally, prisoners endured hard labor, limited freedom, and constant surveillance. The residents of these settlements were subjected to collective punishment and had their movements and access to resources strictly controlled by authorities. The first volume tells the story of Solzhenitsyn's experience in a labor camp in Kazakhstan during *World War II* with his fellow prisoners. The second volume examines how Stalin's policies led to more arrests and harsher conditions for prisoners in the gulags throughout his rule. The third volume focuses on the post-Stalinist rule, looking at how conditions improved slightly for some inmates under Khrushchev's rule, but remained harsh for many others. It also examines how survivors have attempted to tell their stories since being released from prison and what this means for Russia today.

The Gulag Archipelago is a detailed account of life within Russia's concentration camps during Stalin's rule and an exploration of human nature and morality under oppressive circumstances.

288.   Zen and the Art of Motorcycle Maintenance (Robert M. Pirsig, 1974)

> *The real cycle you're working on*
> *is a cycle called yourself.*

— *Robert M. Pirsig, Zen and the Art of Motorcycle Maintenance*

Zen and the Art of Motorcycle Maintenance is a philosophical exploration of life through motorcycle maintenance. The narrator embarks on a cross-country journey with his son to explore the relationship between technology and values. Along the way, he reflects on his past as an academic philosopher who suffered from mental illness that caused him to leave academia behind for a simpler life focused on motorcycling and philosophy. As they travel across America, father and son visit Mount Rushmore, Yellowstone National Park, San Francisco Bay Area, and other places. They meet people with contrasting views about technology versus humanity's need for spiritual connection. As he rides along highways, both rural and urban landscapes are observed while reflecting upon man's inner struggle between rationality (the *Classical* world) vs. emotion (the *Romantic* world). During their time together, our protagonist begins to understand what it means to be an individual living harmoniously within society – which requires us to balance our intellectual pursuits with emotional needs to find meaning in life itself. He also comes away with an understanding of how important it is for each person to have a unique perspective when looking at any situation so that solutions may be found outside conventional thought patterns. Zen And the Art of Motorcycle Maintenance encourages us to act compassionately towards others and ourselves.

Zen and the Art of Motorcycle Maintenance offers readers an exploration of how they can find peace through a better understanding of themselves and their environment through philosophy.

289.   The Name of the Rose (Umberto Eco, 1980)

> *"Books always speak of other books,*
> *and every story tells a story that has already been told."*
>
> — *Umberto Eco, The Name of the Rose*

In this fascinating novel set in a medieval abbey in 14th-century Italy, we are introduced to the brilliant mind of Guglielmo da Baskerville, a Franciscan monk, and his young novice Adso da Melk. Together, they venture into the abbey's walls to unravel a series of complex deaths shrouded in secrecy. Fear of an unknown and sinister assailant lurks among them, meticulously selecting specific targets for unknown reasons. Determined to uncover the truth, William investigates the depths of the abbey, where hidden corridors and the enigmatic library hold the key to the ongoing mystery. During their investigation, the duo learns of a coveted and valuable book called *The Name of the Rose*. It becomes apparent that the entire monastery is consumed by the ardent quest to possess this ancient tome. As they move closer to unlocking the secrets veiled in the book's pages, they encounter formidable adversaries who will stop at nothing to hinder their progress. In a gripping atmosphere, William reveals the chilling truth: the murders are part of a diabolical plan orchestrated within the abbey. The culprit seeks access to an ancient secret, one of immense power and consequence, hidden within *The Name of the Rose*. In a race against time, William must employ his cunning intelligence to overcome those who conspire against him while safeguarding justice and preserving his life in a world cloaked in darkness and despair.

The Name of the Rose is an extraordinary journey that takes readers through the intricate labyrinth of the medieval abbey while blending mystery, history, and philosophy into a masterful narrative. Umberto Eco's eloquent prose envelops us in a compelling tale that explores the depths of human nature and the constant struggle between light and darkness.

The Name of the Rose

290.   Midnight's Children (Salman Rushdie, 1981)

> *"What's real and what's true*
> *aren't necessarily the same."*
>
> —— *Salman Rushdie, Midnight's Children*

The novel revolves around the life of Saleem Sinai, whose fate is intertwined with that of his nation. Born at the stroke of midnight on August 15, 1947, just as India was celebrating its hard-fought independence from British colonial rule, Saleem's life displays as a mirror of the evolving identity and challenges of his beloved homeland. From his earliest years, Saleem discovers that he possesses remarkable abilities that connect him to a group of extraordinary individuals known as the *children of midnight*. They share a mystical bond, having been born in the magical hour of independence, giving them telepathic powers and a unique connection. Through their collective consciousness, they navigate the complex landscape of a post-colonial India, trying to make sense of their place in a society undergoing immense transformation. As Saleem's journey unfolds, so does India's turbulent history. He witnesses the political upheavals, wars, and social unrest that shape the nation. However, tragedy strikes when Saleem loses his telepathic abilities amid the horrors of the civil war between East and West Pakistan. Deprived of his extraordinary powers, he embarks on a quest for *fragmented identity* as he grapples with the profound changes India undergoes under the rule of Prime Minister Indira Gandhi. Throughout his odyssey, Saleem traverses the diverse landscapes of India, searching for meaning and a sense of belonging.

Rushdie's masterful narrative deftly weaves history, magical realism, and political commentary into an enchanting tale that illuminates the universal quest for self-discovery and belonging. Saleem's journey is a metaphor for India's struggle to define itself among the forces of globalization, immigration, and the tension between tradition and progress.

291.   The House of Spirits (Isabel Allende, 1982)

"You can't find someone who doesn't want to be found."

— *Isabel Allende, The House of the Spirits*

This epic novel introduces us to Esteban Trueba, a young man from a decayed aristocratic family who rebuilds his family estate and marries Clara del Valle, a woman with mystical powers who had predicted her own marriage to Esteban when she was a child. Their marriage is the foundation of the Trueba family, around which the story is built. The couple has three children: Blanca, Jaime, and Nicolás. As the Trueba family navigates through life, Chile undergoes significant transformations that shape their destinies. Esteban, driven by conservative beliefs, builds a political career, which sets the stage for a clash with his daughter Blanca, who becomes involved in a secret romance with a revolutionary named Pedro Tercero García. In the meantime, Jaime becomes a doctor devoted to helping the poor, and Nicolás seeks a bohemian life. Clara's mystical abilities and connection with the *spirit world* are also essential to the story, as her powers often serve as a sanctuary and source of wisdom for the family. As the political climate in Chile changes and turmoil ensues, the Trueba family faces trials and tribulations, with Esteban's stubborn and often tyrannical behavior playing a significant role in their struggles. The story spans several generations, including that of Blanca's daughter, Alba, who also becomes embroiled in political unrest. Throughout the novel, the Trueba family's experiences are meshed with elements of *magic realism*, as the characters' lives reflect Chile's social and political changes.

The House of Spirits intricately weaves together the personal struggles of the Trueba family with the backdrop of a nation in flux. By delving into the complex dynamics of love, power, and resilience, Isabel Allende skillfully explores the indomitable strength of the human spirit in the face of adversity.

292.   Baltasar and Blimunda (José Saramago, 1982)

> *"A man must earn his daily bread*
> *by some means some-where,*
> *and if his bread fails to nourish his soul,*
> *at least his body will be nourished*
> *while his soul suffers."*

> — *José Saramago, Baltasar and Blimunda*

Baltasar and Blimunda is set in 18th-century Portugal amid the looming shadow of the Inquisition. The protagonists Baltasar and Blimunda symbolize a beacon of defiance against societal norms. Baltasar, an ex-soldier who sacrificed his hand in the Spanish War of Succession, is joined by Blimunda, a young woman gifted with unique abilities. Together, they construct an airship, symbolizing their collective desire for liberation from oppressive social circumstances. Along their path, they face a series of hurdles, such as destitution and religious oppression, yet their resilient spirits triumph as they successfully build their dream machine. As they navigate these challenges, their bond deepens, fortifying their relationship in the face of adversity. The book also provides a critical commentary on religion's potential to wield control over individuals through fear and manipulation rather than offering comfort or fostering hope. This theme is vividly portrayed through the Inquisition's ruthless use of torture to extract confessions from individuals accused of heresy or witchcraft, regardless of the validity or justice of such accusations. Their story is a testament to the power of love and unity in overcoming formidable barriers.

Saramago expertly explores the human capacity to challenge oppressive systems, irrespective of one's circumstances. The novel provides a detailed portrayal of this period in Portuguese history, riddled with violence and injustice, while simultaneously highlighting glimpses of hope through its characters' personal narratives. The opening quote "...if his bread fails to nourish his soul..." reflects and underlines the struggle of Saramago characters.

293.　The Lover (Marguerite Duras, 1984)

> *"Suddenly, all at once, she knows,*
> *knows that he doesn't understand her, that he never will,*
> *that he lacks the power to understand such perverseness.*
> *And that he can never move fast enough to catch her."*

> —— *Marguerite Duras, The Lover*

The Lover is a semi-autobiographical novel about a young girl's coming-of-age story. Set in French Indochina during the 1930s, it tells the story of a 15-year-old unnamed protagonist and her affair with an older Chinese man. The girl comes from a poor family and has been sent to Saigon for education; she meets her lover on one of her trips back home. The two become enamored with each other as they explore their physical relationship while learning more about themselves emotionally. At first, they keep their relationship secret due to the social stigma associated with interracial relationships at that period. Still, eventually, they decide to go public despite all odds being against them. As the affair progresses, it becomes increasingly difficult for the couple to maintain their relationship due to financial constraints and cultural differences between them. Eventually, both are forced apart when he leaves his job in Saigon without any explanation or goodbye, leaving her heartbroken and alone once again. Throughout this journey of self-discovery, we see how The Lover explores themes such as forbidden love, poverty, and gender roles in colonial society, which still resonates today.

The Lover is an exploration of the complexities of forbidden love and its consequences on the human psyche. Duras captures the nuances of a young girl's passionate affair with an older Chinese man in colonial Indochina through her spare yet poetic prose. Duras's masterful use of language to evoke emotion imbues each scene with poignancy and intensity; she simultaneously reveals how these emotions can be liberating and oppressive. The novel leaves readers contemplating what it means to surrender to desire.

294.   The Unbearable Lightness of Being (Milan Kundera, 1984)

> *"The only relationship that can make both partners happy*
> *is one in which sentimentality has no place*
> *and neither partner makes any claim*
> *on the life and freedom of the other."*

— *Milan Kundera, The Unbearable Lightness of Being*

Milan Kundera's philosophical novel brings to life the intertwined destinies of four individuals during the tumultuous 1968 Soviet invasion of Czechoslovakia. The narrative follows Tomas, a surgeon known for his serial affairs; Tereza, his wife, loyal yet tormented; Sabina, an artist cherishing freedom above all; and Franz, captivated by Sabina. Each character wrestles with dilemmas of morality and identity amid the brewing political chaos. Tomas's relationship with Sabina leads him to deeply explore his obligations to himself and others. Concurrently, Tereza confronts challenging choices concerning faithfulness and trust in her marriage. While cherishing her freedom, Sabina must decide whether to uphold her loyalty to those around her, even when she feels constrained by them. Franz, on the other hand, must reconcile his deep affection for Sabina while resisting oppressive external forces from government officials and military police due to his anti-government stance. Each character experiences life's unpredictability, discovering that moments of beauty can emerge even in the face of darkness or tragedy. As the story continues, they demonstrate how love can yield joy and sorrow, how decisions cast long shadows on oneself and others, and how life retains lightness regardless of its burdens.

In The Unbearable Lightness of Being, Milan Kundera creates an unforgettable story about human connection amid chaos, a powerful reminder that life will never cease to exist without mystery regardless of circumstance.

295.   Beloved (Toni Morrison, 1987)

> *"Definitions belong
> to the definers,
> not the defined."*
>
> — *Toni Morrison, Beloved*

Sethe, a former slave, resides with her daughter Denver in Cincinnati after escaping from Sweet Home, a plantation in Kentucky run by a man called Schoolteacher. Eighteen years prior, Sethe made a difficult choice to kill her infant daughter to spare her the horrors of slavery when the Schoolteacher's posse came to recapture them. The word *Beloved* is etched on the child's gravestone, a touching motif that permeates the novel, representing Sethe's overwhelming guilt and grief. A mysterious young woman who calls herself *Beloved* arrives at Sethe's home at 124 Bluestone Road. She is enigmatic and knows things only the deceased infant would know. It gradually becomes evident that Beloved is the reincarnation of Sethe's slain daughter, who has returned seeking closure and retribution for the pain she endured. As Beloved insinuates herself into the household, Sethe becomes consumed by her. Several characters, including Paul D, a former slave from Sweet Home, Baby Suggs, Sethe's mother-in-law, and the community of formerly enslaved women, play crucial roles in battling the oppressive presence of Beloved. United, they manage to release Beloved's hold, which seemingly dissipates into the air and leaves behind a household in search of healing, especially Sethe who is ravaged by her past actions.

The Pulitzer Prize winner Toni Morrison explores the psychological and physical effects of slavery on African Americans. Combining magical realism with historical accuracy and emotional depth, Beloved is a powerful testament to personal resilience and collective suffering.

296.   The Alchemist (Paulo Coelho, 1988)

"When we love,
we always strive to become better than we are.
When we strive to become better than we are,
everything around us becomes better too."

—— *Paulo Coelho, The Alchemist*

The Alchemist is a novel about an Andalusian shepherd boy named Santiago who embarks on a journey to find his *Personal Legend* – representing the individual's destiny in harmony with the *universe's intentions*. Throughout the story, Santiago's *Personal Legend* serves as his *guiding force*, inspiring his actions, fueling his motivation, and warning against possible calamities. He meets many people, including an old king and an alchemist, who help him realize that he must follow his dreams to fulfill his destiny. Along the way, Santiago learns important lessons about life and love. He also discovers that the universe conspires to make something happen when one truly desires something. By trusting himself and following his heart, Santiago finds what he has been searching for – his true purpose in life. Santiago's story teaches us that we should not be afraid to pursue our dreams no matter how difficult they may seem; with determination and faith, anything is possible. We should learn from our mistakes but never give up on ourselves or our goals because they are always worth fighting for if we want them badly enough. The Alchemist reminds us of the power of positive thinking and understanding how each person has their unique path towards achieving success and happiness. It is a powerful reminder that taking risks can lead us closer to fulfilling our greatest desires if we stay focused on what matters most – following our hearts without fear or hesitation.

The Alchemist by Paulo Coelho is a timeless classic full of wisdom and insight into discovering one's true potential through courageously pursuing one's dreams despite any obstacles encountered – it encourages readers worldwide to have faith in themselves so they can manifest their greatness.

297. A Brief History of Time (Stephen Hawking, 1988)

*"We are just an advanced breed of monkeys
on a minor planet of a very average star.
But we can understand the Universe.
That makes us something very special."*

— *Stephen Hawking, A Brief History of Time*

A Brief History of Time covers topics ranging from black holes and relativity to quantum mechanics and explains how these ideas are related. Hawking begins with an overview of astronomy discussing the Big Bang theory and its implications for our understanding of time and space. He then discusses more complex concepts such as general relativity, thermodynamics, entropy, quarks, and strings. Hawking also touches upon some philosophical questions, such as whether there is a God or if life has any ultimate purpose. He concludes by discussing what we may be able to learn about our universe through future research projects such as the Large Hadron Collider in Switzerland and other experiments designed to probe further into subatomic particles and their effects on reality as we know it today. Through careful examination of current scientific theories combined with thoughtful speculation, Stephen Hawking succeeds in providing readers with a comprehensive look at where humanity stands among the stars today – offering hope that perhaps one day we will unlock even more secrets hidden within our ever-expanding universe.

A Brief History of Time is a comprehensive exploration of the Universe's origins, structure, and fate. It provides a unique insight into cosmology. Through accessible expositions on topics such as black holes, thermodynamics, and quantum mechanics, Hawking delivers a lucid account of some of science's most complex concepts. Its global success highlights its universality in bridging disciplines, making it essential to our understanding of our place in the cosmos.

298.   Harry Potter and the Sorcerer's Stone (J.K. Rowling, 1997)

"Fear of a name increases fear of the thing itself."

— *J.K. Rowling, Harry Potter and the Sorcerer's Stone*

Harry is a young orphan with extraordinary heritage as a wizard. As he begins his magical education at Hogwarts, he befriends Ron Weasley and Hermione Granger, forming an inseparable trio. Together, they navigate the challenges and wonders of the wizarding world. However, Harry soon learns of a dark and treacherous force that haunts his past – Lord Voldemort, the evil wizard who killed his parents and left him with a lightning-shaped scar. Prophecies and ancient legends reveal that Harry is the *Chosen One* destined to confront Voldemort (this becomes more prominent later in the series). Harry embarks on a dangerous quest to prevent Voldemort from obtaining the powerful *Sorcerer's Stone*. Along their journey, Harry, Ron, and Hermione encounter enchantments and dangers within Hogwarts' hidden chambers. Their path is obstructed by obstacles designed to guard the Sorcerer's Stone, including a massive three-headed dog, a life-sized chessboard, and even a troll lurking in the depths of the school. Unbeknownst to them, the treacherous Quirinus Quirrell, once a seemingly harmless teacher, has become an instrument of Voldemort's evil plans. With guidance from the wise and benevolent Albus Dumbledore, Hogwarts' headmaster, Harry confronts Quirrell and the resurrected Voldemort in a thrilling climax. Through courage, resourcefulness, and the strength of their friendship, Harry and his companions emerge victorious, ensuring that the Sorcerer's Stone remains out of Voldemort's grasp.

J.K. Rowling's debut novel features the creative use of magical elements such as spells, potions, enchanted creatures, wands, and broomsticks that bring this imaginative world to life. The magical elements combined with the clever plotting have made it a worldwide success.

Harry Potter and the Sorcerer's Stone

299.   Life of Pi (Yann Martel, 2001)

> *"The world isn't just the way it is. It is how we understand it, no?*
> *And in understanding something, we bring something to it, no?*
> *Doesn't that make life a story?"*

— *Yann Martel, Life of Pi*

His schoolmates hilariously interpret his name Piscine, and he establishes the mathematical constant π as his *real* nickname. The story opens as Pi's family, who runs a zoo, embarks on a journey to Canada, seeking a new life. Accompanied by their beloved animals, they set sail on a Japanese freighter. Tragedy strikes when a violent storm sinks the ship, and Pi finds himself in a lifeboat, *the only human survivor*, sharing his limited space with an orangutan, a hyena, a wounded zebra, and a fearsome Bengal tiger named Richard Parker. The harsh reality of the situation comes to light as the animals start killing each other for survival, leaving only Pi and Richard Parker alive. Against all odds, Pi forms an unlikely bond with the tiger, which becomes his primary threat and sole companion. Alone in the vast expanse of the Pacific Ocean, Pi turns to his faith and spirituality to understand the meaning of life. Pi's odyssey leads him to the shores of Mexico, where he is rescued from the confines of the lifeboat. In a startling revelation at the novel's end, Pi offers a different account of his odyssey, *substituting the animals with human characters*. In this version, Pi's mother assumes the role of the orangutan, a malevolent cook represents the hyena, a seasick sailor is portrayed as the zebra, and Pi stands in for Richard Parker. The investigators who listen to Pi's account *can choose which story they prefer* – the one with the animals or humans – a twist giving a deeper meaning to the novel.

Yann Martel's Life of Pi is a profound exploration of human resilience, faith, and the transformative power of storytelling. The narrative underscores our capacity for survival but also highlights the ability to perceive and shape our realities, adding a rich philosophical dimension to an extraordinary tale.

Life of Pi

300.   The Kite Runner (Khaled Hosseini, 2003)

"It may be unfair,
but what happens in a few days,
sometimes even a single day,
can change the course of a whole lifetime."

— *Khaled Hosseini, The Kite Runner*

In Kabul, privileged Amir yearns for the affection and approval of his father Baba. His loyal friend Hassan, the son of their family servant Ali, remains constantly supportive. However, Amir's jealousy over Baba's seeming fondness for Hassan peaks during a kite-flying tournament. To win his father's approval, Amir decides to not intervene when Hassan is assaulted by neighborhood bullies, hauntingly betraying his friend. Years pass, and Amir, now settled in California, is far removed from his past. However, a call from Rahim Khan, his father's old business partner, lures him back to Taliban-ruled Afghanistan. Compelled to seek redemption, Amir attempts to rescue Hassan's son Sohrab from an abusive orphanage. Facing the perils of war-torn Afghanistan, Amir's determination leads him to Sohrab. But their reunion is overshadowed by a violent encounter with Assef, Hassan's tormentor from years ago. Overcoming adversity, Amir triumphs, securing Sohrab's freedom and promising him a better life in America. This chapter of their lives is marked by hope, yet the scars of Sohrab's trauma, evident after his suicide attempt, remind them of the arduous healing that lies ahead of them.

Khaled Hosseini's The Kite Runner intricately explores human relationships, the far-reaching repercussions of our choices, and the persistent power of hope. The novel underscores that the road to healing often necessitates confronting our most challenging experiences and finding the courage to seek forgiveness for ourselves and those we have wronged.

CONCLUSION

Engaging with humanity's diverse *classics* requires us to move beyond the transient clutter of information we are routinely exposed to, focusing our attention instead on *enduring* literary gems – those masterpieces refined by the passage of time and safeguarded across generations.

The *written word* stands as a formidable medium of expression, adept at sculpting our worldview and linking us to the wisdom of past intellectual giants, who have tackled the manifold moral, aesthetic, and religious dilemmas that persistently color our existence.

The spectrum of literature I have analyzed for this compilation has been vast: a mosaic of ideas and perspectives from around the globe. Each narrative's unique message contributes to an intricate understanding pattern, offering precious insights into our shared past. Fascinatingly, despite the diversity, a common thread emerges recurrent motifs spanning eras and geographies that hint at a unified undercurrent of human experience.

The selection represented here aims to offer an inclusive and balanced cross-section of significant literary milestones. It includes works from a multitude of cultures and epochs, acknowledging their critical role in shaping our collective consciousness. To counter the bias of the *Western Canon*, I have made a concerted effort to honor contributions from *non-Western* literary traditions, particularly from Japan, China, and India. Despite this, I am aware that my grasp of the richness of non-Western cultures remains limited, especially concerning contemporary literature. This represents a significant lacuna, for which I seek your understanding and patience.

I sincerely apologize for any inadvertent inaccuracies or omissions in this book. The task of encapsulating expansive and complex works into succinct summaries is immense, yet it is my earnest hope that I have retained the *essence* of the original texts, paying tribute to their significance through memory and thoughtful critique.

This guide seeks to spark your curiosity, inspiring you to explore these literary masterpieces more deeply. Through this immersive experience, I hope you will uncover the extraordinary beauty and power embedded in these texts, appreciating the rich legacy of intellectual pursuit that has kindled human progress through the centuries.

By recognizing these influential narratives, we align ourselves with countless seekers throughout history, unearthing nuances of the human condition and decoding our intricate relationship with our universe.

ESSENTIAL BIBLIOGRAPHY

1. "How to Read and Why" by Harold Bloom (2000, Scribner)

2. "The Western Canon" by Harold Bloom (1995, Riverhead Books)

3. "The Literary Canon: A Modern Guide to the Best Books of All Time" by John Sutherland (1999, Oxford University Press)

4. "The Great Books" by David Denby (1996, Simon & Schuster)

5. "The Modern Library: 200 Best Novels in English Since 1950" by Carmen Callil and Colm Tóibín (1999, Modern Library)

6. "The Best American Essays of the Century" by Joyce Carol Oates and Robert Atwan (2001, Houghton Mifflin Harcourt)

7. "The Best American Poetry of the Century" by Robert Hass and David Lehman (2000, Scribner)

8. "Why Read the Classics?" by Italo Calvino (2001, Vintage)

9. "The Pleasures of Reading in an Age of Distraction" by Alan Jacobs (2011, Oxford University Press)

10. "A History of Reading" by Alberto Manguel (1996, Viking)

11. "The Philosophy Book" by Will Buckingham, and others (2011, DK Publishing)

12. "The Anatomy of Influence: Literature as a Way of Life" by Harold Bloom (2011, Yale University Press)

13. "The Art of the Novel" by Milan Kundera (1988, Grove Press)

14. "The Uses of Literature" by Italo Calvino (1986, Harcourt Brace Jovanovich)

15. "The Hero with a Thousand Faces" by Joseph Campbell (1949, Pantheon Books)

16. "The Critical Tradition: Classic Texts and Contemporary Trends" by David H. Richter (2007, Bedford/St. Martin's)

17. "A Short History of English Literature" by Ifor Evans (1967, Penguin Books)

18. "The English Novel: An Introduction" by Terry Eagleton (2005, Wiley-Blackwell)

19. "A Handbook of Critical Approaches to Literature" by Wilfred Guerin, et al. (2017, Oxford University Press)

20. "Literary Theory: An Anthology" by Julie Rivkin and Michael Ryan (1998, Blackwell Publishing)

21. "The Bedford Introduction to Literature: Reading, Thinking, and Writing" by Michael Meyer (2013, Bedford/St. Martin's)

22. "The Norton Introduction to Literature" by Kelly J. Mays (2019, W. W. Norton & Company)

23. "The Norton Anthology of World Literature" by Martin Puchner (2018, W. W. Norton & Company)

24. "The Norton Anthology of English Literature" by M.H. Abrams (2006, W. W. Norton & Company)

25. "The Norton Anthology of Classical Literature" by Bernard Knox and others (2014, W. W. Norton & Company)

26. "The Oxford Companion to English Literature" by Margaret Drabble (2006, Oxford University Press)

27. "The Oxford Handbook of Philosophy of Science" by Paul Humphreys (2016, Oxford University Press)

28. "The Cambridge Companion to World Literature" by Ben Etherington and Jarad Zimbler (2018, Cambridge University Press)

29. "The Cambridge Guide to Literature" by Dominic Head (2010, Cambridge University Press)

INDEX OF TITLES

THE MIDDLE AGES

THE RENAISSANCE

THE 17TH CENTURY

THE 18TH CENTURY

THE 19TH CENTURY

THE FIRST WORLD WAR ERA

THE SECOND WORLD WAR ERA

THE POST-WAR ERA

THE CONTEMPORARY ERA

INDEX OF AUTHORS

Disclaimer:

Although the author has made every effort to ensure that the information in this book is correct, and while this publication is designed to provide an accurate summary regarding the matter covered, the author assumes no responsibility for errors, inaccuracies, omissions, or any other inconsistencies herein and hereby disclaim any liability to any party for any loss, damage, or disruption caused by errors or omissions, whether such errors or omissions result from negligence, accident, or any other cause.

Made in the USA
Las Vegas, NV
12 December 2023

82395031R00238